Modernism

and the

Nativist

Resistance

Sung-sheng Yvonne Chang

Modernism and the Nativist Resistance

Contemporary

Chinese Fiction

from Taiwan

Duke University Press

Durham & London

1993

© 1993

Duke University Press

All rights reserved

Typeset in Joanna by

Tseng Information Systems.

Library of Congress Cataloging-

in-Publication Data appear on

the last printed page of

this book.

Contents

	Preface	vii
ONE	Introduction	1
TWO	The Rise of the Modernist Trend	23
THREE	Appropriations of Literary Modernism	50
FOUR	Modernists Reaching Maturity: Cultural Critique and Textual Strategies	88
FIVE	The Nativist Resistance to Modernism	148
SIX	Conclusion: Entering a New Era	177
	Notes	189
	Select Bibliography	209
	Sources of English Translations of Literary Works from Taiwan	223
	Glossary	227
	Index	239

Preface

The Hsien-tai wen-hsüeh yün-tung (Modernist literary movement) of Taiwan's post-1949 era represents one of three extensive efforts made by Chinese writers at active appropriation of Western literary modernism.[1] Just as China's first modernist trend of the 1930s was interrupted by the Sino-Japanese War and virtually discontinued by the Communist Revolution, the recent surge of interest in modernism and postmodernism among writers in the People's Republic of China has also markedly declined since the T'ien-an-men Incident in 1989. Taiwan's Modernist literary movement, therefore, has had the greatest longevity of the three, and it may also claim the most impressive artistic output.

Since the mid-1980s, the richly intricate implications of a "Chinese modernism" have generated much interest among scholars inside and outside China. The historical disconnectedness of the three waves of Chinese modernism, however, poses certain difficulties for theorizing attempts. Although resonances between the Chinese modernist art and literature of the thirties and the eighties undoubtedly exist, direct connections are hard to find because of the intervention of half a century's officially enforced "socialist realism." There are, however, immediately traceable links between the first two waves of Chinese modernist literature, for some of the modernists of the thirties moved to Taiwan with the Nationalist government around 1949 and played crucial roles in initiating the Modernist literary trend there. A comparative study of the latter two movements also promises interesting results, as both are still viable artistic currents and mutual interactions are inevitable, given the increasing contacts between writers from Taiwan and the People's Republic.

Although Modernist fiction in Taiwan bears unmistakable imprints of China's pre-Revolution periods, it must also be considered a product of the unique historical reality of Taiwan over the last forty years. The present study, treating the subject from both the Chinese and the Taiwanese perspectives, is, above all, a scholarly examination of the complex phenomenon of the proliferation of literary modernism in a non-Western context. For, in a serious sense, Taiwan's Modernist literary movement in the 1960s and the virulent Nativist resistance to it in the 1970s are exemplary of world literary history in the twentieth century, a significant component of which is the global spread of Western social and cultural values along with the expansion of capitalism.

Several of the Modernist writers discussed in this book have been my longtime mentors and good friends. Although I have constantly tried to reassess Taiwan's Modernist literary movement in terms of new theoretical perspectives, I am convinced of the worth of these writers' endeavors and share certain values endorsed in this movement—values that have sustained changes in public opinion and shifting intellectual trends. Writing this book in English is part of an ongoing, collective effort to place contemporary Taiwan's fine literary product on the map of twentieth-century world literature. This larger task could never have been accomplished without the pioneering work of such outstanding scholars as C. T. Hsia, Joseph Lau, Leo Lee, and Howard Goldblatt, who have contributed not only critical writings but also translations and editorial work. To them my study is heavily indebted. In particular, if I had not been asked to write on Taiwan's literature for two special issues of *Modern Chinese Literature* in 1984 and 1988, I would have continued my research on medieval Chinese poetry, the subject of my doctoral work. As I am now convinced that my work in contemporary Chinese literature meets a more urgent demand, I am especially grateful to the journal's founder and general editor, Howard Goldblatt, for bringing me into the field.

The unreserved confidence that Reynolds Smith at Duke University Press has shown in this project is heartily appreciated. The Asian Collection of the University of Texas General Library and the unfailing help of its director, Kevin Lin, were also indispensable for the completion of this work. The Pacific Cultural Foundation of the Republic of China supported the final stage of my work on the manuscript with a writing grant in addition to providing a publication subsidy. I would also like to express my gratitude to my friend and colleague Jeannette Faurot, who had to shoulder extra teaching and administrative responsibilities while I took a research leave between 1989 and 1990. Finally, the inexhaustible patience and high-spirited support from my husband Fred Wang and our son Eric have made the process of writing this book a truly memorable experience in my family life.

Unless otherwise indicated, translations of passages from the Chinese originals are my own.

Dates of Major Authors

Ch'en Ying-chen (b. 1936)
Ch'i-chün (b. 1917)
Ch'i-teng Sheng (b. 1939)
Chu Hsi-ning (b. 1926)
Li Ang (b. 1952)
Li Yung-p'ing (b. 1947)
Lin Hai-yin (b. 1919)
Huang Ch'un-ming (b. 1939)
Ou-yang Tzu (b. 1939)
Pai Hsien-yung (b. 1937)
P'an Jen-mu (b. 1920)
Wang Chen-ho (1940-1990)
Wang Wen-hsing (b. 1939)

CHAPTER ONE

Introduction

The death of President Chiang Ching-kuo of the Republic of China on Taiwan in 1988 marked the end of an era in postwar Taiwan. This era began in 1949, when China's Nationalist government, led by Chiang Kai-shek, retreated from the mainland to settle on the offshore island-province of Taiwan after being defeated by the Communists in the civil war. The forty-year period under the autocratic rule of two presidents from the Chiang family was characterized by remarkable continuity and homogeneity in the social, political, and cultural spheres. Drastic structural changes, however, began occurring at all levels of the society in the mid-1980s following momentous political changes initiated by Chiang Ching-kuo during his last two years—the lifting of martial law, the recognition of an opposition party, the removal of the ban on founding new newspapers, and the resumption of communication with mainland China at the civilian level. New intellectual and artistic currents have emerged, many with the explicit or implicit motive of reexamining existing orders. The present moment, therefore, offers an ideal opportunity to reassess the literary accomplishments of writers from Taiwan in the forty-year period as an integral historical unit.

With China split into two political entities with different sociopolitical systems since 1949, the tradition of the Chinese New Literature (Hsin wen-hsüeh) has also been traveling along divergent paths in the two Chinese societies.[1] On the one hand, writers in post-1949 Taiwan have been selective in developing their literary heritage; whereas revolutionary literature and "critical realism" were suppressed, the more inoffensive, lyrical-

2 Modernism and the Nativist Resistance

sentimental strand of New Literature has enjoyed great popularity. On the other hand, from the anti-Communist propaganda of the cold war decade of the 1950s, through the Modernist and Nativist literary movements of the 1960s and 1970s, to the expression of today's pluralism and burgeoning market-oriented mass culture, literary currents in post-1949 Taiwan have closely mirrored the country's larger sociopolitical transitions.

The elitist, Western-influenced Modernist literary movement of the sixties and the populist, nationalistic Hsiang-t'u wen-hsüeh yün-tung (Nativist literary movement) of the seventies may appropriately be regarded as "alternative" and "oppositional" cultural formations in Taiwan during this period, using terminology from Raymond Williams (112–114). As the Modernists adopted literary concepts developed in Western capitalist society, they simultaneously longed for an ideological transformation, taking such bourgeois social values as individualism, liberalism, and rationalism as correctives for the oppressive social relations derived from a traditional system of values. The inherent skepticism of the Modernists toward the dominant culture's neotraditionalist discourse, acted on fully in the later phase of the movement, was beyond any doubt potentially subversive.

The Nativist literary movement, in contrast, with its use of literature as a pretext to challenge the dominant sociopolitical order, may be properly considered counterhegemonic. The movement was triggered by the nation's diplomatic setbacks in the international arena during the 1970s. It provided a forum for native Taiwanese intellectuals to vent their discontent with the unbalanced political power distribution between mainlanders and native Taiwanese and with the socioeconomic problems that had accompanied the country's accelerated process of industrialization since the 1960s. The pronounced oppositional nature of this movement is evident in all three of its proclaimed goals: to destroy the political myth of the mainlander-controlled Nationalist government, to denounce bourgeois capitalist social values, and to combat Western cultural imperialism, which was thought to be exemplified by the Modernist literary movement.

For different reasons, each movement dominated Taiwan's literary scene only for a relatively brief period of time. By the late 1970s and early 1980s, the influence of both the Modernists and the Nativists had sharply declined, and some of their inherent shortcomings had become obvious with the passage of time. As most of the Modernist writers advocated artistic autonomy and were politically disengaged, the subversive elements of their works were easily coopted by hegemonic cultural forces and their critical impact consequently diluted. The more radical subscription to aestheticism by certain writers, moreover, was deeply at odds with the predominantly lyrical sensibility of ordinary Chinese readers. Even though the essential dynamics of the Modernist movement were not entirely exhausted with the loss of popular favor, both critics and general readers received the movement's most mature output in the 1980s with a disheartening nonchalance. In the meantime, the militant political agenda of the Nativists both threatened and bored middle-class readers, who were largely satisfied with the status quo. The resistant activities of the more radical Nativists, moreover, were increasingly channeled into direct political involvement. The subsiding of these contending literary voices thus paved the way for the rise of a "serious" literature more popular in nature and a resurgence of the lyrical and sentimental strain in the eighties. The younger generation of writers of this decade assimilated the technical sophistication of the Modernists and displayed a social awareness as a result of the Nativist influence. Their vocational visions, however, significantly departed from those of their mentors and were much more deeply conditioned by the market logic of Taiwan's increasingly commercialized cultural setting.

Critical discourse on Taiwan's literature of the last two decades has been deeply factional, and studies of Modernist writers, many of whom were heavily stigmatized in the overheated literary disputes of the 1970s, have been particularly scanty. In the United States, since C. T. Hsia observed in the preface to his *A History of Modern Chinese Fiction* (1971, second edition) that "Taiwan since 1961 has enjoyed a minor literary renascence of genuine promise, even though few Western readers are yet aware of its existence" (vii), scores of serious critical essays have been written about this literary phenomenon, and a collection of articles on Taiwan fiction, which included some seminal studies of the Modernists, was published in 1980 (Faurot). Nevertheless, no substantial scholarly treatment of the Modernist literary movement that covers both the early and late phases of its development has appeared in Chinese or English.

The present study, intended to fill this gap, examines this movement from several different perspectives. Chapters in this book separately treat the following subjects: the artistic reorientation of the Modernist writers that significantly distinguished their work from older forms of modern Chinese literature, represented in Taiwan by an older generation of writers active in the 1950s; the various ways in which the Modernists appropriated Western literary modernism; cultural criticism and textual strategies found in works of the mature stage of the movement; and, finally, the contesting voices of the Nativist critics in reaction to the Modernist project.

Western literary influences on Chinese writers and transformations of various literary "-isms" in Chinese hands have been favorite subjects of study in the field of twentieth-century Chinese literature. By arguing in this book that certain literary practices in Taiwan during the Modernist literary movement may be defined, in a specially qualified sense, as "modernist," I hope to engage in dialogues with scholars of Chinese modernist trends who confront similar issues of literary history.

The Modernist Literary Movement

The event commonly considered as having inaugurated the modernist trend in Taiwan's fiction was the publication of the literary magazine Hsien-tai wen-hsüeh [Modern literature] (1960–1973; 1976–), founded by a group of young writers who were at the time still undergraduate students in the Department of Foreign Languages and Literatures at National Taiwan University. In addition to creative work by Chinese writers, the magazine also published translations of creative and critical works from the Western modernist canon, featuring such writers as Franz Kafka, James Joyce, Virginia Woolf, William Faulkner, Thomas Wolfe, and D. H. Lawrence. Initially, the magazine served only as a creative writing workshop for a score of precocious, talented students of Western literature, whose artistic vision closely reflected that of their dearly respected mentor, Professor T. A. Hsia. Soon, however, it turned into a reputable center for literature loosely defined as "modernist," and, in the next two decades, the outstanding achievements of its founding members lent it even greater prestige.[2] In the preface to an anthology of works selected from the magazine, Pai Hsien-yung could proudly claim that the collection included work by nearly all of Taiwan's promising writers active during the thirteen years when Modern Literature was published (Ou-yang, Hsien-tai 15–17).

Although not all of the successive editors of Modern Literature, who included several established writers and students of traditional Chinese literature, necessarily shared the vision of the magazine's founders, the editorial policy of the magazine was clearly to introduce new modes of art distinct from the prevailing ones. Deserving of particular attention is the justification offered for this undertaking in the foreword to the first issue of the magazine, which serves as a de facto manifesto of the Modernists: "We feel that old forms and old styles are insufficient in expressing the artistic sentiments of modern people" (Lau, Foreword 2). The presumption of the statement, that there is a necessary correlation between the artistic form and the *episteme* of a particular historical moment, is reminiscent of claims made by Western modernists, especially British ones, in the early part of the century, explaining their literature as a radical break from the past.

Although one cannot be certain that Taiwan's Modernists indeed share the belief of many Western modernists that a rupture in human history in the modern age severed them from the entire past of human civilization, themes and techniques developed in response to the societal modernization of the last two hundred years—mainly in the West—have appeared repeatedly in their writings. Although these appropriations may have assisted certain Taiwan writers in coping with the onslaught of capitalism in their own society, nevertheless a considerable disparity exists between this Chinese version of modernist literature and its Western models. This disparity is a result of profound differences in historical and cultural preconditions between the West since the mid-nineteenth century and Taiwan during the 1950s and 1960s.

Scholars and critics of post-1949 Taiwan literature have fervently debated the adequacy of such a term as "Chinese modernism." Those sensitive to the derivative, imitative nature of Taiwan's Modernist literature have argued that the superficial modernist traits of most of this literature are not intrinsically motivated. Lacking the animating spirit of modernism that underlies its Western models, it "becomes ultimately more form than content, more stylistic and technical showmanship than a doctrine of profound philosophical implications" (Lee, "Modernism" 20). Underneath the modernist surface are thematic concerns of a very local nature or even feigned, unauthentic sentiments. In sum, the implied criticism is that the Modernists' appropriations of Western modernism only occurred at the linguistic and stylistic levels, with the cultural and historical content largely displaced.

The more negative critics, mainly from the Nativist camp, displaying a bias against modernism similar to that of Georg Lukacs, dismissed literary technique as something superfluous in itself, a formal diversion that prevents writers from engagement with truly important contemporary issues. Motivated by both socialist and nationalist ideas, these critics were primarily concerned with preventing Western capitalism from taking root in Taiwan, and they regarded the Modernists as heralding precisely that process. Thus they have emotionally castigated the Modernists for having voluntarily imposed on themselves, out of vanity, such spiritual disease as the alienation syndrome, existentialist despair, and nihilistic moral depravity—all symptoms of the malaise of capitalist societies not yet endemic in Taiwan. As the Nativist critic Yü T'ien-ts'ung humorously put it, the Modernists have just "sneezed at seeing someone else catching a cold."

Although these arguments contain valid points to receive attention in due course, both views are strongly evaluative, reflecting the Chinese critics' sense of anxiety about the movement's implication of a master-slave relationship between the Western and the Chinese. In fact, this anxiety is rooted in precisely the same external conditions that motivated the Modernists to adopt Western models; holders of these views come mostly from the same generation as the Modernists. The present study, from the vantage point of a later historical moment, intends to point out, however, that the question of whether Chinese Modernist literature is "genuine" or "fake," or whether it renders a perfect simulacrum of literary modernism in the West half a century earlier is insignificant. What really matters and makes the movement worth studying is that the modernist influences have in fact produced significant consequences in Chinese literature and culture from a national perspective.

The significance of Taiwan's Modernist literary movement, therefore, deserves assessment primarily in terms of its generation of new dynamics among contemporary Chinese writers and its redirecting of their artistic mode of expression. Such an assessment is the task undertaken in the central chapters of the book. The present chapter examines the cultural and intellectual context of this movement along two lines of inquiry.

First, the Modernist literary movement is seen as another instance of the larger project of Chinese intellectuals' emulation of Western high culture. Ever since the end of the nineteenth century, shocked by the devastating effect of China's encounter with hegemonic Western culture, modern Chinese intellectuals have embarked on various programs of cultural rejuvenation, the most potent formula for which consists in assimilation of Western cultural products. Taiwan's Modernist literary movement, as one of the latest in a series of such programs, inevitably displays some of its essential characteristics. Second, an important link is perceived between this movement and the liberal strand of thought in China's pre-Revolution era, especially that of the Anglo-American wing of intellectuals.[3] Taiwan's Modernists particularly stressed the principle of artistic autonomy, among other liberal conceptions of literature, and, by and large, have more thoroughly adhered to this principle than their pre-1949 liberal predecessors.

An Elitist Program for Cultural Rejuvenation

Scholars have often attributed the unusually strong influence of Western literature on Taiwan writers of the post-1949 era to the inaccessibility of the literary heritage of their own immediate predecessors. According to this argument, the banning of works by most pre-1949 New Literature writers created a vacuum that forced young writers in Taiwan to turn to foreign sources for literary inspiration. The more political interpreters of this phenomenon, however, have stressed the effect of the ubiquitous workings of cultural imperialism, contending that the prominent American presence in post-1949 Taiwan necessarily fostered excessive zeal for American cultural products.

While the arbitrarily created breach in modern Chinese literary history is regrettable, placing too much weight on the apparent discontinuity between literature in Taiwan and pre-1949 traditions sometimes unduly lures our attention away from certain consistencies in Chinese intellectual attitudes toward the West in both the pre- and post-1949 eras. Despite the different strategies adopted, similar patterns are discerned in the way Chinese intellectuals from different periods cope with their ambivalent feelings about hegemonic Western culture. The way founding members of *Modern Literature* perceive and justify their pro-Western position, for example, draws its strength from the persistently recurring hsi-hua (Westernization) discourse.[4]

The specific logic of the Westernization discourse entails an acknowledgment of the wretched condition of contemporary Chinese affairs and an enlightened acceptance or active assimilation of positive features of Western civilization for the ultimate purpose of self-rejuvenation. Thus, in the foreword to *Modern Literature*'s inaugural issue, Joseph Lau says that the editors do not want to deceive themselves by taking pride in China's past glory but instead would "face our own backwardness" (2). In assuming a self-critical stance, Lau goes on to declare that "the territory of the New Literature is desolate, if not entirely barren" (2). In a later issue, Wang Wen-hsing also claimed that the dissatisfaction with the current decline of art had motivated the young college students to devote their energy and time to the prospect of a "Chinese Renaissance" ("Hsien-tai" 4).

Editors of *Modern Literature* apparently conceived their efforts at invigorating modern Chinese literature with a liberal vision. Lau states in the same foreword that he and his colleagues would pursue their causes with "sobriety, wisdom, receptiveness, and modesty." Even Wang's more iconoclastic editorial note aims ultimately to beseech an attitudinal change among the conservatives. With a sprightly analogy, Wang compares in this note the potential opponents of the Modernists to tyrannical fathers who forbid their offspring to play ball, sing songs, ride bicycles, and listen to the radio—simply because these activities are all "Western" ("Hsien-tai" 6). The seemingly radical assertion of the supremacy of Western civilization in modern life is, after all, intended to elicit open-mindedness.

Such determined liberal efforts to maintain a receptive attitude eased the tension of the East-West confrontation somewhat and thus made the particular version of Taiwan's Westernization program less painful than some earlier ones. The Modernists, for instance, have been comparatively free of the sense of guilt and self-denial that tormented some advocates of Westernization in the May Fourth period.[5] As latecomers, they seem to have accepted the necessity of Westernization as a premise and to have perceived their own mission to be realizing its goals with dedication and intelligence.

The surge of the Westernization discourse is always motivated by specific historical circumstances. The 1960s in Taiwan in many ways resembled the 1980s in the People's Republic of China, when dynamic interactions with Western countries were endorsed by the government and the effects were visible at all levels of the society. For the intellectuals, closer communication with the West not only increased their knowledge of current Western thought but also incited an earnest desire to catch up with what was happening in the rest of the world. That literary modernism came to signify the latest, most advanced artistic development in the world, the "mainstream," was a direct consequence of its recent canonization in Western academia and an effect of the growing global influence of the West in the postwar years. As Western cultural products masqueraded under the guise of cosmopolitanism, the illusion that national boundaries might be in some sense obliterated was reinforced by the conception of the universal existence of a "modern condition." The vision of an artistic community in which absolute artistic criteria apply to every one of its members regardless of nationality was particularly appealing to young Chinese writers in Taiwan, who could not but be keenly aware of the backwardness of the cultural conditions in their own country and of Taiwan's peripheral status in the international scene.[6]

The function of modernist literature as a potent sign of progressiveness in Taiwan was a phenomenon shared with many other Asian countries in the postwar years. At the same time, aspiration for membership in the international elite frequently implied latent nationalistic motives, as the individual's artistic accomplishment would presumably also bring glory to his or her people. For these reasons Taiwan's Modernist literature departed from its Western counterpart in certain aspects. Most notably, seeing themselves as intellectuals in a developing country, Modernist writers in Taiwan typically did not share, except in a perfunctory sense, the disparaging view of modernity of twentieth-century Western modernists. Even in their bleakest moments, they never expressed such profound discontent with human civilization as Lionel Trilling described in his famous essay "On the Modern Element in Modern Literature."[7] Rather than participating in the modernist program of "cultural negation," these Chinese intellectuals often displayed unreserved confidence in the positivistic vision of Matthew Arnold, which, ironically, has been cited by Trilling as demonstrating a spirit categorically rebuked by Western modernists in this century. Arnold's optimistic view of modern culture as one that "signifies certain timeless intellectual and civil virtues" found many subscribers in Taiwan, such as the most influential critic-scholar of the 1960s, Yen Yüan-shu (Trilling 70).[8] In fact, the majority of Taiwan's postwar-generation intellectuals actively supported the country's modernization through technological advancement, regarding this process as indispensable for improving the cultural environment. The project of modernity as they conceived it may be very similar to what was described by Jürgen Habermas in the following words: "The project of modernity formulated in the 18th century by the philosophers of the Enlightenment consisted in their efforts to develop objective science, universal morality and law, and autonomous art according to their inner logic. . . . The Enlightenment philosophers wanted to utilize this accumulation of specialized culture for the enrichment of everyday life—that is to say, for the rational organization of everyday social life" (9). Although such ideals were extremely enticing for Taiwan's most Westernized postwar generation, they at times became dangerously deceiving. In Wang Wen-hsing's soul-searching novel Chia-pien [Family crisis] (1973), for instance, the visionary projection of a rationalized modern society characterized by "the ideal of order, convenience, decorum, and rationality" is in fact the basis for the hero's unjustifiably harsh criticism of the traditional Chinese family system. The young hero's fanatic belief that this utopian human relationship has already been realized in the "genuinely civilized" European societies of the nineteenth century, based on a crude understanding of some novel he has read, is apparently naive. Yet such an extremist position is a product of unexamined assumptions and prevailing myths about Western civilization unconsciously endorsed by many intellectuals in Taiwan.

Elitist Western modernist literature has performed another important function for Chinese intellectuals because of its potential to become a substitute for the aristocratic high art in classical Chinese tradition. In contrast to writers in many other parts of the third world, whose fetishization of a "national culture" reflects an intense fear of its doomed lot of erasure from history, modern Chinese intellectuals often suffer from a different kind of psychological complex, one deriving from an inflated cultural identity. Yet classical literary education in post-1949 Taiwan cannot be said to be of a very high quality. The euphoric rhetoric of the government's wen-hua fu-hsing (cultural renaissance) program, moreover, frequently performs a disservice to traditional Chinese culture by creating pretentious, kitsch images of it. Nevertheless, for contemporary Chinese intellectuals, the desire to live up to China's past glory proves to be a common psychological need, even though the ways in which the Modernists attempted to achieve this goal were very different from the methods of the traditionalists.

With their superior stylistic sensibility, the Modernists were unwilling to deceive themselves about the viability of traditional literary forms in a modern setting. Most of these traditional forms carry with them distinctive characteristics of their gentry class origins, which no longer find justification at the present moment of history. Even though the traditional literary style is still being practiced and is still appealing to certain readers, its lyrical refinement has degenerated with popular use. The worn-out poetic diction, often used as mere embellishment, coupled with May Fourth sentimentalism resulted in a florid but exceedingly anemic prose style. Literary modernism's vigorous demand for complexity and refinement in structure and language, in contrast, promised to meet the serious writers' need for a "new artistic idiom" in their attempt to create a modern Chinese "high art."

Despite their drastically different ideological content, modernist Western and classical Chinese literatures have certain affinities in terms of their aesthetic outlook. Some of Taiwan's Modernists, at least in their maturity, have been increasingly inclined to stress such points of convergence. The most obvious examples are such famous poets as Yü Kuang-chung and Yang Mu. As far as fiction writers are concerned, Pai Hsien-yung is an eminent example. Aside from the traditionalist view of history and culture found in his *Taipei jen* [Tales of Taipei characters] (1971), his latest novel, *Nieh-tzu* [Crystal boys] (1983), directly incorporates symbolism and worldview from his favorite classical novel, *Hung-lou meng* [Dream of the red chamber].[9] Wang Wen-hsing, too, has invoked concepts of classical Chinese poetic and ethical traditions to justify theoretically his Herculean project of language experimentation. His own style in "Wu-sheng yin-hsiang" [Impressions of five Chinese provinces] (1990) is vividly reminiscent of classical lyrical prose. Both writers, furthermore, have displayed exquisite connoisseurship of traditional genres of art and literature, such as k'un-ch'ü, the classic novel, and the lyrical prose of the late Ming Kung-an and Ching-ling schools. Therefore, although the strategy of the Westernized Modernists in dealing with the indigenous Chinese tradition consisted initially of ostensible self-criticism and self-denial, it is nevertheless underscored with an utopian ideal of synthesis, of eventually combining the "best" of both the Chinese and the Western traditions.

It is true that, in practice, before the movement entered its more mature stage, the bulk of Taiwan's Modernist works were only "modernist" in a superficial sense, in which "the outer mannerisms and traits of the modern are faithfully echoed or mimicked but the animating spirit has disappeared," to borrow from Irving Howe (22). Nevertheless, the intellectual orientation of the Modernist project has led Taiwan writers to terrain unknown to their Chinese predecessors, thus creating significant mutations in the thematic conventions of modern Chinese narrative.

If, as expressed by the frequently cited epithet of C. T. Hsia, the moral burden of modern Chinese writers (mainly referring to writers of the pre-1949 period) consists in their excessive "obsession with China," concerns with national destiny have played a much less significant role in writings of Taiwan's Modernists. Instead, the majority of the Modernists have been inordinately obsessed with "depth," as manifested in their preoccupation with psychological exploration, their fascination with the uncanny, and their general predilection for expressing the "truth" through symbolic methods. These writers have frequently ventured into forbidden zones, dealing with themes of sexuality, incest, and guilt; and they are undoubtedly at their best when grappling with such morally compelling issues as the ethical responsibility of the individual, fate, and the meaning of human suffering. This philosophical inclination is especially noteworthy for its departure from the largely pragmatic tendencies in traditional Chinese narrative as well as for its having compensated—or perhaps overcompensated—for the lopsided sociopolitical emphasis of pre-1949 modern Chinese fiction.

Artistic Autonomy and Liberal Ideals

The Modernists writers have been widely recognized—and have even received compliments from their opponents—for the refinement of their literary techniques. This accomplishment, in a sense, is a direct consequence of the Modernists' adherence to the principle of artistic autonomy. In particular, the belief in the autonomous status of art, in the intrinsic value of literary work independent of social use, has enabled the Modernists to effectively resist pressures to write according to political and moral prescriptions, pressures that, as scholars have repeatedly pointed out, constituted the most formidable hindrance to modern Chinese writers' cultivation of artistry. As a result, Taiwan's Modernist writers procured for themselves space for unconstrained artistic imagination almost unprecedented in modern Chinese history. On this account alone, the movement has implications reaching beyond its immediate context of post-1949 Taiwan history.

The way in which the Modernists conceived the notion of artistic autonomy and the various aesthetic principles ensuing from it is unquestionably derived from Western models. The American New Critics' formulations of such doctrines in particular have played crucial roles in shaping the literary outlook of Taiwan's Modernists, as several of them studied in American graduate schools during the 1960s. Here, rather than postulating their essentially formalist conceptions of literature, I will concentrate on unraveling some of their basic ideological assumptions.

The Modernists' belief in literature's nonutilitarian character and its possession of "intrinsic" rules and values may be seen as derived from Enlightenment rationalism, from the notion that aesthetics, constituting a distinct sphere of experience, must be allowed to develop according to its own inner logic. Despite the Nativists' disparagement of the Modernists' artistic view as decadent and escapist, evidence shows that the attraction of Western modernism for Taiwan's Modernists goes beyond the "art for art's sake" tenet and rests much deeper in its ideological assumptions. More specifically, the Modernists have perceived exceptional worth in the ideology precisely because of its promise to help them redress their own cultural deficiencies.

In his essay "Modernity—an Incomplete Project," Jürgen Habermas says that Max Weber "characterized cultural modernity as the separation of the substantive reason expressed in religion and metaphysics into three autonomous spheres," namely, science, morality, and art (9). The differentiation of these three distinct spheres, he continues, was a result of the disintegration of the unified worldviews of religion and metaphysics (9). Given the indisputable differences between Chinese and Western varieties of metaphysics, one may nonetheless argue that in the course of industrialization and modernization in Chinese society, a process similar to that of the collapse of religion in the West has occurred, which may be summed up, in an oversimplified manner, as the disintegration of neo-Confucianist moralism and the terms of interpersonal relationships stipulated according to the model of family hierarchy. With a common theme of father-son conflict, two of Taiwan's Modernists' most significant novels, Pai Hsien-yung's *Crystal Boys* and Wang Wen-hsing's *Family Crisis*—both of which will be discussed in greater detail in Chapter 4—have provided powerful testimony to the horrendous effect of this process on the individual conscience.

By offering bitter protests against the traditional ethical norms that are crystallized in the Confucianist notions of *chung* (loyalty) and *hsiao* (filial piety), these two novels have called into question fundamental underpinnings of the superstructure of contemporary Taiwan society. Notably, in both works, the battle against the social retention of traditional values is waged with the aid of Western conceptual frames. *Family Crisis* features as its central theme the conflict of bourgeois individualism with the concept of filial piety in a financially strapped modern Chinese family. That the hero is portrayed as a fanatic rationalist shows the degree to which the author is skeptical of the real efficacy of such an ideological transfer. *Crystal Boys* projects a more idealistic vision that recalls the countercultural movement of the sixties in this country, with its anarchic assertion of the emancipatory power of the Dionysian impulse, its celebration of youth and beauty in their ephemeral physical forms, and its romantic affirmation of the redeeming virtue of love. The author has further enriched the symbolic level of this book by infusing this vision with mythical themes from the Chinese classic *Dream of the Red Chamber*. The underground homosexual community of New Park in *Crystal Boys*, like residents of the Ta-kuan yüan (Prospect Garden) in the famous traditional novel, is ruled by the supreme order of *ch'ing* (sentimentality) and *hsin* (the heart), which can be both salvational and damning. This microcosm, however, is extremely vulnerable, as it is forever overshadowed by the law of the father—the dominant order of the patriarchal, Confucianist society outside the garden. The prominence of the father-quest motif in both *Family Crisis* and *Crystal Boys*—heroes in both novels are constantly searching for paternal surrogates—betrays their authors' anxiety over the general corruption of the terms governing human relationships in contemporary Taiwan society, terms that in history were solidly built on the patriarchal order.

In their attempts to transform this anxiety into art, Enlightenment rationalism has functioned for these writers at both the artistic and the ideological levels. At the artistic level, the notion of aesthetics and morality as separate spheres has provided them with the distance necessary for their relentless self-analysis, as both writers have made extensive use of autobiographical raw material of a profoundly disturbing nature. At the ideological level, visions of alternative cultural models conceived with emancipatory ideals have been used against pressures from neo-Confucianist ethical prescriptions. Even though both writers may still be somewhat skeptical about the new myths they have valorized, as a careful reading of their texts readily reveals, their strong desire to free themselves from the shackles of tradition while still maintaining moral decency—the primary virtue sought in the Western ideology in question—has been manifestly expressed.

In his illustration of the thesis that the detachment of art from the praxis of life is a historically determined process closely tied to the development of bourgeois society, Peter Bürger, in his book *Theory of the Avant-Garde*, cites Habermas as follows: "Autonomous art only establishes itself as bourgeois society develops, the economic and political systems become detached from the cultural one, and the traditionalist world pictures which have been undermined by the basis ideology of fair exchange release the art from their ritual use" (qtd. in Bürger 24).[10] It is true that an essential condition for the development of bourgeois society, the democratic political system, has yet to be instated fully in Taiwan. Yet, as revealed by such terms as "soft authoritarianism" or "totalitarian pluralism," coined by social scientists to characterize the hybrid nature of Taiwan's political practice, the state-society relationship in Taiwan departs from the commonly assumed model. For my purposes, it is important to point out that, under the state-monitored process of modernization, a bourgeois society with all its essential characteristics has been rapidly taking shape in Taiwan and that the Western-influenced liberals have served as an important driving force of this process. Before their setback in the 1970s with the rise of more radical political activists, the liberals presented a considerable threat to the authoritarian government, which was evidenced by the famous crackdowns on the magazines *Tzu-yu Chung-kuo* [Free China] and *Wen-hsing* [Literary star] in the sixties and *Ta-hsüeh tsa-chih* [The intellectuals] in the early seventies.[11] The Modernists, sympathetic with liberal ideals, had also been surreptitiously undermining the government's neotraditionalist cultural discourse by endorsing capitalist social values in their works.[12]

The Modernists' support for the principle of artistic autonomy is therefore in step with the larger direction of the overall social development in Taiwan. However, the confirmation that the Modernists' aesthetic doctrines are natural products of the society's contemporary development still leaves the more complicated problems pertaining to literary history. The extent to which the specific development of aesthetic features in this movement corresponds to the much longer evolutionary process of Western modernism is often debated but seldom carefully examined. It may be determined by tracing the stage-to-stage development of a prominent modernist trait, the shifting of emphasis from content to form and the conscious refinement of literary technique.

It is frequently noted that the Modernists have devoted exceptional attention to craftsmanship and exhibited unusual consciousness of language. It has been insufficiently observed, however, that, in the later stage of the movement, writers such as Wang Wen-hsing, Wang Chen-ho, and Li Yung-p'ing took a rather extreme aesthetic stance by ascribing an almost transcendent value to artistic language. These writers' dedication of many years' assiduous effort to the refinement of fictional language places them in the Flaubertian tradition of professional artistry. This phenomenon, following Marxist theories of modernism, can be perceived as reflecting the objectification of art in bourgeois society. As Jochen Schulte-Sasse summarizes Peter Bürger's points in the foreword to the latter's book, during the second half of the nineteenth century, in the period of aestheticism and symbolism, artists became increasingly self-conscious about "writing techniques, how material is applied, and its potential for effect." These concerns can be explained as resulting from the writer's desire to be in greater control of the means of production. Correspondingly, therefore, this period also witnessed "the aesthetic sensitizing of art's audience," presumably to prepare qualified customers for the commodity "art" (xiii).[13]

It is arguable that although Taiwan's Modernist literary movement has taken place in a "postmodern" period—since the 1950s and 1960s—and although many newer artistic trends and techniques have been incorporated by the Modernist writers into their work, the dominant tendency of this movement nevertheless is closest to the early phase of Western modernism, the late nineteenth century and early twentieth century. In other words, in the extremely compressed timetable of Taiwan's Modernist literary movement, one nevertheless discerns features such as the reversal of the conventional content-form hierarchy and the radical rejection of traditional writing techniques that can only be the result of a burgeoning skepticism about language and meaning. Most of the Modernists' explorations of language unmistakably reflect Western influences. However, more original experiments have also been done that are results of a new awareness of the unstable relationship between language and its referents as well as of a reawakened sensitivity toward the ideographic nature of the Chinese language. These experiments, especially those found in Wang Wen-hsing's two novels *Family Crisis* and *Pei-hai te jen* [Backed against the sea] (1981), and Li Yung-p'ing's latest story series *Chi-ling ch'un-ch'iu* [Chronicle of Chi-ling] (1986), which mark the apex of the development of modernist aestheticism in contemporary Chinese literature, merit more scholarly attention than they have received.

In asserting that the dominant tendency in the Modernist literary movement corresponds to the aesthetic phase of Western modernism, I am at the same time trying to refute the common belief that part of this movement is avant-garde. The theoretical basis of this argument is again taken from Peter Bürger's book, which offers a new perception of the avant-garde movement as something radically different from modernism. In Bürger's view, "modernism may be understandable as an attack on traditional writing techniques, but the avant-garde can only be understood as an attack meant to alter institutionalized commerce with art"; the two movements thus have drastically different social roles (Schulte-Sasse xv).[14] The extreme popularity of works with characteristically avant-garde stylistic features in the initial stage of Taiwan's Modernist literary movement was short-lived. Many writers who practiced the style later dismissed this tendency as superfluous, and some even reverted to extremely conventional narrative methods. As the principle of artistic autonomy soon became a subject of dispute and writers of the Modernist generation were busily engaged in either its defense or its criticism in terms prescribed by the socialistically inclined Nativists, there was no further development of the particular form of protest entailed by the avant-garde enterprise. At least for the Modernist generation, the informing spirit of the Western avant-garde movement, the radical turning "against the institution 'art' and the mode in which autonomy functions," has never been of any recognizable significance.

Given the argument that no distinct avant-garde tradition has been established in Taiwan, I would nonetheless point out that at least one important factor that laid the foundation of the avant-garde and other antiaesthetic trends in the West, namely, the recognition of the inconsequentiality of art in modern society, had a profound impact on the Modernists. The rational acceptance of art's ineffectuality in modern society by Taiwan's Modernists can ultimately account for a critical difference between them and the pre-1949 Chinese writers, including their liberal predecessors who fought heartily for the independence of art from politics. I will return to this point after examining another topic of interest, the precarious development of artistic autonomy within the larger historical context of modern Chinese literature in this century.

In the last two decades, critics of the Modernists have invariably blamed them for an escapist, decadent, and "ivory tower" mentality; it is perhaps time to look at these preponderant inclinations of the Modernists as effective means in their resistance of prevailing social and political constraints. There is perhaps no need to elaborate on the illegitimate, coercive, and frequently violent political impositions on Chinese writers in the last half century. However, it must still be stressed that moralists have imposed no less pressure on the writers by frequently criticizing them for indulging in depictions of "immoral behavior" or for failing to fulfill the "proper functions" of literature.[15] The struggle of modern Chinese writers for greater freedom from these constraints did not start, of course, with Taiwan's Modernists but has a history as long as the history of modern Chinese literature itself.

It is well known that modern Chinese literature came into being largely through the efforts of such eminent intellectuals and political activists as Liang Ch'i-ch'ao, who saw in Western fiction the potential to strengthen China. From the very beginning, therefore, this literature has been burdened with such great missions as "national self-strengthening" and "cultural transformation." The polemics of literary debates between groups of different ideological persuasions throughout the May Fourth period and the thirties generally centered on how to accomplish such tasks rather than whether they were beyond the proper domain of literature. Modern Chinese writers are exceptionally susceptible to political involvement partly because literature, once a required subject in the civil service examination, remained throughout China's imperial period an integral part of the education of the gentry class, from which the country's officials were selected. Although literature's practical functions for an individual's career advancement in the traditional system were largely dismantled with the founding of the Republic in 1911, the residual elements of the gentry code, which gave literature an important social role, have remained strong even to this date. The country's political leaders have repeatedly exploited this tradition as an efficient means to enlist intellectuals' support. Before the effectively totalitarian Communist government was established in 1949, however, voices against this particular form of abuse were often heard. Anglo-American liberal scholars, for example, played an important role in this protest.

Because members of the Hsin-yüeh she (Crescent Moon Society) known for their promotion of apolitical views of literature, served as an important link between the pre-1949 liberal tradition and that of post-1949 Taiwan, it may be useful to briefly examine the similarities and differences between their ideas about literature and those of the Modernists. Liang Shih-ch'iu, whose criticisms of the shifting demands of radical politics and leftist dogma were made known by his debates with Lu Hsün around 1924, is probably the most prominent figure of this liberal group. As Liang's writing documents, however, despite their distrust of the extreme utilitarian view of literature, the pre-1949 liberals never went so far as to sponsor the aestheticist view, which entails a more or less complete dissociation of art from the function of moral edification.[16] Liang's position to a great extent also represents that of Taiwan's liberal intellectuals, notably those of the Modernist generation. Yen Yüan-shu, for example, is known to have propounded the function of literature as "criticism of life." The difference between the pre- and post-1949 liberal literary scholars is that the latter tend to borrow authority more from the Western liberal-humanist tradition (represented by Matthew Arnold and F. R. Leavis) and less from the Chinese classics than their predecessors did.

The Modernist writers, too, have inherited from the Western liberal-humanist tradition the concept that literature's ultimate goal is to represent the timeless qualities of the human condition. Pai Hsien-yung, in his defense of Ou-yang Tzu against the Nativist attacks, has argued that the primary function of literature is to impart knowledge about "universal human nature" (Mo-jan 41–42). Wang Wen-hsing, despite his strong aesthetic tendencies, also sees the difference between serious and popular literature as resting in the former's power to "tell something about the meaning of life."[17] Insofar as they have viewed art as a privileged form of interpreting reality, the Modernists must still be considered to have endorsed a fundamentally moralistic view of literature.

What has significantly distinguished Taiwan's Modernists from their pre-1949 liberal predecessors is their pessimistic recognition of the inconsequentiality of literature in modern society. The seam between liberal ideals and the reality of bourgeois society has so widened in the course of Taiwan's social development that the Modernists could not but acknowledge the social limitations of their literary endeavors, although they may console themselves with the belief that art's positive functions apply to a select group.[18] The most pointed expression of the Modernists' views about literature's social function is found in a famous (or notorious, from the Nativists' perspective) speech, "Hsiang-t'u wen-hsüeh te kung yü kuo" [Merits and mistakes of Nativist literature], given by Wang Wen-hsing at the height of the Nativist literary movement, at Taipei's Tien Education Center in 1978.

In this speech, Wang Wen-hsing said that he believes the only purpose of literature is "to give pleasure"—nothing else (520). This pleasure, of course, is not defined in the hedonist sense. For morally inclined readers, he argued, pleasure is to be derived precisely from good literature's potential for moral gratification (521). Whereas his opponents argue that "good literature caters to the taste of both the naive and the sophisticated, low-brow and high-brow readers," Wang responds that "art by definition carries a class distinction" (522). A timeless masterpiece like *Dream of the Red Chamber* does not actually appeal to readers of all classes in the same way; some readers can see nothing but the love story between Pao-yü and Tai-yü, whereas others are enlightened by its intellectual themes and its insights about human nature (524). The self-styled proletarian writers are only deceiving themselves in believing that they write for the working class, since working class readers never enjoy reading their works. "They as a rule like to read stories that are as far removed from their real lives as possible" (521).

Wang's arid humor and profuse use of rhetorical irony succeeded in irritating his audience, many of whom sympathized with the Nativists' ideal of an egalitarian society. While Wang's speech revealed the fundamental conflict between the Modernists and the Nativists, it also made it evident that the artistic beliefs of the Modernists presumed such liberal notions as "social stratification" and "cultural pluralism," which precluded the grand scheme of nationwide cultural transformation envisioned by the pre-1949 writers.

Perhaps the critical difference between the Modernists' conception of literature's limited social use and similar propositions found in the pre-1949 era may be illuminated by a comparison of the Modernists and Chou Tso-jen. In his essays written during the 1930s and 1940s, Chou Tso-jen denied that art has any practical use and refuted the didactic *tsai-tao* tradition in favor of the expressionist *yen-chih* tradition.[19] Although there is a similarity in Chou's and Wang Wen-hsing's protest of the illegitimate use of literature by their adversaries, Chou's reassertion of the nonutilitarian aspect of art is clearly conceived in a traditional way. David Pollard has put it this way: "There was an underlying conception of the role of literature which arose naturally from his [Chou Tso-jen's] background. It was not something that made epochs, not the particular province of the exceptionally gifted man, but a normal activity for an educated man" (47). In traditional Chinese society, the function of literature is closely tied to the lifestyle of Confucian literati, who are supposed to engage in the cultivation of an ideal personhood as a daily routine. Chou Tso-jen's shift from writing "progressive" essays in the 1920s to writing on such subjects as flora, fauna, and local customs is generally perceived as a sign of the frustration of a man of letters deeply aware of his own powerlessness. From another perspective, this behavior may be compared to the wise man's "hibernation" in unfavorable times according to the long-standing tradition of the recluse, a tradition that has functioned negatively to consolidate the Confucian system of rule. It can even be argued that Chou's traditional familiar essays on trivial subjects are built on the Taoist metaphysical presupposition of the existence of a unitary principle underlying all animate and inanimate beings in the cosmos, which implies a passive but nevertheless optimistic worldview.

By contrast, the Modernists are more fundamentally pessimistic. Their concession to the inefficacy of literature under the totalizing social system of modern times leads to a rational resignation, a withdrawal from the public sphere and a devotion to writing that, though it may be understood as affirmative, is not without a tragic resonance. The Flaubertian commitment to creative art as craft presupposes the institutionalization of art as a specialized profession in bourgeois society. In the Modernists' dedication to perfecting their craftsmanship, therefore, rests an overriding concern with effect on readers, which suggests a writer-reader relationship radically different from the model of traditional men of letters who treated writing as part of the lifelong project of self-cultivation.

Nonetheless, viewed from another perspective, the Modernists' preoccupation with the aesthetic use of language still in the final analysis enables them to come to terms with the sociological dimension of prose fiction. According to M. M. Bakhtin, "All languages of heteroglossia, whatever the principle underlying them and making each unique, are specific points of view of the world, forms for conceptualizing the world in words, specific world views, each characterized by its own objects, meanings and values" ("Discourse" 292). In such later works as Wang Chen-ho's *Mei-kuei mei-kuei wo-ai-ni* [Rose, rose, I love you] (1984) and Wang Wen-hsing's *Backed Against the Sea*, which I consider a masterpiece of Taiwan's Modernist literary movement, the principle of heteroglossia is consciously explored. Both authors' extensive parodic use of language is targeted at the unexamined ideological assumptions in contemporary Taiwan society, many of which come from residual worldviews from the past. Together with *Crystal Boys* and *Family Crisis*, these works are specific historical products of the cultural transition (or, in Fredric Jameson's term, the bourgeois cultural revolution) of Chinese society in Taiwan in the course of modernization, products that perform the function of "decoding" older value systems. The latent violence that underscores the seemingly relaxed East-West confrontation finally surfaces in the works of the Modernists' mature stage.

CHAPTER TWO

The Rise of the Modernist Trend

Writers active in the forty-year period discussed in this book are usually divided into three "generations," or *tai*—an approximate translation of "generation," although *tai* are only ten to fifteen years apart. Most of the Modernists discussed in this work, with the exception of Li Ang and Li Yung-p'ing, belong to the "middle" generation, who were in their early teens around 1949 and who started their literary careers under the modernist influence in the 1960s. As not uncommon universally, there was a tendency for the Modernists, as newcomers on the literary scene, to define themselves in contradistinction to their older contemporaries. The differences between the two generations of writers as perceived by the Modernists themselves have by and large been accepted by critics and commentators.

First, it is widely assumed that the Modernist literary movement reacted against the anti-Communist propaganda in literature in the 1950s. True, the Modernists' liberal tendency caused them to object to government-sponsored "combat literature" and to disapprove of writers who lent it their service. However, such an objection is directed more toward the politicization of literature than to the government's political stance itself. As will be demonstrated in later chapters, most Modernists were in fact staunch anti-Communists themselves, even though they did not necessarily endorse their own government's authoritarianism. The fact that the older generation of writers was more willing to compromise is partly explained by the tighter political control during the 1950s. Moreover, since many of them were mainlanders who followed the Nationalists to Taiwan around 1949,[1] these writers were in general more easily mobilized in the state-sponsored cultural programs.

Second, in addition to political propaganda, writers of the fifties are frequently faulted for their amateurism, which is partly the product of a special institution in Taiwan, the *fu-k'an*, or literary supplement to newspapers. The *fu-k'an* undeniably has been the most significant sponsor of literary activities in contemporary Taiwan; nevertheless, with its large demand for works with immediate popular appeal, it at the same time fostered casual, lightweight writings as well as middle-brow literary tastes. As literary writing became less professional, the distinction between artistic and journalistic genres was often blurred. It is understandable that the Modernists, who had a propensity for orthodox generic concepts and treated literature as a form of high art, were largely dissatisfied with the mediocrity that typifies writings produced in this environment.

Although the general climate in the 1950s was not conducive to the production of serious art, works of considerable artistic merit by a number of writers deserve greater critical attention than usually given to them. Even more pertinent to this study, the conventional artistic outlook in such works offers a context for understanding the range of changes that the Modernists have brought to Taiwan's literary scene. The first part of this chapter thus deals with two broad categories of writings by these older-generation writers, traditionalist prose and realistic fiction, represented by four authors: Ch'i-chün, Lin Hai-yin, Chu Hsi-ning, and P'an Jen-mu. The second part, then, explores various new artistic orientations ushered in by the Modernists, with illustrations drawn from the work of Ou-yang Tzu.

Writers of the Older Generation and the Dominant Culture

Traditionalist Prose

Contrary to the situation in the People's Republic of China, where gentry literature of China's feudal past was sometimes renounced for ideological reasons and where numerous political idioms designed to mobilize the masses were added to the vocabulary, the prose style in post-1949 Taiwan tended to be more literary, retaining a great many more archaic expressions and allusions to classical literature. This phenomenon is apparently a direct result of the cultural policy of the Nationalist government, which promoted traditional culture partly as a means to assert its own legitimacy as a Chinese government. In practice, the dominant culture's selective emphasis on the lyrical strand of New Literature from the pre-1949 era veered the stylistic development of literary writing in specific directions. The selection of works by such writers as Hsü Chih-mo and Chu Tzu-ch'ing for middle-school textbooks, for instance, contributed to the popularity of the former's exotic, flamboyant, European-flavored aestheticism and the latter's genteel, refined, traditional Chinese sensibility. Such styles, however, easily deteriorated with overuse by writers of lesser caliber.

The Modernists started their movement by launching harsh criticisms at the contemporary literary style, faulting it as heavily loaded with trite phrases and excessive embellishment, thus lacking in precision and originality. Much of their own language use, therefore, was conceived precisely to correct such tendencies. The success of their "language revolution" varies from writer to writer, but the Modernists' challenge of contemporary stylistic practice points to a deeper disagreement between their aesthetic conception and that of the traditionalists.

As the eminent sinologist Jaroslav Průšek put it, traditional Chinese literature is a refined, sensitive form of polite writing, one in which "all experiences had to pass the censorship of beauty[,] only what was *wen* or 'beautiful' being allowed to pass into the temple of literature, also designated *wen*, while all evil and ugly emotions were excluded" (10). Although more than half a century has passed since the New Literature replaced the old, traditional aesthetic assumptions and the "censorship of beauty" are still prevalent among Chinese readers and writers, especially among older people. Such readers inevitably find the modernist aesthetic disturbing. The Modernists have too frequently used the ugly, the sensational, and even the scandalous to shock. They are obsessed with the hidden darkness of the human psyche, and their exposure of conflicts in ethical relations is deemed both subversive and indecorous. A brief comparison of the thematic treatment of the father-son relationship in two well-known literary works, Chu Tzu-ch'ing's essay "Peiying" [Reflections of my father] (1926?) of the New Literature's lyrical strand and Wang Wen-hsing's Modernist novel *Family Crisis*, may bring into focus the fundamental difference between the traditionalists and the modernists. That both Chu's and Wang's works are to a certain extent autobiographical makes these works especially interesting, as they reveal ways in which these authors explore available literary conventions to cope with some deep personal concerns.

The narrator of "Reflections," at the time of writing, is tormented by a gnawing sense of remorse as he recalls his own insensitivity toward his father on an earlier occasion, when the latter saw him off at the train station. The son's annoyance at the father's inefficiency, clumsiness, and other signs of old age, while being vividly and honestly portrayed, soon becomes the subject for self-reproach. And the father's deteriorated state of health is quickly recognized as the consequence of his lifelong sacrifice for the family.

The son in Wang Wen-hsing's *Family Crisis* is so intensely enraged by his father's feeblemindedness and senility that he will not let him finish his birthday meal. After the miserable father runs away from home, the son, distressed and guilt-ridden, goes on a long search, only to come to the realization that, in the father's absence, mother and son have actually led a much happier and healthier life.

That in Chu Tzu-ch'ing's story the slight deviance from the norm of a filial relationship is hurriedly put into a "proper" perspective is dictated by the traditionalist literary convention, which endorses a moralistic worldview. The way Wang Wen-hsing dissects the love-hate relationship between father and son with a relentless candor, in contrast, reveals a modernist ideology: the ugliness of the son's emotion is used to demystify the socially constructed sacrosanctity of parenthood, and to acknowledge rationally the dehumanizing natural and economic laws that govern our lives.

The Modernists' radical use of literature to explore human reality upset the sense of propriety of the more traditionally inclined readers and writers. For them, literary writing served a different set of functions, which are best exemplified by the work of Ch'i-chün.

The proliferation of traditionalist prose in Taiwan during the 1950s, in the forms of the familiar essay and the hybrid genre of essay-fiction, was apparently a continuation of an earlier trend on the mainland during and after the Sino-Japanese War.[2] Although a number of writers (such as Chang Hsiu-ya, Chung Mei-yin, and Hsü Chung-p'ei) earned literary reputation as essayists, none of them is a match for Ch'i-chün, who has continued to be prolific and popular for more than thirty years. The subject matter of Ch'i-chün's writing is unusually repetitive: a striking number of works collected in her twenty-odd volumes are childhood reminiscences centering on a few characters and events. Even in works that resemble fiction, such as "Chi" [The Chignon] (1969), "Ah Yü" [Ah Yü] (1956), "Ch'i-yüeh te ai-shang" [The sorrow of July] (1971), and "Chü-tzu hung le" [The oranges are red] (1987), the autobiographical element remains strong. In fact, as nicely suggested by the title of a book on Ch'i-chün, Ch'i-chün te shih-chieh [The world of Ch'i Chün], the unfailing appeal of Ch'i-chün's work rests precisely in the authentic aura of the stories' persona, perceived to be Ch'i-chün herself.

The daughter of an illustrious scholar-official of the early Republican era, living in a country estate with her mother, Ch'i-chün had a childhood typical of the rural gentry, with which many older middle-class mainlanders identified. Many such readers saw in Ch'i-chün's works their own pasts recaptured: childhoods in the countryside, large households filled with the exhilaration of seasonal festivals, and the toil of classical lessons with austere family tutors. Then came the move to a larger city to attend Western-style schools and the hardships and separations during the Sino-Japanese War. Ch'i-chün's parents, the main characters of her works, also represent familiar types. Her father was a traditional scholar-official in an age of transition. Although open-minded enough to send his daughter to college, in his own home he was a patriarch who married twice and neglected his first wife, Ch'i-chün's mother. The mother, then, was a devout Buddhist who endured life's adversities with traditional female virtues. The attraction of Ch'i-chün's work for readers in post-1949 Taiwan is thus closely tied to the nostalgic sentiments of Taiwan's mainland expatriates.

In addition to nostalgia, the literati lifestyle depicted in Ch'i-chün's work embodies the older ideal of gentility: reading a book during sleepless nights ("When I had a dream at midnight, I took a book as my pillow" is actually a book title of hers),[3] relishing poetry over a pot of hot tea during a friend's visit—in short, treating everyday, ordinary events with cultured sensitivity and thus deriving aesthetic delight. Her literary competence distinguishes Ch'i-chün from numerous other writers on similar subjects. Her prose style is lucid and spontaneous, mixing classical erudition with the subtle musicality of natural language. Ch'i-chün's pedigree, the fact that she has studied under the famous scholar of *ts'u* (the "lyric," a subgenre of traditional Chinese poetry) Professor Hsia Ch'eng-t'ao and had a learned Buddhist recluse for a childhood tutor, further elicited respect from her readers.

The thematic aspects of Ch'i-chün's works are also pronouncedly traditional, as I will illustrate with a highly acclaimed story of hers, "The Chignon." "The Chignon" is a simple autobiographical story in which the author/narrator reminisces about a series of past events in which she sensed a tension between her mother and her father's younger and prettier second wife. She recalls how the latter's ornate hairstyle, an S-shaped chignon, was a constant reminder of her mother's inferiority in their competition for the husband's affection. The animosity between the two women, however, is dissolved after the husband's death, when they "become friends in their mutual suffering." At this time, the daughter's sense of indignation is also assuaged. After both her parents have passed away, she lives with her father's second wife and is then capable of empathizing with the aging woman who no longer wears fancy hairdos. The story concludes with a lament on the transience of life and the futility of the human struggle.

Both the narrator and her mother adhered to the principle of passivity. Instead of identifying the oppressor in an unjust system, here polygamy, the story evokes the virtue of *wen-jou tun-hou* (geniality and sincerity) and relieves personal grief with the Buddhist and Taoist principle of nonaction. The extreme popularity of this work is undoubtedly an effect of its potential to fulfill modern Chinese readers' yearning for certain residual cultural ideals. In this sense the work may be compared with two other memorable traditionalist works in modern Chinese literary history, Chu Tzu-ch'ing's "Reflections of My Father" and Yang Chiang's *Kan-hsiao liu chi* [Six chapters from my life "downunder"] (1983) (the latter is a PRC woman intellectual's touching memoir of her experience in a "cadre school" during the Cultural Revolution). Although all three authors harbor a sense of grief, they consistently refuse to view the cause of suffering from a sociohistorical perspective. The human wrongdoings that inflict pain on others, be they the grievance of a neglected wife, the loneliness of an aging father, or the more atrocious crimes committed during the Cultural Revolution, are absolved in the authors' dignified state of mind, best characterized by the phrase *ai er pu shang*—genuinely sorrowful and commiserative, but without rancor.

Although the lyrical works of Chi-chün are remarkably successful, her attempts at writing realistic modern fiction are, with few exceptions, full of blunders. In her short stories collected in *Ching chieh* [Sister Ching] (1956), for example, visions similar to those found in her essays are conveyed at the expense of oversimplified human relationships and idealized characters, giving her work a heavy dose of sentimentalism and didacticism. Evidently, the traditional mind-set, the ideological force behind the popularity of Ch'i-chün's essays, is inherently in contradiction with the very generic conventions of the modern short story that the Modernists endeavored to consolidate.

Realistic Fiction

Having in their formative years been exposed to works of Lu Hsün, Mao Tun, Pa Chin, and Lao She, writers of the older generation by and large carried on the Chinese "realist" tradition—a somewhat atrophied version of nineteenth-century European realism—established during the May Fourth era and the thirties. For political reasons, however, they consciously or unconsciously modified those realistic conventions that might have been offensive to the dominant culture of the post-1949 Taiwan: revolutionary and proletarian themes were taboo, and references to class-consciousness were also to be avoided. Nevertheless, the nature of literary conventions is such that their suppression can never be as complete as it appears on the surface. From a scholarly point of view, the textual strategies employed by these writers to transform subtly highly tendentious Chinese realistic conventions in order to fulfill a different set of ideological requirements are of great research interest.

The 1950s saw the publication of several well-written, "anti-Communist" realistic novels, such as *Yang-ko* [Rice-sprout song], *Hsüan-feng* [The whirlwind], and *Ti-ts'un chuan* [The Ti village]. Although important in their own right, the fact that these stories were set exclusively in pre-Revolution China and their authors either never resided in Taiwan (e.g., Eileen Chang) or were marginal to Taiwan's literary scene (e.g., Chiang Kuei and Ch'en Hsi-ying) diminishes their significance to Taiwan's post-1949 literary history. Far more relevant are such writers as Wang Lan, Meng Yao, P'an Jen-mu, Lin Hai-yin, Nieh Hua-ling, P'eng Ko, Chu Hsi-ning, Tuan Ts'ai-hua, Ssu-ma Chung-yüan, and Chung Chao-cheng, writers who established their literary reputations around the mid-1950s and who have ever since played prominent roles on Taiwan's literary scene.[4]

Although these writers' fiction works are also filled with nostalgic recollections of the mainland past, they are nevertheless unique products of the contemporary cultural and political environment. On the one hand, unmistakably, the emancipation ethos, a legacy of pre-1949 realist literature, has informed a number of their writings set in the past on subjects such as the oppression of women, the repressive nature of the traditional Chinese family system, and the pathetic condition of working-class people and domestic servants. On the other hand, the realistic codes have been rewritten and the critical messages mitigated or displaced: rightist political convictions and active support for the present government frequently caused these writers to domesticate the revolutionary spirit with counterdevices and to shift the thematic focus from the sociohistorical to the private domain.

Extrinsic political motives and conformist spirit have considerably stigmatized the work of writers of the older generation in the eyes of serious literary critics. The following discussion of three representative writers of this group, by no means adequate to redress this critical bias, will nevertheless concentrate on a commonly misunderstood aspect of their works, namely, the way in which ideological messages are expressed—or, rather, suppressed—and the frequently adverse effect of their ideology on their art.

An English anthology of Taiwan fiction, *The Unbroken Chain*, includes a story by Lin Hai-yin, "Ch'un-chiu" [Lunar New Year's feast] (1953) (68–73), which satirizes the snobbery and a certain "transit passenger" mentality of some well-to-do mainlanders in Taipei, whose privileges were closely tied to the Nationalist bureaucracy.[5] Although this story shows Lin at her best as a realistic writer, its explicit criticism of contemporary social reality is by no means typical of her work as a whole. Much more frequently found in her work is a healthy, forward-looking attitude toward life, best exemplified by such lighthearted domestic comedies as "Lü-tsao yü hsien-tan" [Green seaweed and salted eggs] (1956), the title story of an English translation of Lin's work.

The private domain of life has been a focus of attention in literature of the liberal camp of writers throughout modern Chinese history. The Wen-hsüeh yen-chiu she (Association for Literary Studies), for instance, advocated a "literature for life's sake"; and members of the Crescent Moon Society are known for their delicate taste for humor and their subtle appreciation of the "joy of life." At times, Lin's pragmatic spirit reminds one of the May Fourth woman writer Ling Shu-hua, whose heroines, when tested by life's adversities, often find recourse in the virtues of moderation and prudence. Many of Lin's stories that deal with the hardships of middle-class families in the 1950s are also underscored by a compromising spirit.

In stories that are set in the past, Lin sometimes displays a critical edge comparable to that of the best realistic writers of the thirties. Two such stories, "Chu" [Candle] (1962) and "Chin Li-yü te pai-chien ch'ün" [Golden carp's wedding gown] (1964), deserve special attention for their dramatic plot structure and effectively conveyed feminist theme of protest.

The protagonist in "Candle" is the mistress of a mandarin family in the earlier part of the century. When her husband takes a servant's daughter, Autumn Girl, as concubine, she fakes an illness and becomes bedridden. The mistress's withdrawal from her normal life and household responsibilities has a malicious, vengeful edge—Autumn Girl must shoulder all the domestic chores in addition to waiting on the invalid. When after a long day's hard work, Autumn Girl retires to her bedroom where their husband is waiting, the mistress, wide awake, would listen attentively with gnawing jealousy to their flirtatious laughter. Eventually, the bedridden mistress outlives everyone to become a nuisance to her son's family. Always huddled in a dark corner of her bedroom, the aged woman is seen with a small section of burnt-down candle, an apt symbol of her self-consuming pains.

Golden Carp, the heroine of another story, is a slave girl who at the age of sixteen has been taken by the master of the house as a concubine. She soon gives birth to a son, which is seen as a woman's highest accomplishment in life, comparable to a man's passing the imperial examination. Whereas the son comes to enjoy a high status as the only male offspring of the house, Golden Carp remains a lowly concubine, no more respected than a bond-maid. When the time comes for her son's wedding, however, Golden Carp feels that her real status should finally be acknowledged. Now that it is the Republican era, she ponders, people should be entitled to a certain degree of freedom. She quietly orders for herself a resplendent outfit, a skirt of "a hundred plaits," made of bright red brocade, embroidered with golden magpies and plum blossoms. According to the old custom, however, such magnificently decorated dress is only to be worn by the real ladies of the house, and Golden Carp's presumptuous attempt at elevating her own status is easily defeated: the mistress suddenly announces that on the wedding day the women in the family will all dress in the modern-style ch'i-p'ao, which is, after all, the latest fashion in town.

Lin has written several other stories on similar subjects, such as "Hsün" [Buried alive] (1957)—in which the virgin widow, a willing victim of the feudal chastity code, substitutes for conjugal love a secret admiration of her brother-in-law—and several episodes in Lin's autobiographical story series, Ch'eng-nan chiu-shih [Old stories of south Peking] (1960), but their critical messages are much more implicit. "Candle" and "Golden Carp's Wedding Gown" are distinguished by their tragic overtones. The characters' resistance to a dehumanizing system, though ultimately futile and self-destructive, is nevertheless a gesture of defiance. Moreover, by registering the complexity of domestic politics in China's patriarchal society, the author exposes the mechanisms by which women are made their own worst enemies. She has thus effectively criticized the oppressive social system without making any particular class the scapegoat.

However, the framework of these stories potentially disqualifies them from consideration as works of "critical realism." Both works begin and end with the presence of a grandchild of the heroine, which relegates her story to one of a bygone age. The children's ignorance of the wretched condition of women of their grandparents' generation, while being a source of dramatic irony, also serves to reassure the reader that the historical conditions responsible for such unjust treatment of women no longer exist. The new society, if unaware of the evils of its own past, is nevertheless more civilized and enlightened. Therefore, instead of criticizing social ills or the feudal remnants in contemporary Taiwan society, the author reinforces the reader's contentment with the present. One can perceive a subtle affinity between the thematic device in these stories and that of the more blatantly political i-k'u (remembering the hardship of the past, namely, the days before "Liberation") motif in the People's Republic of China: in both cases, criticism of China's feudal past serves to ratify the present sociopolitical order.

Born to a Christian gentry family in northern China, Chu Hsi-ning served in the Nationalist army from the time of the Sino-Japanese War and has been Taiwan's best-known military writer since the mid-1950s. The majority of Chu's early fiction, collected in *Lang* [Wolf] (1963), *T'ieh-chiang* [Soup of melted iron] (1963), and *P'o-hsiao shih-fen* [At daybreak] (1967), is set against the background of China in the 1930s and 1940s, especially in the rural areas. Although Chu has admitted that these stories are built on rather hazy memories of his mainland hometown, which he left at a rather young age, several critics have remarked that Chu's fiction could easily be taken for works that were written in the thirties. This comment powerfully attests to the notion of intertextuality, to the fact that literary texts are primarily produced by other literary texts rather than reflecting the authors' observation of an "objective" reality. However, although on the surface Chu's work closely resembles the realist literature of the thirties, its ideological content is almost opposite in nature.

The historical and geographical settings of many of Chu's stories are strongly reminiscent of Mao Tun's "Spring Silkworms" and Wu Tsu-hsiang's Anhwei stories. Their rural characters, too, seem to suffer from the same social ills prevalent in that particular period of modern Chinese history: bandits, landlords, corrupt officials, and a collapsing rural economy. However, the registration of such disturbing social conditions in Chu's fiction seldom leads to logical inquiry about the complex historical factors behind them. Typically, disasters are explained in terms of personal eccentricity, moral conflict, or the capricious workings of fate. The frequent employment of a naive narrator also conveniently serves the purpose of evading political judgment.

For example, the rampant bureaucratic corruption and moral degeneration of the land-owning gentry class in "P'o-hsiao shih-fen" [At daybreak] (1963) is not criticized as a historical phenomenon but presented with dark humor, and it merely serves as the background of the young hero's initiation into an unconvincingly portrayed adult world. The amusing short piece "Lo-ch'e shang" [On the mule cart] (1957) mentions nothing about the imperialism, capitalism, class exploitation, or foreign aggression that have apparently forced Chinese peasants like the Ch'e family to sell their land at a loss. Instead, it focuses on a simple didactic message: in bad times, a gentleman goes out of his way to help a neighbor in need. It seems that the chivalric spirit of the individual alone is sufficient to redress the wrong and to teach a lesson to the greedy landlord. "Hsiao Ts'ui yü Ta Hei-niu"

[Little Jade and Big Black Ox] (1960) deals with a young man's frustration with his family-arranged marriage when he secretly admires his cousin, but the potential marital tragedy is displaced by an implausible comic ending. Finally, although Chu's well-known story "T'ieh-chiang" [Soup of melted iron] (1961) may well be a story about the country folk's reaction to the onslaught of a modern economy, as Cyril Birch has suggested, its emphasis on the turning of the wheel of fortune and its exaggeration of the extremity of an outmoded heroic code clearly makes individual eccentricity, rather than realistic comment on the historical process, its explicit thematic focus. At times, therefore, it becomes evident that Chu is deliberately rewriting the realistic conventions to express his disagreement with the leftist ideological messages inscribed in them.

Viewed from today's vantage point, two salient features of Chu's fiction may also be observed. First, in a significant sense, Chu's re-creation of an image of pre-Revolution China and his intertextual references to its realist tradition without its original ideological inscriptions have sprung from a young soldier's nostalgia for a lost homeland, and the motivation behind his evocation of the pre-1949 literary tradition is more sentimental than artistic.[6] In one of his early stories, "Yeh shih tzu-wei" [It's a different taste] (1963), Chu included a rather incongruous comment that randomly associates hung-kuei, a Taiwanese rice cake dyed with red food color, with a "hot steamed bun dipped in human blood to cure tuberculosis," alluding to Lu Hsün's "Yao" [Medicine]. As the analogy serves absolutely no thematic purpose in the story, it should rather be taken as a gesture of memory.

Second, although Chu has frequently displaced the critical themes of realist literature with more purely literary effects—suspense, dramatic tensions, imaginative plots inspired by folk legends, and vividly rendered dark humor, even burlesque—he seems to be also consciously developing his own ideological system. Whereas one sometimes discerns in Lin Hai-yin a self-conscious evasion of sensitive topics and a voluntary compliance with political guidelines (her stories, for example, satisfy well the government's demand for the depiction of the "brighter" side of society), Chu Hsi-ning is a more self-motivated conversative. Over the years, Chu has evolved an ideological outlook that goes beyond the government-imposed doctrines and combines Christian moralism, cultural sinocentrism, and a nativism that presumes an undivided China: the name of a literary club formed by Chu and his younger protégés in the late 1970s, the "Double-Three Bookclub," for example, is explicitly ideological (the two "threes" stand for the Christian Trinity and Sun Yat-sen's Three People's Principles, respectively); a 1981 essay collection by Chu, *Wei-yen p'ien* [Chapters of minced words], features a sentimental cultural chauvinism that extols everything Chinese;[7] and Chu's nativism, while different from the Taiwanese regionalism advocated by the Nativists, shares with it a tendency to romanticize the more primitive values of an agrarian community and to condemn modernization for its threat to the pastoral lifestyle.

The ambition to develop an ideological system of his own seems to be already discernible in "Lang" [Wolf] (1961), an early story that received a great amount of critical attention. "Wolf" describes how an orphan boy's childless aunt, who mistreats the boy because she was offended by the boy's reluctance to call her "mother" on the first day she adopted him, is able to repent her wrongdoings after being remonstrated by the family's dismissed hired hand, Big Axle. The relationship between the aunt and Big Axle parallels the latter's battle with a shrewd wolf that repeatedly attacks the family's herd. The symbolic dimension of this story apparently makes reference to the Christian notion of the battle between goodness and evil, represented by Big Axle and the aunt, respectively. These characters are unmistakably allegorical; while Big Axle's uncompromising hatred of the wolf is lauded as an expression of moral righteousness, the aunt embodies a variety of sins—lack of mercy, dishonesty, and adultery. The ending, however, seems to alter the nature of the spiritual battle by unconvincingly revealing that the aunt's wickedness, especially her sexual promiscuity, is entirely motivated by her overwhelming desire to have male offspring. Thus the upholding of a time-tested community value, here the importance for a woman of having a son, is able miraculously to redeem the woman's other sins. Consciously or not, this ending seems to be adapted from the ending of Shen Ts'ung-wen's famous story "Hsiao Hsiao," in which the birth of a male child, though conceived by adultery, is so welcomed by the family of the child bride's young husband that she is spared punishment.

Chu's story has several obvious weaknesses: the implausible psychological transformation of the aunt, the poorly integrated thematic lines, and the fascinating but digressive dramatization of plot (for instance, episodes about the battle between Big Axle and the wolf are well written but unsubstantiated by thematic demand). None of these, however, is as disconcerting as the awkward attempt to ascribe transcendent value to the indigenous customs of old China.

Chu's slightly unorthodox version of the neotraditionalist conservatism of the dominant culture, although overly sentimental to the point of becoming an artistic liability, is nevertheless widely supported by a special social group in post-1949 Taiwan, the country's middle-class mainlander expatriates. It provided the basis for the development of a vital cultural trend during the 1980s, the "cultural nostalgia" trend, in which second-generation mainlander writers ardently participated.[8]

P'an Jen-mu's expressly anti-Communist novel *Lien-i piao-mei* [My cousin Lien-i] (1951), which deals with the activities of underground leftist students on a college campus in China on the eve of the Sino-Japanese War, at once shares specific formal features with the realistic literature of the thirties and differs from that literature by virtue of the ways in which it evades representation of the crude reality of history. Written in the realistic form used by such revolutionary writers as Mao Tun and Ting Ling, the novel tries to offer an ideological interpretation of a complex historical phenomenon, and is among a few post-1949 literary attempts to explain the traumatic loss of China in the fierce struggle between the Nationalists and the Communists. Exemplary of the cold war spirit, it attacks the Communists for illegitimately using the patriotism and vanity of young college students as instruments to usurp political power. And, to the extent that it tells a partial truth based on preconceived political views, the novel suffers from the same deficiency as many other works in the Chinese realist tradition.

It is therefore not the ideological committment itself that is at fault in this work. In fact, P'an's indignation toward radical politics on behalf of the ordinary Chinese citizen, as represented by the father in the novel, is certainly legitimate;[9] such law-abiding middle-level officials, who typically espoused moderate political reform, were precisely those most cruelly persecuted during the years when the Chinese mainland was ruled by an ultraleftist government. (P'an's assertion of the mainstream Confucianist philosophy of government, a philosophy that relies heavily on the good conscience and the moral rectitude of scholar-officials, in her other stories on contemporary subjects, such as "Ai-le hsiao t'ien-ti" [A small world of sorrow and happiness] and "Nao she chih yeh" [A night with the snake], further underscores this conservative political stance. In those stories, the characters' recourse to old gentry virtues to withstand hardship in difficult times, reminiscent of characters in Shen Ts'ung-wen's literary sketches written during the Sino-Japanese War, seems to be motivated not merely by political allegiance to the Nationalist government, but also by a belief in certain positive qualities of the Chinese intellectual tradition.) That this novel has largely failed to live up to the promise of historical representation is more appropriately explained by P'an's "middle-brow" artistic vision, very much conditioned by the commercialized urban environment of Taiwan, which, in turn, is a continuation of that in the big cities of pre-Revolution China. With her delicate sensitivity to the irrational forces of life and to human perversity, and her strong inclination to interpret experience in terms of its unpredictability, P'an shows a close affinity with such urban women writers of the 1940s as Su Ch'ing and Eileen Chang, who frequently treated history as mere background for their stories of romance.[10] P'an's serious intentions in *My Cousin Lien-i*, therefore, are often trivialized by recurring bathos, witty but frivolous dialogues, and a melodramatic plot. If, as C. T. Hsia has observed, realistic novels of the thirties frequently suffer from ideological dogmas, unimaginative dialogues, and excessive length, then the problem of *My Cousin Lien-i* is precisely opposite: it is the generic traits of middle-brow popular fiction that have deflated the work's capacity to represent history.

P'an's fondness for coincidence and melodramatic plots has occasionally achieved positive artistic effects in her short stories collected in *Ai-le hsiao t'ien-ti* [A small world of sorrow and happiness] (1981). One best example is the frequently anthologized piece "Yeh-kuang-pei" [Jade cup that glistens at night] (1963), which, by focusing squarely on the chance element in life, manages to create a sense of irony reminiscent of Maupassant.[11]

In sum, although works by writers of the older generation are not without artistic merit, their ideological outlook is deeply embedded in the conservative dominant culture of Taiwan's post-1949 era. The rise of the young Modernists, with their liberalism and new aesthetic conceptions, challenged not only these older writers' artistic visions, but also the dominant culture's ideological control over creative writers. The changes brought forth by the Modernists in the artistic realm, discussed below, formed the basis for more radical cultural critiques to be dealt with in later chapters of the present study.

New Artistic Formulations of the Modernists

The Modernist literary movement created significant impact on contemporary Chinese fiction from Taiwan in both form and subject matter. In subject matter, the Modernists' endeavors to explore new spheres of human experience beyond the confines of traditionalist literature continued the efforts of their early-twentieth-century May Fourth predecessors and even surpassed them in depth.[12] To comprehend and analyze the complexity of human experience in the modern world, they generally favored rationalism, scientism, and serious, if at times immature, philosophical contemplations. In form, since, as some scholars have recently observed, the attempts of earlier modern Chinese writers to offer realistic portraits of life were frequently hampered by the dominance of the subjective voice in the work's rhetorical structure, the Modernists tried to redress this deficiency by introducing a new "objective form." They were especially fond of manipulating narrative points of view to convey a relativistic view of morality. As such formal devices were primarily modeled on modern fiction of the West, writers from the *Modern Literature* group, being students of Western literature, naturally played a leading role.

Commenting on fiction writers of the *Modern Literature* group, Pai Hsien-yung, Wang Wen-hsing, Ou-yang Tzu, and Ch'en Jo-hsi, Leo Lee thus observed: "Judging from their early works, there is no doubt that all four of them demonstrated a stylistic consciousness inspired by modern Western fiction. Wang Wen-hsing, in particular, was a conscientious, though not always successful, practitioner of style and form" ("'Modernism'" 17). The radical experiments with language in Wang Wen-hsing's fiction will receive fuller treatment later. For a general understanding of the new narrative form that was introduced by the Modernists and widely assimilated by writers in Taiwan during the last three decades, no one serves as a better example than Ou-yang Tzu.

Ou-yang Tzu's total output of fictional work consists of less than a score of short stories written between 1960 and 1967, collected in *Na ch'ang t'ou-fa te nü-hai* [The girl with long hair] (1967).[13] However, her focus on the aberrant social behavior and psychological crises of alienated individuals and her punctilious observation of the technical rules of modern fiction as propagated by the literary departments in American academe has made her a pioneer of Taiwan's Modernist fiction.

It is interesting to note that, according to Ou-yang herself, she was initially attracted to the lyrical-sentimental style. Among her favorite writers in her earlier days were Ping Hsin and Chang Hsiu-ya, who appropriately represented the May Fourth lyrical strand and the traditionalist prose of the 1950s. After attending the eye-opening lectures of Professor T. A. Hsia in her freshman year, however, she was converted to "modernist fiction." T. A. Hsia's well-taken criticism of the sentimentalist tendency in modern Chinese literature was rooted in intellectuals' reactions against aspects of the May Fourth style that had already become popular in the pre-Revolution years.[14] Thus, one may argue that Taiwan's Modernist literary movement is intricately linked with the New Literary tradition of Modern China. Under Hsia's influence, the Modernists were not only sensitized to the romantic idealization and sentimentalism of May Fourth literary writing, but they also proceeded to consolidate Western-influenced literary forms based on their knowledge of Anglo-American formalist theories, thus bringing to fuller realization these forms' internal dynamics.[15] As the technical principles propagated by the Modernists played important roles in shaping the works of fiction produced in Taiwan since the 1960s, it is worthwhile to take a close look at Ou-yang's succinct run-down of these principles in the preface to her short story collection *The Girl with Long Hair* (*Na Ch'ang-tou-fa* 1–4).

The preface starts with a firm denunciation of sentimentalism as the patent flaw of modern Chinese literature as a whole. Having identified the human psyche as the focus of her thematic interest, Ou-yang Tzu proceeds to postulate several technical rules to be followed in short story writing. Citing Henry James' scenic method and the Aristotelian "three unities," she stresses the key role played by "structure" in a literary work, apparently privileging dramatic presentation over authorial narration. Then, using examples from her own stories, she advocates economical use of language and advises avoiding hackneyed expressions and allusions. The plots of her stories, she maintains, are carefully trimmed of irrelevant details and are seldom built upon improbable coincidence.

The remaining part of the preface concentrates on introducing the rhetorical technique of "objective narration." After asserting that the "tone" of the narration is the means through which the author conveys his or her attitude toward the subject matter and characters, she suggests that her attitude is mostly neutral and unbiased and that readers must not take the characters' point of view as hers, nor should they think it represents the "correct" view. Finally, she illustrates this nonjudgmental stance of the author with one of her own stories, "Chin huang-hun shih" [As the dusk approaches] (1965), in which three accounts of the same story from different perspectives are juxtaposed, but none of them is completely right or wrong. Readers are asked to compare them carefully, using their own judgment, in order to "correctly uncover the truth of the matter" (Na ch'ang tou-fa 4).

This preface implies that its author believes it is both possible and desirable to present an impartial picture of reality so that readers may be given the privilege of forming their own opinions and moral judgments. These ideas are more reminiscent of the realists' concept of literary representation than the modernist view of literature as self-referential discursive practice. Throughout the 1960s, in fact, the majority of critical writings introducing Western literary concepts focused on basic technical rules and critical criteria that have long been naturalized and taken for granted in the West. Authoritative U.S.-trained scholars and critics such as Yen Yüan-shu, Chu Li-min, and Wai-lim Yip systematically expounded the fundamentals of a whole set of Western literary codes, and their influence on creative writing and practical criticism in Taiwan was immeasurable. Such a phenomenon is actually not very difficult to understand, given that literary genres of the short story and the novel (in the strict sense) have been imported from the West only in this century. That Chinese writers aspire to excel in these genres on their own terms and are eager to learn their original formal requirements is witnessed not only by writers of Taiwan in the 1960s but also by writers in the People's Republic of China in the 1980s, when "modernist fiction" once again became fashionable.[16] It is also true, however, that the appropriation of foreign literary codes always goes beyond the mastery of basic techniques and necessarily involves larger, more complicated networks of artistic and ideological systems. One of the major arguments of the present study is that, in the Modernist literary movement of Taiwan, a few dedicated writers have actually appropriated literary modernism at a deeper, ideological level and assumed aesthetic views that are far more complex than those set forth in Ou-yang's preface. This phenomenon will be the central focus of the third and fourth chapters. For the moment, my concern is with the more general impact of the technical principles introduced by the Modernists, which I will discuss from two angles: first, the establishment of a set of thematic conventions that supposedly incorporate advanced knowledge of human behavior made available by the modern sciences and, second, the replacement of older formal conventions by new ones, especially privileging the "objective" narrative form in fiction writing.

The Psychological Paradigm

A number of new Modernist themes came into fashion because of their broad appeal to young writers eager to explore the dark forest of human heart. However, as many writers of the 1960s were relatively sheltered middle-class college students, the tendency to substitute categories of abstract knowledge obtained from book reading for the actual observation of life was exceedingly strong. Apparently influenced by popular versions of Freudian psychoanalysis, Ou-yang was particularly fascinated with abnormal interpersonal relationships. Several of her other stories have focused on the scandalous revelation of an abnormal psychological trait. The mother in her "Mo-nü" [The bewitched woman] (1967), for example, is revealed in the end as a lifelong slave of a possessive passion for her lover, which makes her incapable of any normal relations in life. The revelation shocks because she has successfully deceived everyone with the image of a loving mother. The young wife in "Wang" [Net] (1962) cannot marry her former lover because of a masochistic tendency shared by both: both parties are too eager to sacrifice, too sensitive to the other's feelings, so that they torment each other to an unbearable degree. Ou-yang was by no means the only writer that has demonstrated an interest in the abnormal. Most other young Modernists have written stories featuring imaginary post-Freudian middle-class spiritual dilemmas: Wang Wen-hsing's "Mu-ch'in" [Mother] (1960), for example, deals with a psychotic mother who has an incestuous attachment to her teenage son; Pai Hsien-yung's "Hsiang-kang, 1960" [Hong Kong, 1960] (1964) tells the sad story of a high-class woman refugee in Hong Kong who has degenerated to the most depraved form of sensuality and humiliated herself by taking a rascal as a lover; and the list goes on to include Shui Ching's "Mei-yu lien te jen" [A man without face] (1962), Ch'en Ying-chen's "Wen-shu" [Documents] (1963), and many others.

The Modernists' consciousness of form and their treatment of the literary text as primarily self-referential were not fully developed until some time later. Works produced at the early stage of Taiwan's Modernist literary movement, such as the ones mentioned above, were mainly conventional stories with unrealistic subject matter, too closely inspired by literary or nonliterary texts from Western sources. With her usual candor, Ou-yang admitted that "The Bewitched Woman" was adapted from an American television soap opera and that "As the Dusk Approaches" was written right after she completed a term paper on Faulkner's *As I Lay Dying*.[17] From the historical point of view, such quasi-psychological fiction is certainly not as enduring as the Nativist works that took contemporary life in Taiwan as their model.

Nevertheless, from the point of view of technical advancement, the Modernists must be given credit for having called attention to mechanisms involved in transforming raw material into art and thus preparing for more sophisticated formal innovations. Pai Hsien-yung has cited T. A. Hsia in asserting that "what to say" in a literary work is not as important as "how to say it." Wang Wen-hsing has even more aggressively contended that the writer should be solely concerned with how to manipulate the reader's response. The significance of these artistic conceptions must be comprehended in the proper context, namely, in view of their drastic departure from the more traditional expressive view of literature and narrative conventions. Whereas critics may accuse the Modernists of devoting too much energy to craftsmanship, to the extent that they have neglected the thematic content of their work, it may also be argued that the narrative paradigms of psychological fiction established during the early stage of the Modernist literary movement actually nourished such major works as the later novels of Wang Wen-hsing and Pai Hsien-yung with significant sociological implications. In a positive sense, vicarious knowledge about life acquired from translations of Western classics and the academic study of Existentialism and Freudian psychoanalysis lent the Modernists vocabulary and conceptual frameworks for in-depth psychological exploration that were not readily available to modern Chinese writers before.

Moreover, as any writer's fictional imagination necessarily reflects his or her private fantasies, which have roots in problems encountered in the process of the individual's socialization, even the artistically less mature works by the young Modernists reveal serious attempts by individual authors to come to terms with troubling psychological obsessions. In the work of Ouyang Tzu, for example, the disparity between one's self-image and a social persona seems to be a private concern repeatedly projected into dramatic moments of great emotional intensity. Her "The Bewitched Woman," "Panko wei-hsiao" [Half a smile] (1960), and "Tsui-hou i-chieh k'o" [The last class] (1967) all center on a traumatic anxiety about the unexpected public exposure of one's private, ignoble thoughts. This motif is easily seen as a projection of the author's own latent fear, so that the compelling effect of Ouyang's much celebrated story "Hua-p'ing" [Flower vase] (1961), superficially about a madly jealous husband's struggle to overcome his inferiority complex with desperate schemes that were uncovered to his utter humiliation, may be interpreted as a masochistic enactment of a haunting nightmare.[18] Wang Wen-hsing's stories that deal with a boy's initiation into adult love, fate, sexuality, and mortality—such as "Ch'ien-ch'üeh" [Flaw] (1964), "Ming-yün te chi-hsien" [Lines of life] (1963), "Han-liu" [Cold currents] (1962), and "Jih-li" [Calendar] (1960)—invariably foreground an obsession with the existential "meaning" of life. Such obsession receives a more forceful treatment in his later work. Pai Hsien-yung, as C. T. Hsia has suggested, has borrowed literary idioms from Western classics to express intimate aspirations that spring from experiences of a personal nature. In the case of another fine Modernist writer, Shui Ching, the recurring motif of humiliation registers the author's sensitive response to an alienating social environment as well as a wish to reassert human decency in a modern world governed by values of utility.

Thus, if most early Modernist stories lack originality in thematic conception, they reflect certain highly personal realities of their authors' lives. Although such psychological exploration is rather commonplace and cannot be said to have offered powerful new interpretations, the young Modernists' sincerity and bold, honest self-analysis broke new ground in Taiwan's cultural context: such efforts have redefined boundaries of normality in human behavior and thus have presented challenges to conventional ethical prescriptions and the conservative middle-class mentality that have been the backbone of the dominant culture of post-1949 Taiwan. It is in this sense that the early Modernists have paved the way for the more radical cultural reexaminations found in works of the movement's mature stage.

The Ideal of Objectivity

The most noteworthy formal feature popularized by the Modernists is the widened distance between author and text. In a sense, the Modernists' efforts to emulate Western modern fiction may be seen as having continued the general trend in modern Chinese literary history away from the traditional expressive view toward the mimetic view of literature. With their denunciation of sentimentalism and their express interest in the hidden complexities of the human psyche, personal emotions are no longer treated as the source or origin of literature, but rather as objects for detached observation.[19]

Having been immersed in sophisticated Western literary conceptions, the Modernists not only reject the simplistic notion that literary representation consists of edited records of either personal experience or observed human activities, but also underscore the more abstract idea that writers "re-create" events based on universal laws governing human behavior. Thus, Ou-yang Tzu writes, "The content of my work usually depicts the kind of reaction a person may have under specific circumstances and the kind of choices he would make when confronted with certain dilemmas. That he reacts in a particular manner, makes a specific choice, has a definite reason, and this reason can be traced and inferred from his environment, his past, or his personality" (Na ch'ang t'ou-fa 2). This clinical model of fiction as case history naturally produces works substantially different from those still influenced by traditional artistic assumptions.

Many scholars have pointed out that modern Chinese fiction writers, including such revered ones as Lu Hsün, favored thematic closure because they felt the author is to some extent obliged to endorse explicitly certain moral visions. The Modernists, however, consider any kind of explicit didacticism an insult to the reader's imagination and constantly endeavor to open up the narrative closure. One way is to stress the disparity between the author's and the characters' points of view; Ou-yang Tzu thus feels the need to remind her readers that "the character's point of view does not represent mine and is not necessarily correct" (Na ch'ang t'ou-fa 3).

While insisting that a good piece of literary representation is nonjudgmental and "objective," the Modernists are fully aware that this objectivity is only an artistic pretense. True, stories should be allowed to unfold without the intrusive authorial presence and direct preaching, but every single detail is still ultimately manipulated by the author, and the technical manipulation, mainly of plot and symbolism, has the final goal of effectively communicating specific messages. Although these messages cannot be characterized as moralistic in a superficial sense—since one major thematic import of the Modernist work is precisely to expose the relativity of conventional morality—they nevertheless always pertain to the moral sphere of human behavior.

It is crucially important to keep in mind that thematic indeterminacy and moral disinterestedness, which are characteristic of certain strands of Western modernism, are not prominent features of works by Taiwan's Modernists. Perhaps symptomatic of a consciously adopted rational worldview, many of Taiwan's Modernists, at least in their early careers, have had a strong tendency to define objective representation in terms of ways in which factual information is released or mechanical processes by which the represented reality is unfolded in plot. They thus frequently appear to be rather insensitive to the "epistemological incertitude" that has been foregrounded in works of early Western modernists. I would like to illustrate this point with Ou-yang Tzu's story "As the Dusk Approaches."

"As the Dusk Approaches" juxtaposes three different accounts of an intended murder resulting from a complex triangular relationship among three people—a young man in his early twenties, Chi-wei; his soft-skinned, fair-looking friend Yü Pin; and his no longer young but still attractive mother, Li-fen. Yü has an affair with Li-fen but intends to leave for another city. After Yü discloses his decision to Li-fen, Chi-wei, who is waiting for him outside in the garden, has a quarrel with him and finally strikes Yü near his genitals with a carving knife. The reader is presented with three monologues, by Li-fen, Chi-wei, and Nanny Wang, a witness of the accident, offering three disparate versions of the story.

Li-fen is bitter that another of her younger lovers has deserted her after learning from her the art of love, although, compared with her other lovers, Yü Pin seems to be more passive and lacking in passion. Her monologue also reveals that her life of self-abandonment is a consequence of the trauma of her elder son's death at a young age. Feeling that recently Chi-wei has been watching her and Yü with "cold, hateful eyes," she is inclined to interpret Chi-wei's attempt to kill Yü as a gesture of hatred and revenge toward herself.

Chi-wei's account discloses that instead of resenting his mother for never having loved him, Chi-wei apparently has an Oedipus complex and has pleaded with Yü not to leave this lonely woman. He and Yü Pin were homosexual lovers before the affair. Yü apparently started the affair with Li-fen to prove that he could live a normal, heterosexual life, and Chi-wei seems to have been vicariously having a relationship with his mother through his friend Yü. His attempts to keep Yü from leaving having failed, he again pleaded with Yü to "return to the old relationship." But Yü rejected both. Driven by despair and envy, Chi-wei apparently tried to castrate Yü rather than to kill him.

In Nanny Wang's interpretation, Chi-wei was justified in trying to kill his best friend out of his indignation over the illicit love affair and as an attempt to protect his father's reputation. Her account provides extra details that confirm the reader's suspicions about Li-fen's narcissism—that she loved her eldest son because he inherited her beautiful features whereas Chi-wei resembles her husband.

The story has apparently adopted the popular *Rashomon* device to drive home the message that reality has many phases.[20] With this device, Kurosawa offers the philosophical insight that the "truth" is forever lost in time, as a result of the impenetrable subjectivity of the three speakers in the film who give different versions of the story. The fact that each of them "lies," either intentionally or involuntarily, is not merely a result of ignorance. Rather, such untruths are dictated either by self-interest or by egoism, convincingly portrayed as universal human traits. Therefore, by stressing the ultimate inaccessibility of truth to individual consciousness, the film intensifies the "existential anxiety" and conveys a profound epistemological doubt.

Although Ou-yang Tzu also stresses that everyone's interpretation of the episode was inevitably conditioned by certain predispositions, the structure of her story is actually that of a detective story, in which the "true story" may be recovered as long as sufficient information is provided. In each of the three accounts, a partial picture is presented either because the narrator is ignorant of certain crucial facts or because the narrative account itself is elliptical. By drawing together the scattered clues, the reader can easily patch together a complete story, which is nothing less than "the truth of the matter." Ou-yang's belief in the existence of an original story reveals that she is more interested in the empirical process of storytelling than in the epistemological question involved in the human perception of reality or the narrative act itself. Since unearthing this original story is all that is required to understand the cause and effect of the actions depicted, the reading process offers the reader intellectual satisfaction rather than provoking philosophical contemplation.

The narrative device of Ou-yang Tzu, of course, serves its own thematic functions. Most of her stories, like the three individual pieces in "As the Dusk Approaches," are told from a single narrative perspective, with a unitary linguistic consciousness—mixed points of view are consciously avoided, and alternative perspectives are introduced largely through other characters. This narrative device facilitates the presentation of Ou-yang's favorite theme, the self-deceiving, self-alienating individual confined by limited visions of reality. This limitation, unlike the universally entrapping egoism in Kurosawa's film, is a pathological trait. Thus, although the actual contour of "reality" is hidden from a certain character's conscious knowledge, it is nevertheless readily accessible to other characters or to any uninvolved spectator. The dramatic effect of her stories thus comes from the tension between a known (or easily known) truth and the unenlightened individual blinded by specific, often excessive forms of psychological obsession. The author, as creator of the story, enjoys absolute power and does not seem to be bothered by the problems involved in the process of generating meaning.

The early Modernists have consciously invested narrative form with thematic implications and manipulated the narrative point of view. Though hardly a uniquely modernist concern, the correspondence between form and content has been so thoroughly explored by the Modernists that a new territory has been charted for Chinese fiction writers. In *Family Crisis*, for example, Wang Wen-hsing has communicated significant thematic messages through formal design—two intersecting story lines—and through the deliberate confusion of the hero's and the narrator's points of view. The extensive use of parallelism in the stories of *Tales of Taipei Characters* serves a key function in the author's construction of his elaborate symbolic system. To be sure, something remains slightly disturbing: as these writers take unusual fancy to dramatic plot creation, they have shown surprisingly little uneasiness about the author's arbitrary role in the act of literary representation, which must account for the inordinately mechanical quality of some of their plots. The same consciousness of form eventually enabled the more ambitious Modernists to accomplish greater artistic feats, to create more "writerly" than "readerly" texts, and finally to veer away from the mimetic model and take the dichotomy between the literary text and its referent as a basis for more radical innovations.

Impact on the Literary Scene

The thematic and formal conventions effectively disseminated by the Modernists have all but monopolized serious fiction writing in Taiwan since the 1960s; the new fictional form has thus considerably marginalized the more lyrical form of prose writing. Even while prose writers from the same generation as the Modernists, such as Lin Wen-yüeh, Chuang Yin, Chang Hsiao-feng, Fang Yü, Wang Hsiao-lien, and others, more or less stay with the traditional style, the lion's share of creative talents are devoted to practicing the new type of fiction. Even in the case of more socially conscious writers who openly castigate the modernist ideology, such as Ch'en Jo-hsi, Ch'en Ying-chen, Huang Ch'un-ming, and Wang Chen-ho, the preference for dramatic presentation free from explicit authorial intrusion and the predisposition to explain human behavior in terms of psychological motivations are commonly shared.

The literary scene in Taiwan since the late 1970s has become increasingly pluralist, yet the overall impact of the Modernist literary movement is everywhere observable. Younger writers of the baby-boom generation, such as Li Ang, Tung-nien, Huang Fan, and Ku Chao-sen, have elaborated on the theme of conflict between the realization of individual values and conventional ethical norms, and are still marginally interested in themes involving the sense of being and existentialist anxiety. Even though, unlike the early Modernists, these younger writers no longer treat creative writing as an "intellectual project," they have nevertheless thoroughly assimilated the literary techniques introduced by the Modernists, especially the "objectivity principle." In many cases, the structural refinement of their work surpasses even that of their predecessors and well deserves the label of "well-wrought urn."[21]

Another notable impact of the development of Modernist fiction has been the polarization of taste between the elitist and the popular, the modernist and the traditionalist. Although the Modernists for a decade or so contributed frequently to newspapers, as some of them developed stronger aestheticism, the gap between them and the general public widened. Although a group of baby-boom-generation writers had come to enjoy great popularity by publishing in the literary supplements of newspapers since the late 1970s, the serialization of Wang Wen-hsing's *Backed Against the Sea* in *Chung-kuo shih-pao* [China Times] at about the same time was discontinued because its "vulgar" language offended the sense of propriety of middle-class readers. The tension between the traditionalists and the Modernists is subtler and less publicly acknowledged. There is little doubt, however, that a fundamental disagreement on the criteria for literary excellence exists among the best critics from the two camps. Ou-yang Tzu, in a private conversation, mentioned a revealing incident: her freshman composition in the florid, sentimental style was heartily praised by her Chinese teacher but was met with scorn by Professor T. A. Hsia. The traditionalists' almost unanimous negative response to Wang Wen-hsing's *Family Crisis* and *Backed Against the Sea*, moreover, attests to this unbridgeable gap in literary taste.[22] Such a bifurcation of critical opinions among qualified critics attests that an aesthetic reorientation has occurred in Taiwan's post-1949 literature as a consequence of the Modernists' appropriation of a new system of compositional and thematic conventions governing the production and reception of literary texts.

CHAPTER THREE

Appropriations of Literary Modernism

The previous chapter has suggested that the Modernist literary movement produced significant changes in both rhetorical and thematic conventions of narrative prose in Taiwan, fundamentally transforming the artistic assumptions of writers and readers of an entire generation. This chapter will further examine the specific ways in which Modernist writers have appropriated more characteristically modernist literary features. An ideal point of departure for this inquiry is the temporary surge of an "avant-garde" trend in the initial stage of the movement. Although for certain critics the Modernist literary movement is exclusively defined in terms of such radical subversions of literary form, as I shall demonstrate, the avant-garde trend in Taiwan has turned out to be both short-lived and inconsequential, to the point that the label "avant-garde" may be a misnomer. For the sake of convenience, however, I will continue to use the term, albeit in a qualified sense.

The Romantic Avant-Garde Writers

One prominent feature of the self-styled avant-garde writers of the 1960s was their infatuation with the intellectual current of existentialism. As Franz Kafka was introduced early in the movement, the use of obscure plots and bizarre language quickly became a fad, and works by numerous young writers seemed to be dominated by nihilism, agonism, and an anxiety over the absurdity of existence.[1] Predictably, readers and critics alike were at a profound loss about what these writers were trying to say; many of them complained feverishly about their unintelligibility and affectedness. Among such negative critical responses, a piece of informed criticism has come from an overseas Chinese scholar, John Kwan-Terry.

In his 1972 article "Modernism and Tradition in Some Recent Chinese Verse," Kwan-Terry offered a penetrating discussion of problems involved in the "modernist" poetry currently practiced in Taiwan. He maintained that the "modernist" poets' disdain for the "sense" of the poem not only resulted in a pathetic failure of communication between poet and reader on the plane of reference, but also "threatened the breakdown of art."[2] Considering this phenomenon a result of fashion-seeking and blind worship of modern Western artistic trends, he expressed deep apprehension about a cultural crisis. By and large, the arguments posed in this essay applied to the fictional genre as well and seemed to articulate some widely shared opinions. The result was a heated debate on New Poetry, the "Hsin-shih lun-chan" [New poetry debate], which was then followed by a more full-fledged antimodernist movement in the mid-1970s, the Nativist literary movement.

The Nativist critics' forceful demand for social relevance and mass intelligibility in literature successfully stemmed the avant-garde craze for obscurantism in literary style. As writers were now considered spokespersons for the underprivileged and exploited class, tendentious works of social criticism proliferated, and technical deliberations were taken as indicative of a reactionary social attitude. Obscurantism was rejected and replaced by a deliberately uncouth style, purporting to simulate the rusticity of the less educated. In the new climate, some of the once ardent practitioners of the avant-garde style openly denounced their earlier works as decadent and politically incorrect.

Although criticism of the pseudo-avant-garde was largely justified, the upsurge of "aesthetic iconoclasm" in the 1960s represented a significant moment in postwar Taiwan's literary history. The vigorous dynamics of newly introduced artistic conceptions associated with modernism called into question conventional forms and criteria of literary excellence. The more enduring efforts generated by this initial enthusiasm eventually ushered in a new era of modern Chinese literary history. It is precisely with reference to such revolutionary implications that Joseph Lau surveyed the phenomenon of unconventional writings in 1973 in "The Concepts of Time and Reality in Modern Chinese Fiction," still one of the most perceptive critical overviews of fiction of the period.

The works cited by Lau to exemplify the new trend, which he subsumed under the category of parabolic writing, may be further divided into two kinds. The first kind, represented by works of Ch'i-teng Sheng, Ts'ung Shu, and Shih Shu-ch'ing, may be appropriately called avant-garde because of their authors' deliberate "use of anti-form or desecration of established conventions" (Bradbury and McFarlane 30) and because themes of these works are usually obscure and defy rational analysis. The second kind, such as Wang Wen-hsing's "Tsui k'uai-le te shih" [Happiness supreme] (1960) and Shui Ching's "Hi Lili Hi Li . . . ," however, reveal a drastically different artistic conception and are written in lucid, ordinary language, with realistic settings and well-defined thematic messages. Although both kinds of works sufficiently depart from conventional literary practice, they contain seeds for developments in two different directions. The moral parables of the latter kind, on the one hand, with intellectually conceived goals of expressing visionary truth about "human nature," anticipated the broader allegorical tendency with which such Modernists as Pai Hsien-yung and Wang Wen-hsing constructed elaborate symbolic systems in their later works. The semantic ambivalence of writings of the first kind, on the other hand, turns out to be the product of specific psychological motives that characterized the early phase of the Modernist literary movement. Ch'i-teng Sheng, who produced the largest amount of blatantly "obscure and bizarre" writings during the 1960s, illustrates this early phenomenon.

Ch'i-teng Sheng began to attract critical attention with a series of sketches and vignettes that were published in the literary supplement of the *Lien-ho pao* [United daily news] and *Modern Literature* between 1962 and 1964. These writings are primarily based on his own life, skillfully rendered in a deliberately unsentimental style reminiscent of Hemingway's stories with typically alienated heroes. His more characteristically "avant-garde" writings were published between 1964 and 1972, in such collections as *Chiang-chü* [Quandary] (1969), *Ching-shen ping-huan* [The mental patient] (1970), *Chü-hsieh chi* [Giant crab] (1972), and *Lai-tao hsiao-chen te Ya-tzu-pieh* [Ya-tzu-pieh who came to a small town] (1965). These later works may be further divided into two major types. One type of stories, consisting mainly of descriptions with minimal discursive elements, although filled with fantastic episodes and frequently lacking a coherent plot, are appealing for their concrete images and compelling immediacy. The other type of stories, however, typically contain lengthy philosophical deliberations, mostly expressed in the characters' interior monologues, but sometimes also in imaginary dialogues such as the conversation between the character Lao Tai and the statue of a deity in "Cheng-chih" [Quarrel] (1968).

Occidental Exoticism

Joseph Lau once mocked Ch'i-teng Sheng's style as being inflicted with "infantile paralysis" ("Ch'i-teng Sheng" 39–41). True enough, judged by any critical standard, Ch'i-teng Sheng's language is replete with awkwardly distorted, Westernized syntax and unjustified semantic ambiguity. Nevertheless, it possesses a quaint impressionistic vividness and sonorous rhythm. With refreshing imagery, the stories often conjure up an enchanting atmosphere that has a special appeal for those predisposed to the novel and strange. Judging from the fact that several early critics of Ch'i-teng Sheng, such as Yeh Shi-t'ao, Kuo Feng, and Joseph Lau himself, have all compared Ch'i-teng Sheng's works with those of Kafka, Ionesco, and Pirandello, his unconventionality has been provisionally granted the status of aesthetic iconoclasm.

As Renato Poggioli argued in *The Theory of the Avant-Garde*, specific psychic motives may be discerned in avant-garde iconoclasm, "which rarely limits itself to formal and aesthetic suggestions of the deformed and deforming vision (as in Modigliani) but transcends the sphere of art to affirm . . . real impulses of agonism and nihilism" (181). It is precisely at the level of psychic motives that significant disparity exists between Western and Chinese avant-garde writers. On the part of Taiwan writers of the 1960s, the iconoclastic gesture and the refusal to use conventional forms were apparently not an effect of historical pessimism toward modern civilization; instead, they largely sprang from aspirations and frustrations of a highly personal nature. As many critics have pointed out, the young writers' rage for enigmatic art forms and the tendency toward nihilism were part of the cultural syndrome produced by Taiwan's isolation and stagnancy in years following the Retreat. The egoistic rebelliousness that marked Ch'i-teng Sheng's work, especially his demands for unconditional individual freedom, is a product of this specific cultural environment.[3]

The influence on Taiwan's young intellectuals of Western avant-gardism and the new metaphysics popularized by existentialist philosophy may be compared to that of neoprimitivism on the Western avant-garde writers at the beginning of the century. Both influences operated through the effect of exoticism. Poggioli has pointed out how neoprimitivist deformation, or the conscious replication of bizarre images from barbaric art, was used by the Western avant-gardists to desecrate the established artistic norms of Western civilization.[4] In the case of Taiwan's avant-garde writers, the appropriation of the principle of deformation, twice imitated and amply mixed with existentialist nihilism, may be said to have served a similar countercultural purpose. Ultimately, one may treat it as another manifestation of the same yearning for artistic freedom and individual self-fulfillment expressed in *Family Crisis* and *Crystal Boys*.[5] Nevertheless, while Wang Wen-hsing, Pai Hsien-yung, and some other Modernists such as Ch'en Ying-chen and Lin Huai-min offered critiques on some Chinese experiences with the assistance of Western intellectual frames, the avant-gardists expressed their yearnings for alternative cultural values through imaginative creations based on foreign cultural images, which were largely inspired by an influx of Western texts into Taiwan in postwar years. Beneath the thin philosophical veneer is invariably a mass of romantic exoticism. The well-known story "Yüeh-po te mo-i" [The last descendants of Job] (1967?), by Shih Shu-ch'ing, for example, although superficially philosophical with its pretentious biblical allusions, has attracted attention primarily for its exoticism, as the readers of the story would not have been familiar with the metaphysical framework of the Old Testament.

Ch'i-teng Sheng, too, has energetically explored the effects of exoticism. In some works he mimicks the narrative tone and diction of popular translations of Western classics while adding a personal flavor. His settings are frequently strewn with objects utterly alien to the native landscape of Taiwan and more likely to be found in nineteenth-century Europe such as stone statues, marble town halls, and Gothic churches. Even his fables are populated with foreign fairies rather than with Chinese celestials. Some of Ch'i-teng Sheng's characters have unusual names made up of words frequently used to transliterate foreign names, Western or Japanese. All these devices have a disorienting, alienating effect and go hand in hand with the author's efforts to construct an imaginary cultural space that valorizes a moral context different from that familiar to Ch'i-teng Sheng and his readers.

The critical consensus holds that Ch'i-teng Sheng's lifelong obsession has been the struggle against his own disadvantaged social position. Many of his stories reiterate the theme that an "artist"—male, self-centered, defiant, and creative, very much modeled on his own self-image—should be free from all constraints and practical concerns of life. As critics Kao Ch'üan-chih and Joseph Lau have argued, such a willful, egoistic demand inevitably separates "me" from "them"—the latter being the entire society. Some of Ch'i-teng Sheng's early stories explicitly glorify unconventional behavior. In "T'iao-yüan hsüan-shou t'ui-hsiu le" [The champion long jumper has retired] (1968), for example, the aloof, antisocial, even diabolic persona is unconditionally exalted. Similarly, in such stories as "Fang-wen" [Visit] (1970) and "Ssu-kua pu" [Gourd dishcloth] (1971), the hero, in self-righteous indignation, condemns the corruption of other characters without giving convincing evidence of his own moral superiority.

The Borrowed Existentialist Discourse

Ch'i-teng Sheng's 1967 story "Wo ai Hei Yen-chu" [I love black eyes] offers an excellent example of the way the early Modernists appropriated existentialist themes from Western literature. The hero of the story Li Lung-ti has arranged to meet his wife Ch'ing-tzu in front of a movie theater. She is late, and they miss each other; when Li goes to her workplace, she has already left. On his way back, there is a sudden downpour, and the city streets are soon flooded. Showing a deep contempt for the people desperately trying to escape from the disaster, the hero selfishly pushes and steps over them as he begins to philosophize. In order to present the exact contours of the hero's mind-set, I will quote the work extensively:

> Tears came to his eyes. He thought indignantly, "How shameless people who fight for survival like this are. I'd rather stand here and cling to this pillar, and just die with it." . . . He privately mourned that in this world of nature death wasn't even worth mentioning. What harm, then, could human tribulation do to cold, unfeeling, Nature? Face to face with this invincible force of natural destruction, how would the values which

were a man's conviction and what he lived by achieve enduring existence? He was glad that the ill-defined faith that he had established in earlier days now turned out to be of use. It was helping him confront this frightful attack with fortitude. If in ordinary times he had been the type to fight for power and self-interest, how could he have endured seeing those things swept away now by natural forces? . . . A man's existence, then, was the relationship between himself and his environment in the here and now. Under these circumstances could he first identify himself, then love himself? Was he now coextensive with Godhead?[6] (Lau, *Chinese Stories* 67)

After righteously condemning everyone else and congratulating himself for his aloofness, he finally climbs on a rooftop in order to assist a sick prostitute. The next morning at daybreak, although he discovers his wife Ch'ing-tzu on a rooftop close by, separated from them only by a gulf of running water, he refuses to recognize her, but instead consoles the sick girl in his arms and feeds her the bread he has bought for Ch'ing-tzu. In response to Ch'ing-tzu's infuriated protests, the hero thinks to himself:

You say I've betrayed our relationship, but under the circumstances how can we put it back together? The one thing that makes you angry isn't my betrayal, but the jealousy in your heart; you can't bear to see the rights you used to enjoy taken over by another. As for me, I must choose, and choose in the present situation. I must be responsible for what I live for, I didn't come into the world to reap its benefits for nothing. I must take up a duty which would make me proud of my existence, no matter what. This gulf makes me feel that I'm no longer really your husband. Unless there comes a time when this gulf disappears—only then could I come back to you. May God have mercy on you; you're in bad shape. (71)

While the speaker of this passage sounds sufficiently self-centered for the reader to discount his argument, the philosophical support for this peculiar reasoning offered later is even more preposterously pedantic. Listening to Ch'ing-tzu on the other bank talking to herself about the past, the hero responds:

Yes, everyone had a past; pleasant or not, everyone had such experiences. But people often used past circumstances as the basis for making demands in the present, and when they didn't get what they asked for they were hurt, and felt bitter about it. Men were frequently shameless enough to keep deceiving the present with the past. Why was it that they couldn't look for a new meaning for living at each moment of the present? Life was like a stick of burning firewood: although the ashes at the burning end still retained the outward shape of the wood, it couldn't stand being touched, nor could it burn again; only the other end was firm and bright. (72)

The philosophical notion of an existential gap between a person's past and present seems to have fascinated many young Modernists in Taiwan (Ch'en Ying-chen, for instance, in the 1967 story "Ti i-chien ch'ai-shih" [My first case] used an image very similar to the torch in this passage to convey the theme of temporality),[7] but Ch'i-teng Sheng's use of this existentialist concept as the basis for the individual's moral choice appears strained.

The doomsday catastrophe is another frequent motif in existentialist literature. Indeed, the catastrophe scene immediately recalls God's punishment of human beings in biblical stories, and it also symbolizes the cruelty of an unfeeling nature. The device of placing the individual in extreme conditions as in natural disaster enables the writer to question ethical norms and assumptions whose validity in ordinary life is taken for granted. However, loopholes in Ch'i-teng Sheng's plot and his protagonist's reasoning have weakened this thematic function. Despite the hero's assertion that crucial change has been brought about by the flood, the disaster is not presented as plausibly insurmountable. The fact that the flood actually recedes the next day and there is a lifeboat rescuing people makes the hero's insistence on the "impossible gulf" between the two rooftops seem forced. To be sure, Ch'i-teng Sheng would probably dismiss this flaw, if it were pointed out to him. For, it seems that the gulf is in all likelihood a convenient excuse; what has severed the tie between the hero and his wife comes from a highly subjective, arbitrary definition of "present responsibility" and personal dignity, an obsessive moral question that has been haunting the hero all along. His choice of not recognizing his wife is a result of idiosyncratic reasoning, which is a logical development of his melancholic mood and habit of philosophical meditation already established at the beginning of the story. His weird belief that his moral responsibility toward a stranger "at the present" should temporarily nullify marital obligations does not, then, represent a natural human response under unusual circumstances but is the self-willed action of an idealist who devises his own heroic code. The high-sounding philosophical justifications merely provide an excuse for romantic elevation of the self and egoistic self-assertion.

The critical response to "I Love Black Eyes" is interestingly divided. C. H. Wang, on the one hand, affirms the hero's capacity for compassion at the risk of deviating from the ethical norms through a symbolic reading, envisioning the hero's world as a contesting ground for "fantasy" and "reality." Defending the hero, Wang says, "Ch'ing-tzu, separated by the gulf, was merely a notion in his fancy, and was no longer capable of competing with the prostitute in her husband's arms" (199). So the hero "chose to protect the sick prostitute at the cost of the loss of his own wife because it was the only realistic, honest way through which he could demonstrate his moral power" (201).

True, the only way to accept the hero's rationalization at face value is to read the story not realistically but symbolically as a battle of conflicting forces. The majority of critics seem to have taken a realistic approach and faulted the hero for his thinly disguised egoism. Kao Ch'üan-chih and Joseph Lau ("Ch'i-teng Sheng"), moreover, have identified the dilemma of the hero and a number of Ch'i-teng Sheng's other main characters with the author's headstrong endeavor to aggrandize the profession of artist in total neglect of the individual's function in a normal society.

The Romantic Celebration of the Artistic Ego

In the late 1970s, Ch'i-teng Sheng, at a more mature age, finally stepped forward to carve his own public image. Since then he has written about himself extensively in prefaces, afterwords, and chronologies attached to his publications.[8] The biographical information disclosed in these writings incidentally revealed that some of the wildly fantastic, enigmatic scenes in Ch'i-teng Sheng's early stories were based on actual events dressed up with some imaginary details. One may of course be disappointed by their lack of genuinely creative artistic reformulation. Yet they demonstrate that, in a literal sense, Ch'i-teng Sheng has taken his own life as his primary object of observation. T'ang Wen-piao, an amateur critic who ignited the Nativist literary movement in 1973, insightfully suggested that since Ch'i-teng Sheng "has so subjectively projected himself into every single work of his, we may simply take every one of them as an autobiography" ("Yin-tun" 185). The idiosyncratic "avant-garde" style, therefore, is revealed to be motivated not so much by a modernist skepticism about language and form as by a preoccupation with romantic self-portraiture.

In his later works, Ch'i-teng Sheng has more directly registered his capricious temper, sudden bouts of melancholy, uncontrolled malice against what has wronged him personally, and a not-so-sincere disdain directed at the masses. In stories collected in *Sha-ho pei-ko* [The sad music from Sandy River] (1976), *San-pu ch'ü Hei-ch'iao* [Strolling to the Black-bridge] (1978), *Yin-po ch'ih-pang* [Wings over the silver waves] (1980), and *Lao fu-jen* [The old lady] (1984), he discarded the earlier, bizarre style and adopted more conventional forms. Then, after a period of "self-examination," he published *T'an-lang te shu-hsin* [Love letters from T'an] (1985) and *Ch'ung-hui Sha-ho* [Return to Sandy River] (1986), which consist of eloquent letters and diary entries. Since then Ch'i-teng Sheng has openly used unedited biographical materials and has written about personal experiences involving other celebrities in literary circles. Although ethical problems inevitably arise in Ch'i-teng Sheng's works and the author's philosophizing habit at times becomes annoying, there are also moments of genuine eloquence. The influence of Whitman—a writer Ch'i-teng Sheng deeply admired at a young age—has finally been driven home. In his competent treatment of romantic subjects, such as the celebration of the ego, the confession of private eccentricities and fluctuations of moods, and the sensitive appreciation of nature, a classic Romantic seems to have emerged. C. H. Wang, a brilliant poet himself, has even compared "Strolling to the Black-bridge" with prose poems of Wordsworth and T. S. Eliot's "The Love Song of J. Alfred Prufrock" (203). The angry young man who employed the "avant-garde" style as a weapon to criticize upper- and middle-class values has become the tranquil Romantic.

Though not every writer of the avant-garde style shared Ch'i-teng Sheng's romantic vision of the all-important ego, it has nevertheless been common for writers to use the pseudo-avant-garde style to exoticize their personal experiences. Shih Shu-ch'ing professed a youthful craving for adventure, lamenting the fact that she was "born in a peaceful age . . . too late to witness the war" ("Na-hsieh" 182–197). Li Ang argued that her experimental stories of the late 1960s, though fantastic in appearance, were based on actual occurrences in her exotic hometown, the city of Lu-kang (*Hua-chi* 2–3).[9] The fact that the avant-garde style served primarily as a vehicle for vicarious adventures for young writers of the sixties with exuberant imaginations prompts an interest in exploring more serious aesthetic issues.

Commenting on the avant-garde in the West, Poggioli says:

> The linguistic hermeticism, which is one of the avant-garde's most important characteristics of form and style, would be conceived of as both the cause and the effect of the antagonism between public and artist. The problem of obscurity in so much contemporary poetic language is furthermore understood by many modern critics as the necessary reaction to the flat, opaque, and prosaic nature of our public speech, where the practical end of quantitative communication spoils the quality of expressive means. According to this doctrine, the linguistic obscurity of contemporary poetry should exercise a function at once cathartic and therapeutic in respect to the degeneration affecting common language through convention and habits. The quasi-private idiom of our lyric poetry would then have a social end, would serve as a corrective to the linguistic corruption characteristic of any mass culture. (37)

Peter Bürger, in his recent book on avant-gardism, however, argues that such features are not exclusively avant-garde, but are already characteristic of such earlier trends in the nineteenth century as symbolism and aestheticism, which later evolved into modernism proper. In Bürger's perception, the avant-garde movement in the early part of the century should more appropriately be seen as an inevitable consequence of the intensification of the aesthetic tendency, which drove artists to make radical attempts to reintegrate art into practical life.

The avant-garde style as practiced by the Taiwan writers served none of these purposes. Although these writers may have found themselves tempted to assume the posture of a surrealist, a dadaist, or an artist of other avant-garde trends, they have done so mainly because of the attraction of an exotic flair, or, more important, because such a posture always signifies progressiveness. In the historical development of modern Chinese literature there was no well-developed aestheticism prior to the 1960s (the sophisticated aestheticism in traditional Chinese literature has not been a viable artistic trend in the modern period), and the newly awakened skepticism toward language and the relation between form and content has yet to be fully absorbed. The willful playing with language and imagery and the departure from established conventions are therefore often accompanied by a defiant gesture protesting the totalizing tendency of the society, while sanctioning individual self-fulfillment (a similar observation can be made about the writings of PRC writers Liu So-la, Hsü Hsing and Ts'an-hsüeh in the 1980s). Joseph Lau is right in repeatedly emphasizing that the literary trends in Taiwan in the 1960s were indirect, distorted reflections of sensitive young artists' reactions to a stifling sociopolitical atmosphere. That a number of such writers, such as Ch'en Ying-chen and Ch'en Jo-hsi, soon realized the inefficacy of this indirect protest and shifted to more realistic forms of writing to criticize the same cultural conditions not only confirms Lau's point, but also exposes the shallowness of the avant-gardist influence in these writers' artistic conceptions.

With his obsessive concern with the artist's role in society and his romantic belief in the spontaneous overflow of personal emotions, Ch'i-teng Sheng has in fact endorsed an essentially expressive view of literature. He once refuted an editor's suggestions for his grammar in the following words: "It so happens that I do not care about the so-called correctness of grammar; when I am writing fiction, I try to follow the images and the ideas closely with intensive concentration, and to be fastidious about grammar at such a moment is simply improper."[10] By the 1980s, many of the early practitioners of the avant-garde style had become socially engaged writers, actively interacting with the public through more conventional narrative forms. The ease with which they gave up their linguistic hermeticism proves that there has never been a serious antagonism between the public and these artists.

Other writers, however, were more deeply wakened to the prosaic quality of the "language of the market" during the Modernist literary movement. Such writers as Wang Wen-hsing, Li Yung-p'ing, and Wang Chen-ho, by rigorously experimenting with style and, in particular, by trying to enrich fictional language with sensuous detail, developed an aestheticism in an unqualified sense of the term. Their views of language significantly depart from the conventional expressive view that seems to underlie Ch'i-teng Sheng's literary career. Before discussing these more ambitious endeavors in the final section of this chapter, however, I will first call attention to some more rudimentary influences literary modernism has exerted on Taiwan's fiction writers.

Conscious Explorations of Language and Voice

In a 1926 essay on the dominant currents in contemporary Chinese literature, Liang Shih-ch'iu, a liberal scholar of considerable stature at the time, expressed his reservations about foreign influences. He argued that Chinese writers' inordinate enthusiasm for foreign literary modes was fundamentally a "romantic" tendency, a result of their eagerness to break away from and pump new blood into worn-out and enfeebled native traditions. This enterprise, however, lacked a solid foundation and would eventually be abandoned: "The foreign influences, once introduced, immediately prevail with an irresistible force, and their merits and weaknesses are equally honored. The result, then, is inevitably disorder, or even chaos, even though beneath this chaos is usually an extremely lively vital spirit. This disorderly condition will not sustain itself for long; when its dynamism wears out, everything will again be resting on a solid basis" (4–5). Such skepticism toward indiscriminate acceptance of anything foreign was undoubtedly shared by many, but Liang was equipped with a theory that advised the adoption of a "classical spirit" to counterbalance romantic excess: "The 'classical' is what is healthy, for it purports to maintain balance in each component part of the whole; the 'romantic' is what is abnormal, since its essence lies in unrestrained developments of the abnormal. For example, feeling and imagination are both essential elements of literature; if they can be controlled by rationality and receive full development without departing from the norm, then we have the classical. If, however, feeling and imagination each develops in its own path for the purpose of creating the extraordinary effect of wonder, then, it may be called romantic" (232–233).

As a Harvard-trained scholar, Liang wrote about literature with close reference to the Anglo-American literary tradition. To some extent, his views represented the liberal mainstream among Chinese literary scholars and carried considerable weight in the literary circles of post-1949 Taiwan. Liang himself taught at National Normal University until retirement; influential younger scholars, such as T. A. Hsia, Chu Li-min, and Yen Yüan-shu, all by and large shared the same intellectual bearing. Even as literary modernism, another foreign-influenced literary trend, assumed the status of a strange new god, these scholars unmistakably favored the "classical" strand of Western modernism. T. S. Eliot, for example, was probably the most respected Western modernist.

Given such an intellectual climate, it is easy to understand why writers from the *Modern Literature* group, in an attempt to achieve a classical control of literary form, placed great emphasis on reason rather than emotion, on the intellect rather than sentiment. Even the radical individualism of such an iconoclastic writer as Wang Wen-hsing is most closely tied to an inordinate faith in rationality. It is also not surprising that these writers have, generally speaking, avoided exoticism, existentialist agonism, and various "avant-garde" antiforms. They have instead demonstrated a more intellectual concern with the theoretical issues involved in narrative representation, with language, voice, and point of view.

With respect to the Modernists' experimentation with language, too much attention has been paid by critics to the stream-of-consciousness technique, which apparently represents a conspicuous departure from conventional narrative modes. The Chinese writers' appropriation of the stream-of-consciousness technique is for the most part slavishly imitative rather than innovative. In his book *The Stream of Consciousness and Beyond in Ulysses*, Erwin R. Steinberg pointed out that as logical, single-directional, linear language is an inadequate medium for representing the unorganized, multidirectional mental activities simultaneously taking place in the psyche, new sets of narrative conventions have to be created. Such linguistic features as unpunctuated run-ons, truncated sentences, fragmented syntax, and juxtaposition of unrelated details are then used in stream-of-consciousness literature to simulate the unmediated visual impressions, random associations, and abrupt shifts in one's train of thought. However, if one looks at the often-cited works by Taiwan's Modernists that contain stream-of-consciousness passages, works such as Shui Ching's "A Man Without Face," Wang Wen-hsing's "Mother," and Pai Hsien-yung's "Wandering in the Garden, Waking from a Dream," it is evident that their authors merely mimicked the devices that had already been standardized and normalized in Western literature. Although these writers appropriated the techniques with considerable competence, and the outcome usually served the artistic purposes of individual works well, such an appropriation showed no sign of the essential modernist spirit of experimentation and innovation.

"Impersonal Narration" and Single Language Consciousness

Violations of established formal conventions, imitated or not, call attention to some basic facts about literary representation that have been so far taken for granted. In particular, the Modernists' attention was attracted to the mimetic literary concept that presumes a disjunction between fictional discourse and the referential world. The first, most enduring efforts made by the Modernists therefore largely revolved around technical maneuvers directed toward the preservation of the realistic illusion in fiction. The early Modernists energetically promoted "impersonal narration," with a subdued authorial presence and minimally mediated narration and description, in order to achieve a higher degree of verisimilitude. In this type of narrative, by virtue of the inherent disparity between the point of view of the "implied author" and that of the characters, an effect of irony is usually achieved, and this effect has been regarded a hallmark trait of Modernist fiction.[11]

Theoretically speaking, the term "impersonal narration" is necessarily a qualified concept, a technique valorized by specific conventions of modern Western fiction. Even Wayne Booth and Seymour Chatman, scholars who were themselves responsible for promulgating such terms as "impersonal narration" and "overt" and "covert" narrators, remind us that, strictly speaking, "impersonal narration" is a practical impossibility and that all narrative types inevitably contain "mixed points of view," owing to the connotative ranges of individual words and the inherently ambiguous nature of personal deictics in narrative discourse. Bakhtin, working primarily with the nineteenth-century European novel, confronted this issue from a different angle. His theory of discourse suggests that what characterizes novelistic discourse is precisely its resistance to the monopoly of either purely personal or purely impersonal voices. Even the most unitary and direct authorial discourse, which would be closest to the condition of "impersonal narration," is fused with "another's speech"—another's voice, another's accent, another's point of view—through the workings of "internal dialogism" and through "character zones" as well. The discourse in artistic prose is therefore always "polyphonic".[12]

As the Modernists in Taiwan were deeply influenced by Anglo-American rhetorical theories, they made a big issue of how to secure ideal conditions for unmediated, "impersonal" narrative transmission. The most purist attempts made in this direction are found in Ou-yang Tzu's work. She is said to have deliberately shunned ornate, colorful diction. A close inspection of her short stories reveals a rigorously maintained consistency in narrative perspective—her stories are mostly told from a single perspective, and voices other than that of the narrator are only allowed to enter the story through represented inner speeches and dialogues among the characters. Ou-yang's fastidious efforts to eliminate, or at least put under control, the interplay of different voices presuppose the ultimate desirability of making the language of fiction a transparent medium for narrative representation, unobstructed by the subjective feelings of the narrative agent. As a consequence of such meticulous control, the intractable effect of heteroglossia, which Bakhtin sees as the source of the essential dynamics of fictional discourse, is naturally weakened or domesticated. At the same time, the author transfers her energy to plot and action, and thus frequently attains a heightened dramatic intensity.

Indeed, most of Ou-yang's stories excel in conveying heightened dramatic tension. The restrictive effect of the "single language consciousness" of Ou-yang's fictional discourse is not as devastating as it could be. Since she is mainly interested in the psychological drama of the educated middle class, her characters share many of the linguistic habits of the narrator, and the plain, "ordinary" language used in the narration is easily carried over to speech representing the voices of the characters.

Generally speaking, however, the widened distance between author and text allows not only more dramatic presentations but also communication of thematic messages through multiple channels. Even with such a writer as Huang Ch'un-ming, who is allegedly "immune" to certain prominent modernist influences, the imprints of such a technical concept are obvious. In the seemingly natural and straightforward narrative discourse of Huang's stories that vividly capture the linguistic habits of the country folk, for example, the author nevertheless displays great dexterity in the manipulation of narrative perspective, which stays within the sphere of impersonal narration but is free from the rigidity of Ou-yang Tzu. The natural shifts between overt and covert narrative voices in Huang's stories create an intimacy between the narrator and the hero, in sharp contrast to the estrangement effected by Ou-yang Tzu's narrative method. In Huang's works the distance between the author and the text permits the ingenious use of section subtitles to convey sarcasm. The interplay of such subtitles with the content of a story gives his works an extra thematic dimension.

The "Arbitrary Narrator" and the Undermining of Realistic Illusion

If Ou-yang Tzu's faithful adherence to the principle of "impersonal narration" appears conservative and recalls a dated practice in the West, there are also writers who were more attracted to the latest aesthetic trends around the world, such as those found in works of late modernism. Such works often take to task the realistic conventions of narrative fiction and are no longer as concerned with either the "context" or the "text" of the literary work as with the narrative "code," the very process of storytelling. To the extent that the use of an "arbitrary narrator" by Wang Chen-ho often deliberately undermines the realistic illusion, it may be considered as exhibiting the same kind of experimental spirit.

In contrast to the self-effacing narrator of the impersonal narration found in the majority of the fiction of the Modernists, the intrusive narrator in Wang Chen-ho's stories usually calls attention to itself through a distinctive mocking voice, parenthetical authorial comments, and other kinds of derisive remarks. What is more, Wang Chen-ho at times seems to toy with the paradox of the act of narrative transmission. My favorite example of Wang's "modernistic" idiosyncrasy is his uncanny story "Wu-yüeh shih-san chieh" [The thirteenth of May festival] (1967). The story is unexpectedly given a surreal cast when two separate events are narrated nearly verbatim with almost identical details. Two different customers visit a toy shop run by an old couple, one in the morning when the husband is keeping the store and the other in the afternoon when only the wife is present. Curiously, the words used to represent the two scenes are almost identical—not only do the conversations taking place closely resemble each other, but so does the narration itself—as if the narrator were suddenly captured by a capricious desire for self-mimicry.

The liberty Wang takes with his narrative manner foregrounds the fictionality of his fiction and undercuts the realistic illusion that a writer like Ouyang Tzu painstakingly tries to preserve. This arbitrariness of Wang's technique becomes more obtrusive in a few of his later works, such as "Su-lan hsiao-chieh yao ch'u-chia" [Miss Su-lan wants to get married] (1976), "Chi-mo hung" [The lonely redness] (1963, 1971), and "Hsiang-ko-li-la" [Shangri-la] (1979), when he employs devices that recall *Tristram Shandy*, ranging from typographical variations—enlarged or boldface print, for instance—to textual insertions from other genres. In one case the narrator suddenly switches to verse in the middle of a narrative; several other times he inserts a piece of dialogue in the form of a script; occasionally the author provides explanations for obscure dialectical expressions, musical scores for a song that the characters have sung, or a chart to explain the details of the income and expenses of the family in a story. In another story he places a large empty square in the middle of the page to represent the part being omitted in his narration.

Such occasional anomalies in the narration of Wang's stories, which may be taken as lighthearted tampering with the author-reader relationship, had a conspicuously "metafictional" effect long before postmodernist, metafictional devices such as multiendings became a fad in Taiwan. Wang does not follow any set patterns; he is quite free in adopting whatever unconventional techniques suit his whim with a spirited playfulness. Although the experimental energy thus exhibited seems "modernistic," the lack of an aesthetic end frequently diminishes the value of Wang's innovations. Nonetheless, the fact that such devices no longer take for granted a stable relationship between the text and referential reality seems to anticipate the more systematically conceived experiments of the aestheticists.

Development of Language Consciousness: the Conscious Incorporation of Various "Speech Genres"

If attempts to confirm or challenge established narrative conventions are necessary consequences of the writers' consciousness of a widened distance between author and text, there is another important dimension in which the Modernists explore this distance to enhance artistic effects, namely, the incorporation of a diversity of voices in narrative discourse. As Bakhtin has pointed out, each speech type, or speech genre, artistic or extraartistic, "possesses its own verbal and semantic forms for assimilating various aspects of reality" (321). The individual voices incorporated in artistic prose therefore represent particular ways of viewing the world, and the presence of multiple voices broadens the conceptual horizon of artistic discourse (321). Such conscious efforts have helped the Modernists to move even further away from traditional narrative discourse, which usually features a dominant authorial presence.

That Pai Hsien-yung is often considered a masterful stylist has a great deal to do with his colorful presentation of a chorus of distinctive voices, ranging from the dignified conversations between a four-star general and his secretary to the bawdy vulgarities of the whoremaster, in his best-known work, *Tales of Taipei Characters*. As the son of one of the most illustrious generals in the history of the Republic of China, Pai enjoyed a unique advantage in observing people from various social groups. His tales are thus populated with people from many sociolinguistic groups. Even though Pai's talent for mimicking different voices is not exceptional (some of the dialogues in *Tales* and especially in *Crystal Boys* are rather unnatural), the dialogic interplay between the juxtaposed voices and disparate worldviews creates a dynamic that is rarely found in the works of his peers. One example is the brilliant use of the double-voiced narrator in the opening story of *Tales*, "Yung-yüan te Yin Hsüeh-yen" [The eternal "snow beauty"] (1965). The narrator's adoption of a voice from high-society gossip simultaneously creates an enviable image of leisure, comfort, and gentility and communicates a bleak vision of moral decay and doom. The splendor of the decadent world of Taipei's Shanghainese exiles is constantly undermined by a matter-of-fact account of what history has in store for these characters.

A more broadly used technique that involves active exploration of voice is the employment of the Taiwanese dialect, generally thought to have been initiated by Wang Chen-ho. Although this device was apparently conceived to reflect reality, it also provides a powerful means of representing underprivileged social groups through the successful rendering of the language used by Taiwan's peasants and country folk. For this reason, this artistic feature has been exploited, stigmatized, and abused alternately, as Nativists used it to sharpen readers' perceptions of the sociolinguistic differentiation in society, and numerous epigones made a fetish of it for no other reason than that it stood for the latest literary fashion.[13]

The incorporation of speech types and speech genres of course goes beyond the appropriation of voices of special sociolinguistic groups in the simple mimetic sense. The concept of "speech genre," according to Bakhtin, refers not only to types of living social speech (nonartistic genres) but also to texts that are mainly written (artistic genres). The Modernists' conscious appropriation of speech genres from existing literary texts played a notable role in shaping their individual styles and attests to the complex dynamics of the cultural and ideological forces that have forged their literary projects.

It is often mentioned that Pai Hsien-yung's language is heavily influenced by that of *Dream of the Red Chamber*. Whereas most of Pai's generation grew up reading translations of foreign literature, Pai benefited from early exposure to traditional Chinese novels in childhood, and it is readily discernible that the fictional discourse in *Tales of Taipei Characters* is greatly enriched by the narrative style and descriptive vocabulary of vernacular fiction. To cite an obvious example, the gorgeous living-room setting in his famous story "Wandering in the Garden, Waking from a Dream" is presented with the fast-paced enumeration of selected details of the decor and the costumes of the characters that is frequently found in traditional novels. The spectacular atmosphere of festivity, the image of a mundane storyteller who comments on the life and death of his characters with involved detachment, and the passive worldview that ultimately submits to the caprice of fate all readily evoke associations with old China. Thus the nostalgic image of the past is not a realistic recreation but a textual product heavily relying on the narrative conventions of traditional fiction. Such a style in *Tales of Taipei Characters* brings out vividly its presiding theme of the rapidly fading cultural ambience of the past.[14]

The use of peculiarly long and convoluted sentences and redundant sentence-ending particles in the early stories of another writer, Ch'en Ying-chen, suggests an appropriation of Japanese syntax. The style is visibly influenced by the Japanese aesthetic, with its characteristic melancholy as well as a romantic fascination with sensuality. Ch'en's well-known stylistic appropriation of literature of the May Fourth period and the thirties, most evident in such early stories as "Mien-t'an" [The noodle stall] (1959) and

"P'ing-kuo shu" [The apple tree] (1961), betrays an ideological motive, as Ch'en was apparently attracted by the leftist humanitarianism that dominated these periods. Although the opening passage of "The Apple Tree" and the romantic song in the story are vested with a delicate nostalgic beauty, it is preposterous that the Taiwanese father in "The Noodle Stall," a native of Miao-li, addresses his customers with the polite word *nin* in Northern Chinese dialect. Ch'en's replacing *ta* (she) in standard modern Chinese with the more archaic *i* because the latter appeared frequently in pre-1949 literature seems equally obtrusive. In all fairness, however, this attempt to recapture the past through linguistic means does help to create a distinctive personal style, one marked with a peculiar sentimentality that is appealing to some but "embarrassing" to others.[15]

Although these writers' deliberate appropriation of an older or a foreign style is primarily thematically motivated, there are also writers who explore this technique with more purely literary effects in mind. Wang Chen-ho, for example, frequently mixes high and low dictions to create a mock-heroic, parodic effect. In several of his short stories he deliberately juxtaposes quoted lines from well-known classical poems that depict exalted sentiments with descriptions of vulgarities, notably in "K'uai-le te jen" [A happy person] (1964). Wang Wen-hsing, too, in an allegorical story about the Nationalist-Communist civil war, "Lung-t'ien lou" [Dragon tower] (1964–1965), appropriates a number of speech types found in earlier literary texts, ranging from traditional Chinese novels to Western classics, to form a mock-epic style with a touch of black humor. In one episode of the story, for example, the brigade commander's neighbor delivers a lofty speech, in a rhetorical style recalling a Shakespearean play or a Greek tragedy, to relate how the commander's family has heroically resisted and then been brutally killed by the enemy. The apparently intentional exploration of the technique of stylistic parody anticipates the more successful language in Wang's later novel *Backed Against the Sea*.

To demonstrate that the Modernists' studious cultivation of a consciousness of language has in fact distinguished their works from the bulk of Chinese fiction written in the pre-Revolution period and in the contemporary People's Republic, I would like to offer a careful analysis of a much-celebrated short story by Wang Chen-ho: "Chia-chuang i niu-ch'e" [An oxcart for dowry].[16] Even at an early stage of the Chinese writers' appropriation of Western fictional forms, attempts at manipulating narrative voice, through irony and the use of unreliable narrators, for example, were impressive. Such stories as Lu Hsün's "Ah Q cheng-chuan" [The true story of Ah Q] (1921) and "K'ung I-chi" (1919), and Wu Tsu-hsiang's "Kuan-kuan te pu-p'in" [Young master gets his tonic] (1934 or 1935) are only the better-known examples. Nevertheless, when it comes to sophisticated artistic reformulation of speech types and individual voices, the pre-1949 Chinese writers cannot compare with some of the best fiction writers in Taiwan. "An Oxcart for Dowry" provides a good example.

In a sense, Wang may be described as a master of "heteroglossia," or the dialogical interaction between different speech genres within the text, as defined by Bakhtin. As Bakhtin says, "All languages of heteroglossia, whatever the principle underlying them and making each unique, are specific points of view of the world, forms for conceptualizing the world in words, specific world views, each characterized by its own objects, meanings and values" (292). In "An Oxcart for Dowry," the artistic reformulation of language foregrounds socioideological assumptions and thus forms an integral part of the story's thematic dimension.

The story is about a poor villager named Wan-fa, who, because of a hearing problem, finds it hard to keep his family from starving with his job as an oxcart driver. Then a clothes vendor, Chien, moves in as a new neighbor and has an affair with Wan-fa's wife. Chien also provides much-needed financial help by hiring their son in his business. While struggling to save his own sense of self-respect at the expense of an empty stomach, the ill-fated Wan-fa is unexpectedly imprisoned for accidentally killing a child. After being released from prison, he finally must accept the fact that Chien's relationship with his wife is the only means left for his family to survive. Once a week he swallows humiliation along with a bottle of beer that Chien gives him and lets Chien and his wife spend the evening together. Ironically, with money from his wife's adulterer, Wan-fa becomes able to fulfill his lifelong dream of owning an oxcart for himself.

Unlike the humanitarian stories of the thirties, the perennially impoverished villagers in this story are portrayed as rather unlikable, each with a special physical defect. Wan-fa is nearly deaf because during the war he once bathed in unclean water and was unable to find a good doctor. He is, moreover, laughably cowardly in his pathetic struggle to maintain his dignity.

Wan-fa's wife Ah-hao is exceptionally ugly, with a chest like a washboard; she loves to gamble and is unpleasantly garrulous. The adulterer Chien has a bad odor and is constantly scratching his armpits. The author's humanitarian message, therefore, is conveyed not by appealing to the reader's sympathy with innocent, positively portrayed victims, but mainly through ingenious devices at the discursive level.

Throughout the story, the mischievous, double-voiced narrator exuberantly uses witty aphorisms and proverbial phrases to mock and ridicule the wretched conditions of his characters; for instance, he calls the stomach that yearns for food a "bottomless pit." He deliberately employs professional jargon—military, educational, and diplomatic—in describing the ignoble manners of peasants. The villagers who laugh at Wan-fa appear to be "performing a 'Right face!' in response to a drill sergeant" (Lau, *Chinese Stories* 76), and when Ah-hao and Chien make love in the muddy field, they are said to be engaging in "battles and truces." Ah-hao's unsightly posture with her hands on her hips is compared to the shape of a "parenthesis," and as Ah-hao and Chien fight to defend themselves when suspected by Wan-fa, they seem to be at a "recitation contest" of school children. When Wan-fa loses his job and undergoes a period of starvation, he is said to have to "conquer" "one-eighth," "one-quarter," or "one-half" of his hunger, as if someone were measuring his appetite with mathematical precision. Finally, Ah-hao's carefully enunciated sentences are compared to those found in a "diplomatic communiqué." Such language, clearly alluding to respectable middle-class life in civil society, belongs collectively to the entire community of language users, in particular the middle-class, educated readers of this story. Therefore, when readers laugh with the narrator at the characters, they soon find themselves sharing the class snobbery and mean-spirited perversity of the narrator. Through the device of eliciting "ambivalent laughter," the author has intended to criticize his readers by first involving them through their sociolinguistic consciousness.

Narrative voice is considerably less sophisticated in "Young Master Gets His Tonic," in which the reader quickly learns to reverse the meaning of every word the young master has uttered to decode the author's message. Many of the author's views about China's problems and the world economy are conveyed directly through the mouthpieces of the young master's cousin and another old man in the village. Oppressed, poor peasants in

Wu Tsu-hsiang's stories, moreover, are so positively portrayed that they easily earn sympathy. The wet nurse and her family, all decent, honest, and hard-working, are compared by the author with such animals as cows and buffaloes; the woman's breasts are likened to such agricultural products as "pumpkins"; the blue veins on her breast are "rivers on the map," making her a symbol of China.

Wang Chen-ho, however, has succeeded in communicating a more complicated message through his narrator; although his characters are considered despicable by ordinary middle-class readers, that very audience is implicated in these people's misery. Besides, filthy, smelly, and ignorant as they are, these unfortunate people deserve sympathy simply because they share with all other human beings the basic need for food and they have hearts capable of feeling the pain of humility. In this sense, therefore, Wang is more of a humanitarian than many authors of proletarian literature. Wang continued to develop his special narrative technique to express his humanitarian social vision. The tour-de-force of *Rose, Rose, I Love You* lies precisely in the juxtaposition of different social languages—Tung Ssu-wen's pseudo-intellectual rhetoric, the pimps' low-class obscenities, the prostitute's naive way of talking—so that the interplay of different verbal-ideological groups is intensively dramatized.

Culminations of the Aesthetic Tendency

The Modernists' self-consciousness about form, manifested in extreme ways, reflects a skepticism toward language and the relation of form and content. The prolonged, undaunted efforts of Wang Wen-hsing to test "the limits of the fictional form and the functions of the fictional language" (Lee, "Beyond Realism" 74), for example, can only be justified in terms of theoretical precepts of the modernist aesthetic. Although Wang has created a patently self-referential novelistic discourse, the main import of Wang's literary project as a whole is conceived as the expression of a moral vision, a subject that will be addressed in Chapter 4. It is only in the work of a younger Modernist, Li Yung-p'ing, that one finds the absolute domination of aesthetic concerns. Li's highly acclaimed story series *Chronicle of Chi-ling* brought the aesthetic tendency in Taiwan's Modernist fiction to a new height.[17]

The Aesthetic Views of Wang Wen-hsing

Wang Wen-hsing is convinced that "everything a literary work has to say must always be said through language." He has advised his readers to "simply look at the language [of his works] and nothing else."[18] From his academic training in New Criticism, Wang has obtained a firm belief in the formalist idea that literary effect is best attained through a process of "deautomatization," or "dehabitualization." He therefore has strived, with indomitable spirit, to put these formalist principles into actual practice—to create a fictional language that possesses the utmost power to estrange. The result is inevitably a highly self-referential style that calls so much attention to itself that one suspects it may detract from the intended effect of refreshing the reader's perception of the represented objects. The following discussion, however, is neither an analysis nor an evaluation of the linguistic attributes of Wang's style and their effectiveness, since this subject has already been addressed by several competent critics (Chang Han-liang; Ou-yang, "Lun Chia-pien"; Cheng Heng-hsiung; Gunn, "Process"). Instead, it will focus on the aesthetic conceptions behind Wang's experiment in language. Over the past ten years, Wang has offered several explanations of his stylistic practice on public and private occasions. Without being full-fledged theories, these explanations represent thoughtfully conceived, systematically formulated aesthetic views, which are rarely found in modern Chinese literary history.

What significantly distinguishes Wang Wen-hsing's literary experiment from that of other Modernist writers, such as Wang Chen-ho, is its rigorous professionalism. Whereas Wang Chen-ho spontaneously dabbles, sometimes superficially, in different aspects of narrative form, Wang Wen-hsing has concentrated on developing a literary "idiolect" and is apparently convinced that this task requires the same hard work and self-discipline as the training of a good musician or painter. Simply counting the years he has spent writing his two novels *Family Crisis* (from 1965 to 1972) and *Backed Against the Sea* (from 1972 to 1981 on the first part, which has been published, and from 1981 to the present on the sequel) reveals that for well over twenty-five years he has been engaged in the daily travail of this Herculean enterprise.[19] Technically speaking, Wang's experiment consists mainly of syntactical and lexical modifications that foreground certain auditory or visual qualities of the language. But what exactly constitutes his aesthetic vision, and how would one characterize the ideal effect he is striving to achieve? Further, where has he derived the model for his aesthetic language, and by what criteria would he judge its successful attainment?

In a personal interview in 1982, I asked Wang why sentences in his autobiographical novel Family Crisis become increasingly longer, clumsier, and more convoluted as the story proceeds. Wang replied that he envisions a consonance between the style of the narrative discourse and the general "mood" of the story. Therefore, as the inner world of the hero gradually enters a state of turmoil, the speech of the narrator also becomes more and more entangled. Wang added that since the narrator is an "arbitrary" construction of the author, the author naturally enjoys absolute power to determine which style is used.[20]

Wang shares the attitude toward language that has characterized much novelistic experimentation in this century, that is, a heightened awareness of the arbitrary nature of language as a symbolic form. By treating language in terms of its material qualities—in addition to lexicon, prosody, and syntax, the ideographic quality of the Chinese written language lends itself to further manipulations of psychovisual effect—in order to explore its artistic potential, Wang widens, in a sense, the space between language and its referents. This approach easily jeopardizes the basic mimetic function of fictional language as conventionally understood, a not uncommon phenomenon in late modernism. However, the radicalness of Wang's experiment pales beside the more radically antirealistic practices in the West, as his novelistic discourse only departs from the realistic convention by a small breach of the principle of mimetic representation. The less than radical violation of the realistic rules, however, works against him in some ways. For example, his departure from conventional practice at times seems blatantly awkward: as a consequence of his linguistic maneuvers, his characters all seem to share the same set of idiosyncratic linguistic habits, such as preferences for long sentences, certain types of repetition, and excessive punctuation. When the narrator in Family Crisis begins to use convoluted, entangled sentences, both the hero and the hero's brother also speak in the same manner, inevitably upsetting the reader's presumption that their speech is represented realistically.

Wang, however, is apparently not bothered by this flaw; for him, the redeeming virtue of such language lies in its specially conceived "vividness."

He claims that his language use does not follow the realistic principles in a superficial sense. Rather, it is intended to capture the subtle essence of speech manners with its peculiar accents. Language in fiction must be artistically reformulated and, to borrow a traditional Chinese critical notion, must strive at *shen-ssu*, a likeness in spirit or essence, rather than *hsing-ssu*, a likeness in form.[21] He even coins the term "trans-mimetic" to convey his idea of a "heightened" sense of lifelikeness, which constitutes for him a "higher mode" of realism. It is in this sense that he expects his language to be appreciated for its "fluency" and "precision."[22]

As a professor of English literature, Wang is apparently very familiar with the history of realistic fiction in the West. Many conventions of realistic fiction have gone through cycles of being perfected, naturalized, and subsequently parodied, and the world has long seen literary genres whose main import is precisely to undermine such conventions. While Wang undoubtedly sees himself as a realistic writer in the global tradition, he cannot but be aware of the current state of realism. As a latecomer, he is nevertheless determined to bring renewed vitality to a heavily worn-out form. Therefore, on the one hand, he has chosen not to subvert or parody the process of writing as some Western postmodernists have done, but rather to stay within the familiar terrain of realism. On the other hand, inspired by more avant-garde currents in contemporary literature, he has taken the dissociation between signifier and signified as a basis for his own innovative experiment. He is thus fundamentally different from the avant-garde writers in that he considers his violation of the older conventions a necessary evil in his attempt ultimately to achieve the pristine ideal of realistic fictional representation.

Such a rationally conceived project, however, has some inherent problems. The older conventions of realistic fiction and the newer concepts of literary representation are apparently heading in opposite directions: one to create, the other to undercut the illusion of the real. Although this conflict seems to be resolved rationally in Wang's own mind, the resolution is undoubtedly a precarious one. For readers and critics alike, the awkwardness of Wang's innovative fictional language is undeniable. This awkwardness, in a sense, aptly reflects the plight of an original artist who is determined to take part in the modernist project half a century after its heyday.

Despite the problematic nature of Wang's language experiment, Wang's language has a sensuous concreteness that qualifies it as superior art, an accomplishment heavily indebted to the modernist aesthetic. On different occasions, Wang has suggested that his manipulation of language takes as its model artistic forms more abstract than narrative fiction, such as music, painting, and poetry. The writer of fiction has words at his disposal just as the musician has notes or the painter has colors. This analogy cannot but recall Fredric Jameson's argument that the modernist writers' treatment of language primarily in terms of its sensory data is an "impressionistic strategy," whose main function is "to derealize the content and make it available for consumption on some purely aesthetic level" (Political Unconscious 214).[23]

Much evidence exists to demonstrate Wang's inordinate concern with foregrounding the sensuous quality of fictional language, which necessarily results in a tension between its aesthetic and communicative functions. Although the synaesthetic quality of Chinese characters is explored, it is worth pointing out that Wang tends to privilege the psychoacoustic effect. Much of Wang's aggressive manipulation of the ideograms, to the annoyance of many readers, involves an arbitrary use of the semantic element of certain characters for phonetic purposes, such as replacing the "hand" radical with the "mouth" radical to force a softer pronunciation or substituting English letters or phonetic symbols for ideograms, which seems to have a similar effect.[24] The repetitive use of particle and syntactical manipulations, at least in Wang's latest novel, *Backed Against the Sea*, do indeed produce a rhythmic sound pattern that is pleasing to the ear and even, using Fredric Jameson's words, "libidinally gratifying."

Wang tries to persuade his readers to free themselves from the convention of searching for the novel's meaning only in its communicative dimension. Insisting that his language is "musical," he on many occasions urges the reader to read his prose as if it were poetry and to pay attention not only to the "sense" but also to the "sound." To demonstrate that the real essence of his fictional language rests in its sonorous quality, he sometimes recites passages from his works at critical seminars.[25] In his preface to the Hung-fan edition of *Family Crisis*, Wang compares the act of reading to that of listening to classical music, cleverly arguing that just as you cannot rush over a four-movement concerto in ten minutes, so the reading must also be done over a specific length of time. He even suggests that in order to take heed of every nuance, including the punctuation marks, the ideal speed of reading a literary work is one thousand Chinese characters (roughly seven hundred English words) per hour, two hours per day.

Marxist criticism has argued that the modernist aesthetic strategy is ultimately related to the capitalist process of reification and to the artist's attempt to resist standardization in industrialized society.[26] It may be argued that when Wang Wen-hsing launched his career, the stage of Taiwan's capitalist development roughly corresponded to that of late-nineteenth-century Europe. Chinese artists were naturally attracted to the early modernists in the West, who experienced similar kinds of structural changes in daily life in an increasingly fragmented, quantified modern world. It is therefore unsurprising that, although Wang has occasionally made attempts to educate and sensitize his audience, he is inevitably aware of the futility of such efforts. As a matter of fact, Wang has always been conscious of the incongruity of his elitist literary project with Taiwan's highly commercialized cultural environment. He has said that he did not expect the novel *Family Crisis* to be widely read—he had originally planned to photocopy the manuscript to circulate among a small selected group.

However, in perhaps another sign of the inherently utopian nature of the modernist project, Wang also idealistically craves something that seems impossible: he says he has an irresistible yearning to produce a "popular" work in a popular language with Hemingway-like "liveliness," although he would insist on reaching that goal by following the same path that he has until now been taking. Such an almost religious belief in the ideal style is reminiscent of the *le mot juste* principle of Flaubert and of many Western modernist writers' dedication to language in this century. The irony of the situation, however, is that, as a result of the rapid development of a consumer culture in Taiwan, the "Modernist" literary period has been extremely brief. Even before serious artists have had time to publish their mature works, the society surrounding them has already rushed forward to a full-blown mass culture that tends to nullify the very basic assumptions of the Modernist project. The public attention that *Family Crisis* has attracted largely resulted from its iconoclastic content rather than its innovative style. Some cynical commentators have even attributed the surprisingly warm reception of this book to the successful publicity strategy of the editors of *Chung-Wai wen-hsüeh* [*Chung-Wai literary monthly*] in which the novel was serialized. As the fervor over *Family Crisis* soon subsided, the gap between Wang and popular readers has become ever wider.

Until now I have been treating Wang's language program largely in terms of its modernist characteristics as defined in the Western sense. However, even in such a brief modernist moment in postwar Taiwan, a Chinese version of modernist literature can never be a mere duplication of its Western models. Wang Wen-hsing's roundabout journey from an absolute embrace of Western artistic models to the deep contemplation of elements from traditional Chinese culture best proves this point.

In a short essay of 1987, "Wu hsiu-chih te chan-cheng" [A never-ending battle]" (104–105), Wang states that when he was twenty years old, he was once suddenly struck by the realization that his own language was not in any way different from that of any other people. He was then reading Flaubert, Maupassant, and Tolstoy, and he could hear in their works a cadence, a rhythm, like that of a bass orchestra. There was no such music, however, in his own language—it was shamefully "immature, hasty, and flustered." It was not until two years later, when he came across the work of Hemingway, which to his mind was an ideal mixture of musicality and simple vividness, that he plunged into a lifelong struggle with fictional language. He was able to write only a few words a day, and in order not to write too fast, he deliberately wrote from left to right rather than from top to bottom. He revised every sentence more than ten times. Wang admitted that it might seem odd that he has taken Hemingway as his model, as the latter's characteristic simplicity is so drastically different from Wang's own style. Yet he is convinced that there is such a thing as a "resemblance in spirit (*shen*) and a dissimilarity in form (*hsing*)," as stated in a traditional Chinese critical epithet.

Although the initial inspiration for Wang's aesthetic views apparently comes from foreign literature, as Wang probed into the deeper recesses of aesthetic questions, he seems to have turned to traditional Chinese artistic and ethical concepts for theoretical support. The critical term *shen* is a key word used by the "metaphysical school" of Chinese theory of literature, as James J. Y. Liu defines it, the philosophical foundation of which consists of Taoist philosophy and Ch'an (Zen) Buddhism.[27] When Wang declared that he had been striving to emulate the sound pattern of the classical Chinese language, its *i-yang tun-ts'o* (modulation and rhythm), he seemed to be endorsing ideas advocated by the "technical school" of the Ch'ing dynasty.²⁸ Most interestingly, Wang's ideas toward the end of "A Never-ending Battle" seem to suggest a return to the time-honored moralist tradition of Chinese literature. There Wang describes his struggle with language as governed by a principle of "sincerity" and supports this notion with the Confucian motto *hsiu-t'su li ch'i ch'eng* (rhetorical, or stylistic, practice must be based on sincerity or honesty). In a sense, both the doctrines of Western realist literature and traditional Chinese ethics stress the importance of truthfulness to experience, or *ch'eng*. By perceiving his stylistic practice in moral terms and by returning to subjective ethical experience, Wang seems to have found a new anchor for his seriously conceived lifelong literary project.

An Exemplary Modernist Aesthetic Work: Chronicle of Chi-ling

A modernist tendency that universally offends public taste and unfailingly incurs censorship from the authorities and gut-level disapproval from conservatives is what is known as "striving for sensations," described by Irving Howe in the following words:

> The modernist writer strives for sensations, in the serious sense of the term; his epigone, in the frivolous sense. The modernist writer thinks of subject matter not as something to be rehearsed or recaptured but to be conquered and enlarged. . . . He becomes entranced with depths— whichever you choose: the depths of the city, or the self, or the underground, or the slums, or the extremes of sensation induced by sex, liquor, drugs. (31)

It is apparently not coincidental that all important Modernist works published in Taiwan in the 1980s—Wang Wen-hsing's *Backed Against the Sea* in 1981, Pai Hsien-yung's *Crystal Boys* in 1983, Li Ang's *Sha-fu* [The butcher's wife] in 1983, Wang Chen-ho's *Rose, Rose, I Love You* in 1984, and Li Yung-p'ing's *Chronicle of Chi-ling* in 1986—display this tendency in a conspicuous way: In *Backed Against the Sea*, the antihero's erotic imagination has made him a victim of an overly potent prostitute, turning an ordinary prostitution scene into a pageantry of sadism. The vivid rendering of the slaughterhouse pig killing in *The Butcher's Wife* and the butcher's physical and psychological abuse of his wife at home reinforce each other, forming the basic tenor of a story about sexual brutality and vengeful murder. In *Crystal Boys*, along with frequent evocations of an atmosphere of festivity, two kinds of physical desire, hunger for sex and the basic need for food, are mentioned with equal frequency, with the apparent thematic implication of glorifying the body. This idealizing tendency, evident in the sometimes florid discourse, is undercut, however, by the sordidness of sensuous detail, particularly regarding bodily fluids—blood, sweat, tears, and saliva—whether caused by Taiwan's semitropical weather, sexual activities, or human brutality. Lower bodily functions are the primary source for carnivalesque laughter in *Rose, Rose I Love You*—the protagonist farts whenever he opens his mouth to preach. However, none of these works is comparable, in aesthetic intensity, to *Chronicle of Chi-ling*, a work that transfixes with a sinister atmosphere of violence and blasphemy and contains excruciatingly sensational descriptions of murder, animal killing, and sex.

Although the Modernists typically downplay the historical specificity of their works, the writers of most of the above-mentioned novels have intended to use what Bakhtin calls the "underworld naturalism" as a means to communicate some kind of social message (*Problems* 94). Whereas Wang Chen-ho's *Rose, Rose I Love You* can be readily classified as a political satire cast in a parodic mode, the first three, more symbolic works also subordinate sensational depictions to themes clearly conceived to comment on existing social or ethical practices. Their candid treatment of such social ills as violence in the family, prostitution, blue- and white-collar criminality, and, above all, poverty unmistakably points to real problems in contemporary Taiwan. However, the subversive edge of these works comes not so much from their authors' penetrating sociological insights as from the assault implied in their sensational subject matter on the sense of propriety of ordinary readers. *Backed Against the Sea*, when serialized in the literary supplement of *China Times*, had to be discontinued because of pressure from offended readers; controversy surrounded *The Butcher's Wife*, in large part because the explicit depictions of sex were written by an unmarried woman; *Crystal Boys* had to be transformed into a melodramatic film before the public would pay any attention to it.

Ironically enough, *Chronicle of Chi-ling*, by far the most sensational work among them, has not caused any controversy. Perhaps it is precisely because the work is completely devoid of any ideological relevance—or, one may say that the only ideology behind Li's detailed, amoral depiction of morally transgressive behaviors is the "ideology of the aesthetic"—and is so obviously concerned with eliciting "disinterested" aesthetic pleasures that readers of the work have been prescreened. As the work provides few entry points for readers who are likely to misinterpret its theme, those who actually read it tend to be predisposed to appreciate its aesthetic quality. That may be the reason why the few critical reviews it has so far received are all favorable.

Chronicle of Chi-ling is not a novel in the conventional sense but a story series revolving around a criminal event that took place some time before the beginning of the book. A local scoundrel, Sun Ssu-fang, with the assistance of four teenage hoods, rapes and causes the suicide of Ch'ang-sheng, the wife of a coffin maker, Liu Lao-shih, on a night when the townsfolk are celebrating the birthday of the Kuan-yin Bodhisattva. The next day, Liu Lao-shih kills the wife and mistress of Sun and is arrested. From that time, residents of Chi-ling, all of them in some sense accomplices to the crime, are haunted by guilt and uneasily anticipate revenge from Liu on those more immediately involved in the rape. The redressing of the wrong, however, takes a convoluted path, which is not even fully unfolded when the story series ends.

The book's themes are conspicuously "amoral." The long-awaited revenge on the four boys is deliberately detained. When Liu Lao-shih avenges his wife's death, he does not kill the rapist Sun Ssu-fang, but Sun's wife and his mistress Ch'un-hung—the latter dies in front of her five-year-old son, who becomes mentally incompetent as a result of his trauma. Or, if one follows critic Lung Ying-t'ai's explication of the plot and takes the family of four murdered on the river in the story "Ta shui" [Great flood] to be Yen-niang's family—her husband being one of the four hoods that have assisted Sun Ssu-fang in the rape, as we have learned from the other two stories "Ssu-nien" [Missing] and "Man-t'ien hua-yü" [A sky full of flower-rain] ("Yi-ko" 167–168)—the irony of fate is nearly complete, since Yen-niang's husband is the only one out of the four who shows signs of repentance. As every act of revenge inevitably involves the innocent, moral transgression also seems to reproduce itself. The world is presented as an unjust existentialist hell where *t'ien-li*, or heavenly justice, exists only in people's minds, constantly alluded to but forever receding from the characters' grasp.

In Wang Chen-ho's and Wang Wen-hsing's fiction, characters are often victims of blind sociological forces, and the authors' deliberate emphasis on their despicable qualities is a literary strategy aimed to test the reader's capacity for compassion. As aesthetic concerns dominate in *Chronicle of Chiling*, moral transgression is constantly used to elicit sensations of fear and exhilaration rather than moral self-reflection or humanitarian feelings. For example, in the episode "Hao i-p'ien ch'un-yü" [What a nice spring rain], the author's insinuation that Ch'iu-t'ang, an innocent young girl who is probably later raped and sold into prostitution by a villain, is sexually attracted to the "tough guy" criminal suspect, gives an ambivalent touch to the reader's concern for Ch'iu-t'ang's fate (206). Similarly, in the story "Jih-t'ou yü" [The rain from the sun], Hsiao Lo's killing of the dog is depicted in such minute detail that the reader vicariously takes pleasure in the ruthless brutality.

If the reader seldom finds it easy to sympathize with Li's characters in moral terms, he or she is frequently invited to empathize with them in sensuous terms as a result of Li's superlative skill in creating tension and immediacy, building a compelling illusion of the "real." Much of the power of his narrative comes from the brilliant execution of techniques revolving around "impersonal narration." Indeed, Li has brought to near perfection the ideal narrative type aspired to by the formalist group of the Modernists.

The narration in such stories in the series as "The Rain from the Sun," a story that won first prize in the 1979 *United Daily News* short story contest, and "Wan-fu hsiang li" [In the Wan-fu alley], purporting to be untouched transcripts of characters' behavior, best exemplifies the ideal of minimally mediated narrative representation. Because the narrator strictly denies himself the power of free mental access, the narrative in these stories is composed largely of meticulous descriptions of overtly visible physical actions and recorded speech. The control of perception is exceedingly rigorous. Important settings, such as the crimson sun on the horizon and the recurring image of the *kuan-yin* Bodhisattva at the carnival, find their way onto the scene in an inconspicuous manner, by "incidentally" coming into the view of a certain character. As a result, there are many tags that indicate the characters' outwardly discernible perceptions in such phrases as "he saw," or "he gazed at." The narrative act, therefore, is modeled on the workings of the stenographer and the camera—Seymour Chatman's analogy—and the discourse type approaches the pole of "pure mimesis."

As the "nonnarrated representation" discourse type deliberately blocks all conventional channels of direct communication between narrator and readers, the readers of Chronicle frequently find themselves relegated to the role of spectators in a spellbound world. As readers are constantly presented with a composite of visual images, uninterpreted actions, and unremitting suspense, floods of sensation are evoked but not always relieved. The story "The Rain from the Sun" provides an excellent example of how tension is built and finally relieved—but not in a conventional way. Much of the space of "The Rain from the Sun" is devoted to meticulous, vivid descriptions of how Hsiao Lo, one of the four scamps, kills and skins a female dog on a poisonously hot afternoon. Feeling nauseous all the while, Hsiao Lo apparently is affected by the rumor that someone resembling Liu Lao-shih has suddenly appeared under the chinaberry tree somewhere in the town, presumably seeking revenge. After a great amount of tension building, the ending seems anticlimactic: Hsiao Lo finally walks over to the chinaberry tree and confronts the avenger, but the man, who is never actually identified as such, simply departs without a word. The highly equivocal ending is nevertheless given a strong sense of closure through a symbolic shower of rain that suddenly falls as the mysterious visitor takes his leave. By dispelling the unbearable heat that is repeatedly mentioned in the text, the rain also significantly relieves the compelling anxiety of Hsiao Lo and the townsfolk, cleansing their guilt-ridden consciences. It also, to a certain extent, soothes the anxieties of readers, even while leaving them with unresolved suspense on the level of the plot.

The book's aesthetic treatment of animalistic gratification, violence, sacrilege, fear of retribution, and aspiration for grace may be seen as producing therapeutic and cathartic effect on its readers. Critics such as Yü Kuang-chung, Joseph Lau, and Chu Yen, all in one way or another interpreted the work as a moral fable, a story of crime and punishment about a community that has collectively sinned (Yü Kuang-chung, "Shih-erh"; Lau, "Tropics"; Chu Yen). Yü Kuang-chung further suggests that, in addition to dealing with the most basic, instinctive human desires and emotions, the work at the same time offers insight into the deep recesses of the Chinese psyche. This comment surely touches on a most important source from which the work's aesthetic effects are derived.

Whereas the early "avant-garde" writers of the Modernist literary movement explored occidental exoticism to give expression to their romantic fantasies, Li, writing in a post-Nativist decade, has exoticized "native" Chinese regional features for a well-conceived aesthetic project. His sense of nativism, unlike that of Chu Hsi-ning and the Taiwanese regional writers, is derived from his memory of ethnic Chinese communities in Southeast Asia, if not specifically from Sarawak, where he spent his childhood. Although critics have suggested that the setting of Chronicle of Chi-ling may be loosely identified as somewhere on the Chinese mainland in the early twentieth century, there are no sufficiently realistic references in the book to support or refute this suggestion. As a matter of fact, the composite image of old China does not depend on historical identity but is largely a textual product: the language is deliberately adapted from traditional Chinese vernacular fiction; character names, physical landscape, and customs may have specific models but are obviously re-created to evoke vividly the unique ambience of Chinese small-town life before the "modern" period. The fictional world in the stories is therefore at once realistic and fantastic, familiar and strange, in some ways reminiscent of the semilegendary outlaw community in such traditional novels as Shui-hu chuan [The water margin]. One element of the antiquated worldview of such a community, namely, the fatalist folk belief in *yüan* (fated interpersonal relationship) and *nieh* (cyclical retribution), both derived from vulgarized Buddhist concepts, is explored and used as a baseline for the plot of the story.

As Yü Kuang-chung points out, the traditional Chinese moral system ranks *yin* (licentiousness and its worse manifestation in adultery) as the utmost evil and the source of all kinds of wrongdoings. Sun Ssu-fang's rape of Ch'ang-sheng in front of the image of the bodhisattva thus plants an evil seed of *nieh*, as he violates both human and sacred law. The violation is even more atrocious as Ch'ang-sheng is the symbol of chastity—she has never conceived a child—and is in many ways presented as the double-image of the bodhisattva. As the evil seed grows, it is bound to incur a chain of other *nieh*— criminal acts and retributions that would not only involve the violator himself, but also his family, descendants, and other innocent people as well. While the punitive aspect of the Chinese folk belief in *nieh* has the same effect on individual conscience as the Christian notion of divine judgment, the macabre arbitrariness with which *nieh* unfolds reflects a more primitive, irrational fear of the uncontrollable chance element in life. By tapping such a dark corner of the Chinese subconscious and evoking both eerie feelings and an instinctive awe for the uncanny, Li has proven to be more successful than earlier Modernist writers in his realization of the modernist aesthetic with Chinese resources.

The unique structure of Li's work also deserves special comment. Without distinctive thematic lines, many of the stories in the series, when isolated, have the appearance of fragmentary sketches. Li's tour-de-force, in fact, rests precisely in gathering them into a series, yoking them into an integral whole, so that he can ingeniously explore the rich potential of its text syntax. As the stories' central characters and their perspectives differ, the core event is focused and refocused from different angles, and its different phases are illuminated to varying degrees. Each time the murder is mentioned, it is recontextualized within a new sphere of reality, which reverberates with a number of other such spheres in the series that have been "stored" in the story's memory. As individual stories tangentially intersect, one character's fate becomes "entangled" with another's, and open-ended episodes forever anticipate new stories. Therefore, theoretically speaking, the story series may proliferate without limit, although momentarily the narrative merely focuses on what is covered by the spotlight. The overall effect, then, is that, instead of forming a closed semantic system, the final emergence of a hidden signified—something that would imbue the story with moral relevance—in the endlessly extendable story series is forever delayed. Compared with such a story as Ou-yang Tzu's "As the Dusk Approaches," which also involves multiple presentations of the same incident, Li's approach to the epistemological problem seems very different. Instead of affirming the objective existence of a "truth" while doubting its accessibility to individual consciousness, Li seems to be building the aesthetic effect precisely on the indeterminacy of the situation, on the notion that, given the limits of human cognition, the "objective reality" will never emerge with a distinct contour and clearly delimited circumscriptions. As Bradbury and McFarlane once suggested, on recognizing the primary epistemological difficulty, the modernists set out "to redeem, essentially or existentially, the formless universe of contingency" through art (50). Instead of imposing "form" on the chaotic materials of life, Li has taken "contingency" itself—the underlying principle of the notions of *yüan* and *nieh*—as the very organizing principle of his book.

While the syntax of the text of *Chronicle of Chi-ling* points to a new aesthetic mode—the postmodernist?—the narrative method employed in presenting individual episodes undoubtedly achieves the very ideal strived for by the Modernists. The two features combined thus create the unique quality of the "hyper real": with all its semblance of veracity at a local level, the fictional world as a whole is nevertheless clearly an imaginary verbal construct, deliberately situated in a temporal and spatial void. By purposefully undermining the notion of realistic representation of some "objective reality" and by shaping a highly effective aesthetic discourse, Li is, more self-consciously than any other Modernist, trying to create a text that is self-referential rather than referential. It is probably in this sense that one can wholeheartedly endorse Joseph Lau's remark that ranks Li among the few significant writers, including Lu Hsün, Eileen Chang, and Pai Hsien-yung, who have contributed to "expanding the horizon of modern Chinese narrative" ("Tropics" 6). Further, as the artistic potential of a number of techniques introduced by the Modernists are explored to the fullest extent in Li's work, *Chronicle of Chi-ling* may also be regarded as representing a culminating point in the Modernist project of post-1949 Taiwan.

CHAPTER FOUR

Modernists Reaching Maturity: Cultural Critique and Textual Strategies

In this chapter I will discuss four major Modernist works of fiction from Taiwan: *Tales of Taipei Characters* and *Crystal Boys* by Pai Hsien-yung; and *Family Crisis* and *Backed Against the Sea* by Wang Wen-hsing. My aim is not only to identify the specific ways in which these works embody certain strands of the Western modernist aesthetic, but also to demonstrate that as Taiwan's Modernists matured in their artistry, their capacity to incorporate native literary traditions and comment on contemporary social reality also grew impressively, resulting in some monumental contributions to modern Chinese literary history. Since the first work to be dealt with, Pai Hsien-yung's *Tales of Taipei Characters*,[1] has already been thoroughly analyzed in several excellent critical studies by such critics as Ou-yang Tzu, Joseph Lau, C. T. Hsia, and Yen Yüan-shu, my examination will concentrate on one specific feature: the work's indebtedness to traditional Chinese views in terms of thematic conception and ideological outlook.

Tales of Taipei Characters

Though primarily concerned with the younger writers of the 1960s, Joseph Lau's "The Concepts of Time and Reality in Modern Chinese Fiction" identifies a prominent feature of Taiwan literature written in the two decades immediately following the Retreat: the repression of historical representation. Because writings on sensitive topics were easily banned and their authors blacklisted during this period, voluntary or involuntary self-censorship has produced a literature in which contemporary history is strikingly underrepresented. This feature stands out conspicuously in comparison with literature of the pre-1949 period, when Chinese writers displayed an "obsessive concern with China as a nation afflicted with a spiritual disease" (Hsia, "Appendix 1" 533).

Although writers of the older generation inherited the pre-1949 realist tradition of Chinese New Literature, their deliberate avoidance of "critical realism," consciously or unconsciously altering the very conventions of this tradition, was largely an effect of the dominant culture's ideological prescriptions. Most of the younger Modernists, however, did not subscribe to the same ideology. Although they inevitably felt the same kinds of pressure, the downplay of historical references in their works was more aesthetically than politically motivated. Not only was tendentiousness remarkably absent in their literature, but the conception of "history" itself was also different. As Lau observed, almost all the young Modernists had tried writing "moral parables," and "in the hands of these parable writers ... modern Chinese fiction has branched off from the central tradition: instead of the naturalistic 'man-social history,' they are now writing what John Henry Raleigh has called the 'ego-universal history'" (32). Even though the really obscure parable writings quickly went out of fashion and the Modernists soon began to take up the subject of contemporary history, Lau's observation remains valid, as such Modernist works usually claimed to be part of universal human history. Pai Hsien-yung's *Tales of Taipei Characters* provides an excellent example of this tendency.

Addressing the ostrich mentality of Taipei's mainlander émigrés in the 1960s, *Tales* first appeared as a welcome exception to the general lack of historical references in Taiwan's Modernist fiction. C. T. Hsia, for example, commended the work as virtually offering an allegory of the history of the Republic of China ("Pai" 294). Joseph Lau saw in characters of this book "the collective consciousness of Chinese exiles in general" ("Celestials" 410). Yen Yüan-shu also praised Pai for his "strong historical consciousness," even though his own criticism of the book primarily focused on its technical aspect. Furthermore, when leftist critics castigated Pai for his "reactionary" attempt to whitewash the crimes of a decadent social class closely associated with the Nationalists, calling him "a cosmetician for funeral homes," they expressed their concern with the work's historical implications. Nevertheless, from the specific vantage point taken in the present study, the kind of historical representation found in *Tales* conceals an aesthetic strategy that purports to rewrite history in ahistorical, universal terms.

Ou-yang Tzu has most fully expounded the universalist nature of the work in her *Wang-Hsieh t'ang ch'ien te yen-tzu* [Swallows in front of the noble mansions of Wang and Hsieh], a critical study devoted to exegesis of Pai's *Tales*. Stressing the work's multilayered semantic structure—a feature that may plausibly be seen as having developed from the parabolic writings' allegorical tendency discussed by Joseph Lau—Ou-yang argues that the tales are primarily concerned with universal human struggle, with the gap between past and present, the conflict between soul and flesh, and the unresolvable riddle of life and death. Although she identifies the dividing line between Pai's "past" and "present" to be the year 1949, with specific historical reference to the Nationalist Retreat (9), her interpretation of the past-present theme is primarily conceived in universal rather than historical terms. Within the book's particular symbolic system, she argues, the "past" is not merely a temporal reference, but stands for a set of psychological values; an illusion of plenitude plays a crucial role in the characters' involvement in "the eternal battle between soul and flesh."[2] Following this line of thinking, even though the central subject of *Tales* is contemporary Chinese history, it is so in a highly generalized, symbolic way. Ou-yang's analysis is particularly valuable as it makes evident some fundamental assumptions that Ou-yang shares with her former classmate Pai Hsien-yung as, in general terms, both of them have positioned themselves in the Western liberal-humanist tradition.

Despite his reputation as Taiwan's leading Modernist fiction writer, Pai has been moderate in his appropriation of pure aesthetic modernism. Whereas modernist skepticism about the referential quality of literature and the view of the literary text as essentially self-referential are clearly pronounced in the aesthetic views of such Modernists as Wang Wen-hsing and Li Yung-p'ing, Pai's publicly expressed opinions about literature, especially in regard to the hierarchy of form and content, remain largely within the broad humanist tradition and lack a specific emphasis on the autonomous status of language as an independent verbal reality. (For example, his advocacy of artistic autonomy in the past has always placed more emphasis on the importance of freeing modern Chinese literature from political interference.) Still more important, Pai has proven to be more willing as well as more successful in assimilating traditional Chinese literary elements in his work than any of his peers.³ His intricate textual allusions, political allegories, and the strategies he employs to skirt explicit political criticism all seem to be inspired by traditional Chinese literary practices. The central themes of both of his major works, too, are pregnant with references to long-standing Chinese literati traditions as well as to the legacy of Chinese gentry ideology. In *Tales*, such elements are most visible in the stories' treatment of the relationship between history and culture, public and private.

Culture versus History

> The wild grass and flowers on the side of the Vermilion-Sparrow Bridge,
> The slanting sun setting at the edge of the Black-Swallow Alley—
> Birds that in old times frequented the mandarin halls of the noble clans of Wang and Hsieh,
> Are now plunging into the humble residences of plebians of a hundred clans.
> Liu Yü-hsi (772–842, T'ang dynasty),
> "Wu-i hsiang" [Black-Swallow Alley]

The lament of transience and mutability, the theme of this classical poem cited on the title page of *Tales*, is perhaps the most persistent and most widely employed thematic paradigm in traditional Chinese poetry. Besides setting the tenor for the emotional ambience of the book, the poem, with references to the rise and fall of the Six Dynasties and the decline of illustrious noble clans, evokes a time-honored paradox of the relationship between history and culture: Although the Six Dynasties was a historical period marked by political turmoil and weakened central governments under menacing northern barbarians, it is also a period known for its extraordinary cultural vitality and artistic achievements. The poet's express admiration for the beauty and splendor of the cultural monuments produced in a time when national existence was endangered goes against the Confucian moral prescription that associates excessive attention to artistic refinement with the individual citizen's neglect of responsibility toward the state.[4]

This inherently ambivalent view of the relationships between culture and politics and between art and history features prominently in Pai's privately and publicly expressed opinions but is only insinuated within the textual space of *Tales*, where the implied author ostensibly abstains from explicit moral judgment in accordance with the objectivity principle. This technique is best illustrated by the most celebrated story in the series, "Yu-yüan ching-meng" [Wandering in the garden, waking from a dream] (1966). That in this story traditional China is symbolically represented by a group of k'un-ch'ü singers at the Fu-tzu miao (Confucian temple), a public entertainment quarter located in Nanking, the Republican period capital, points to the intimate and by no means innocent relationship between decadence and cultural refinement,[5] as the situation immediately calls to mind, for culturally informed readers, two famous poetic lines traditionally used to condemn those who fail to take proper patriotic action: "Shang-nü pu chih wang-kuo hen, ko chiang yu ch'ang Hou-t'ing hua" (Across the river, the singsong girls, ignorant of the fact that their country has already been overtaken by the enemy, are still singing the decadent love song "Blossoms in the Backyard").[6] Despite the apparent neutral stance taken by the story's narrator, implicit moral judgment is still made, if obliquely. In describing the pompous lifestyle led by Nationalist army generals and their wives, for example, the narrator allows a glimpse of the underside of this glory by telling how, for a sumptuous party of Mme. Ch'ien, "tons of silver dollars had been *sinfully* spent" (my italics). With one intrusive adverb, the entire historical milieu—the extreme disorder, calamities, and hardships of ordinary people in the late 1940s—begins to loom in the background.

Thus, the lack of moral judgment from the sociohistorical point of view in Pai's work is a deliberate "suppression" rather than political blindness. Moreover, perhaps the most prominent strategy used to bracket off such judgments is Pai's dedication of the book to "the generation of my parents, who lived in a time full of grief and disasters." History is thus deliberately presented as sieved through subjective consciousness and treated only in terms of its impact on the individual life. This conversion from the public to the private, from the objective to the subjective, again, is a distinguishing feature of the genre stylistics of Chinese literati literature, in which scholar-officials give free vent to their sensitive, delicate, even decadent sentiments while reserving for practical life their serious dedication to state service.

To a large extent, as Ou-yang Tzu has demonstrated well, Pai is not explicitly critical of the Confucian tradition in *Tales*; at times, he even seems to be indirectly confirming its value. Therefore, even though the book's "apolitical" references to contemporary history could be politically liable—since they are likely to trigger unsanctioned associations of subjects embarrassing for the Nationalists—the work has nevertheless been well accepted within Taiwan's dominant culture and comfortably consumed as history under erasure. Moreover, since the work's cultural assumptions are so highly traditional and characteristically "Chinese," the *Tales* has not only enjoyed unusual popularity among Taiwan readers, modernists and traditionalists alike, but has also been warmly appreciated by readers on the mainland, unaffected by the ideological differences.

Public versus Private

If Pai's perception of the culture-history relationship shows the visible influence of the Confucianist value system, he has also unmistakably displayed discontent with certain aspects of the Confucian tradition. Though most pronounced in *Crystal Boys*, the conflict between public and private already appears in *Tales*. In order to understand this motif, some comment on Ou-yang Tzu's criticism in *Swallows in Front of the Noble Mansions* is in order.

In her interpretation of the thematic structure of *Tales*, Ou-yang has stressed the opposition between the spiritual and the libidinal, soul and flesh—an interpretive scheme perhaps too heavily informed by Western concepts. Because *Tales* was written at a time when the author himself was under similar Western influences, Ou-yang's approach is probably well justified. Nevertheless, on several occasions, Ou-yang, a careful and conscientious critic, has admitted that her critical scheme does not always work.[7] One of these occasions is of particular interest: Although always inclined to stress Pai's assertion of the spiritual over the corporeal, Ou-yang has sensed that, in the story "Wandering in the Garden," Pai has clearly placed his sympathy with the corporeal aspect of love. In order to maintain the consistency of her argument, Ou-yang treats this story as "a rare exception":

Thus the bitter remorse of Mme. Ch'ien, that "I have lived only once," which refers to her affair with Cheng Yen-ch'ing, may even imply a more important theme, the grievance against the repressive ideology imposed on the innate desire of the individual. In the majority of Pai's fiction, the spiritual and the corporeal, and youth and sexual desire are always opposed to each other. The spiritual and the youthful represent "life"; the corporeal and sexual desire are equivalent to "death." That the character Cheng Yen-ch'ing represents both youthful vitality and sexual temptation, that he is endowed with both a spiritual quality and physical attraction seems a rare exception in *Taipei jen*. (255–256)

Ou-yang's perceived dichotomy between the emotional and physical aspects of love is rather typical in Western, psychological criticism; it is also part of her way of asserting the work's universal themes.[8] However, one may easily take issue with this interpretation by arguing that the dichotomy between soul and flesh, spiritual and libidinal is not as clear-cut in the Chinese concept of love, or *ch'ing*, as in the West. *Ch'ing*, originally signifying "the natural disposition of things" and therefore connoting both amorous passion and plain sentimentality, is of course an antonym of *yü*, or animalistic desire. Yet both faculties are seen as having sprung from the natural human physical condition, and they do not have the transcendental implications of the Western concepts used by Ou-yang. In perhaps the characteristically monistic mode of Chinese thought, *ch'ing* and *yü* are also a two-in-one concept. Though differentiable in evaluative terms, they are not exactly seen as opposing each other, but rather appear to occupy different slots on the same continuum.

One major theme of "Wandering in the Garden," as Ou-yang properly states, is "the grievance against the repressive ideology imposed on the innate desire of the individual." This theme implies a cultural criticism that presumes the mutual implications of *ch'ing* and *yü*. The following discussion will sketch this criticism by way of augmenting, and slightly modifying, Ou-yang's analysis.

According to Ou-yang, as the nickname "Jade of the Indigo Field" suggests, Mme. Ch'ien, the former k'un-ch'ü singer married to an aged general, embodies the ideal of traditional ladyship and, by implication, the spiritual essence of traditional Chinese culture. Since k'un-ch'ü, in contrast to the more popular form of Peking opera, is a more refined form of elite pastime, Ou-yang takes the author's allusion to k'un-ch'ü plays as an affirmation of traditional Chinese culture and suggests that the present condition of Mme. Ch'ien—leading an obscure life in the south, away from the cultural center—symbolizes the decline of that tradition. Ou-yang also extends this symbolic meaning to explain why orthodox Chinese culture is neglected in modern times: "Traditional Chinese culture has a past full of glamor. However, just because it is purely aesthetic and purely spiritual, it refuses to be contaminated by vulgar reality. It is thus divorced from everyday life in the contemporary world of ordinary people and consequently no longer appreciated" (265).

Whereas Ou-yang builds her argument on the fact that k'un-ch'ü is a more refined artistic form than hua-pu, a former version of Peking opera that superseded k'un-ch'ü in popularity, another important historical fact about the Chinese drama may also be taken into consideration. As its origin coincides with the rise of the commercial class in the Yüan and Ming dynasties, Chinese drama, just like vernacular fiction, has always remained a less respectable form of art. Over a long historical period, both drama and fiction served as a means for those literati rejected by the mainstream culture to express their discontent and to amuse themselves. Their frequent indulgence in melodramatic sentimentality and their occasional lewd descriptions are typically implied criticism of the excessively ascetic tendencies of the dominant Neo-Confucianist moralism, including the repression of innate feelings and natural desires. Although such popular forms as k'un-ch'ü and vernacular fiction were later transformed into elitist art forms in the hands of several great masters and consequently incorporated into the canon, the erotic elements retained in their content as well as the elevation of the private over the public continued to be deemed subversive by Confucian moralists.[9] One may thus argue that, by alluding to Mu-tan t'ing [The peony pavilion] in "Wandering in the Garden," which anticipates the more extensive textual references to Dream of the Red Chamber in Crystal Boys, Pai has situated himself within a tradition of resistance vis-à-vis the repressive elements of the Neo-Confucian ideology that has a history of several hundred years.

Though still fundamentally conservative, Pai's view of the dominant culture becomes more explicitly critical in his later work Crystal Boys, published nearly twenty years after Tales. Generally speaking, despite an indirect gesture of protest, the stories in Tales tacitly espouse Apollonian reason. The thematic thrust of the novel Crystal Boys, however, may be seen as partaking in the celebration of the Dionysian impulse—libidinal ecstasy and anxiety, the unresolved tension of sexual longing, and an obstinate refusal to be reabsorbed into a bland order. The conflict between public and private now occupies the foreground of the story's thematic domain.

Crystal Boys

Although it has been almost a decade since Pai Hsien-yung's latest novel, *Crystal Boys*, was published, no comprehensive critical analysis of the work has yet been conducted. Although this lack of attention may be indicative of a general loss of enthusiasm in Modernist literature among Taiwan's readers and critics, another factor could be that, for sophisticated readers, the cultural criticism expressed through the lives of a cohort of homosexual boys in the position of social outcasts seems fairly unambiguous, and the message of protest in the novel is also explicitly articulated. This seeming uncomplicatedness, however, is more apparent than real. The serious Modernist treats creative writing as a lifelong intellectual quest, and the moral vision that has emerged in this novel, a product of a mature stage in Pai's personal development, has more substance than is recognizable on the surface. Many of the novel's broad and deep implications for the Chinese cultural landscape, such as its comments on the relationship between the public and the private and on the way paternal authority dominates in the family and in society, moreover, can only be fully comprehended through a careful deciphering of the novel's elaborate symbolic system.

Crystal Boys comprises four books: a one-page prologue, two main sections consisting of thirty-three and thirty chapters, respectively, and an epilogue. In book 1, "Banishment," protagonist A-qing (Ah-ch'ing), a high-school senior and the son of a discharged brigade commander, is driven out of the home by his father after being dismissed from school for homosexual activity with the school's janitor. Book 2, "In Our Kingdom," begins with A-qing's joining an underground gay community that gathers nightly in Taipei's New Park. In the following months, as he survives as a male prostitute, A-qing chances upon a stranger, Wang Quilong (Wang K'uei-lung), or Dragon Prince, who turns out to be the hero of a long-circulated legend in the park. He also gets to see his mother, who many years before eloped with a trumpet player and now, in wretched shape, is painfully awaiting death. Book 2 ends with an incident four months later: A-qing is arrested along with others at the park when a minor crime attracts the attention of a policeman. Book 3,

"The Cozy Nest," is named after the new gay bar founded by Chief Yang, the boys' guardian in the park. The bar replaces the lotus pond of New Park, which is now under curfew, as their new gathering spot. A-qing and three other boys of the park—Little Jade, Mousey, and Wu Min—having been released with the help of a certain Papa Fu, who has been anonymously helping boys of the park, work happily as waiters in the bar. Then Chief Yang sends A-qing to stay with Papa Fu and take care of the old man after his maidservant breaks her leg. Papa Fu dies of illness shortly thereafter, with A-qing waiting at his deathbed. The bar eventually must close because some journalist has published a nasty newspaper article insinuating its existence. The epilogue, "Youth Birds on the Wing," briefly tells how A-qing and his friends are eventually reabsorbed into society, taking ordinary jobs.

Alongside the main story line, the story of two secondary characters, Dragon Prince and Papa Fu, carries special thematic weight. Dragon Prince is the hero of a "legend" that has been told and retold in the park. The son of a high-ranking official, Dragon Prince falls madly in love with a boy of New Park, Phoenix Boy. The latter, raised in the slums, has an unusually fiery temper. Their ill-fated love ends with Dragon Prince killing Phoenix Boy one New Year's eve because the latter refuses to go home with him. Dragon Prince's father promptly sends him abroad to stop the scandal and forbids him to return as long as he is alive.

Papa Fu, a retired general, has a son Fu Wei, a promising young army officer who commits suicide after being caught in a sexual act with another soldier. Actually, Fu Wei only decides to kill himself after his father refuses to give him a chance to explain. The death occurs on Papa Fu's birthday, which becomes a bitter reminder of the son's grievance.

The intricate character system in the novel is apparently an extension of the use of parallelism in *Tales of Taipei Characters*. By clustering the characters sharing common traits in a crisscross manner, Pai succeeds in foregrounding a number of major and minor themes. Among these themes, the ones revolving around Dragon Prince and Papa Fu, the prototypical son and father are of central significance: The first important theme of the novel is the antisocial nature of *ch'ing*. Although the violent consequence of Dragon Prince's irrational passion is matched only by the story of another marginal character, Peach Boy who takes his own life in revenge for his lover's betrayal, the same kind of passion, though less intense, constantly agitates everyone in the park and is at the heart of the inherent incongruity between this private community and the outside world. The second theme is the father-son conflict. As Dragon Prince is renounced by his father, Papa Fu also rejects his son. When Dragon Prince returns after his father's death and through A-qing's mediation pays a visit to Papa Fu, the conversation between the two suggests the possibility of reconciliation between antagonistic fathers and sons. The third theme is the pervasive form of oppression in modern society. Dragon Prince, though originally from a privileged social class, forms associations with the most miserable, victimized members of society: Phoenix Boy is born to a fruit peddler's retarded daughter, who was raped, beaten, and left in a ditch by a gang of hoodlums; during his exile in New York, Dragon Prince runs into numerous homeless boys forced into crime and prostitution. Both Papa Fu and Dragon Prince finally attain spiritual growth through repentance and by helping the poor and helpless: Papa Fu volunteers in orphanages and adopts a child born without limbs; Dragon Prince adopts a crippled boy and helps him cure his foot. Thus, the author seems to be communicating the moral vision that only forgiveness and indiscriminate compassion can alleviate human suffering. The following discussion will elaborate on the significant cultural implications of these themes.

Sensuality and Civilized Society: The Influence of the American Countercultural Movement

The opposition between the passions of the private self and the normative laws of the society that represses the self is poetically expressed in the beginning passage of book 2, "In Our Kingdom."

> There are no days in our kingdom, only nights. As soon as the sun comes up, our kingdom goes into hiding, for it is an unlawful nation; we have no government and no constitution, we are neither recognized nor respected by anyone, our citizenry is little more than rabble. Sometimes we have a leader—a person who's been around for a while, someone who's good-looking, impressive, popular. But we have no qualms about dethroning him any time we feel like it, because we are a fickle, unruly people. The area between our borders is pitifully small, no more than two or three hundred meters long and a hundred meters wide—that narrow strip of land surrounding the oval lotus pond in Taipei's New

Park, on Guanqian Street. The fringes of our territory are planted with all sorts of tropical trees: green coral, breadfruit, palms so old their drooping fronds nearly touch the ground, and, of course, the stand of old cocoanut trees alongside the road that wave their heads in exasperation the day long. It's as though our kingdom were surrounded and hidden by a tightly woven fence—cut off from the outside world.[10] (17)

By suggesting that the gay circle is a "kingdom," a mirror image of the society outside, the author is proposing an alternative value system. In direct contrast to civilized modern society, which upholds the law, the constitution, and reason, the illegal gathering of gays around the lotus pond is described as unruly, anarchical, and carnivalesque. Yet, if citizens of this kingdom are not governed by ordinary rules, they have their own hierarchy of values, which can be summed up as the glorification of the sensuous body. Physical beauty may qualify one as a leader; ancient, primitive passions, symbolized by the tropical weather and plants, lie deep in every bosom; and sensual gratification, suggested by the "breadfruit plant" and numerous food images throughout the book, like sex, is a natural instinct springing from the basic existential condition, the human being's possession of a body. Thus the members of this society are not only social outcasts; insofar as they actively refuse to be indoctrinated in the normative laws of the society, they are also rebels. Yet, of course, in terms of actual power, they are no match for their enemies; they are the oppressed minority, constantly "frightened," warily guarding against the outside world's "invading our territory," and groping in the dark "for a path to survival" (17–18).

The celebration of the sensuous body, especially the homosexual body, seems to hark back to Pai's work of the early period. C. T. Hsia once noted that the mythological figure of Adonis served as an important archetype in Pai's early stories ("Pai" 298–308). In those stories, Pai shows a personal preference for young male characters and treats them as symbols of youth, beauty, and love, as he portrays certain domineering women characters as fleshy, lustful, and threatening. The apparent enlargement of thematic scope in *Crystal Boys* to include sociocultural criticism, however, significantly distinguishes this novel from Pai's more personal early fiction. This change may be plausibly explained by the influence of the antiestablishment spirit, humanist ideals, and emancipatory ethos—the flower child mentality—of the American countercultural movement of the 1960s, which Pai witnessed personally.[11]

Although the impact of this movement on Pai seems undeniable, Pai departs drastically from its more radical participants in his political views. Pai remains a liberal and a vocal critic of communism, as several other Modernists in Taiwan are. The difference between Taiwan's young writers of the 1960s and their Western counterparts writing in the same historical period is perceptively observed by C. T. Hsia, whose views may be summarized as follows: As the progressive young writers in the West discarded Christian civilization and its modern spokesmen, such as Yeats, Eliot, Joyce, Lawrence, and Faulkner, Taiwan's Modernists followed the classic modernism of the Western tradition. Whereas the collective search for a utopian society by the young Western writers caused "the extreme popularity of Herbert Marcuse, who mixes Marxism and Freudian psychology into a new system of thought," the Modernist writers of Taiwan displayed a decisively conservative predisposition ("Pai" 293). Hsia has explained this characteristic in historical terms:

> [The writers from Taiwan,] deeply disturbed by the tragic outcome of the radical rebellions of youths of their parents' generation [during the May Fourth period], which had resulted in the expansion of Chinese Communism, are not likely to take any fancy in the utopian ideals of a socialist revolution. Although they do not write anti-Communist propaganda, their profound love for their mother country has imbued in them a respect for tradition and a conservative temperament. ("Pai" 293)

The relative conservatism and moderate political stance of Taiwan's Modernists, however, do not prevent them from radically protesting against the hegemonic cultural forms of Chinese society. The disintegration of the traditional metaphysics of Christianity in the West has had a counterpart in the collapse of the Neo-Confucianist, feudalist moral code in Chinese society, where the transition from the feudal to the modern mode of thought is still an ongoing process. Selectively drawing from the antitraditionalist legacy of the May Fourth intellectuals, the Modernists in Taiwan have, in their own ways, engaged in serious reexamination of their own cultural heritage. The Modernists' contact with the American countercultural movement at a crucial stage of their creative careers (from around the ages of twenty-five to thirty) seems to have suggested a viable alternative cultural model. The emancipatory ethos of this movement was embraced by almost all important writers of the generation, including the more conservative, such as Ou-yang Tzu, and the more radical, such as Ch'en Ying-chen (although Ch'en did not come to the United States until the 1980s, the influence of the spirit of the sixties is pronounced in the development of Ch'en's political thought, which is explicitly articulated in such stories as the 1978 "Ho Ta-ko" [Brother Hopper]). In the case of Pai Hsien-yung, the glorification of the sensuous body and the discontent with civilized society have formed the basis of his critique of remnant feudal values in Chinese society.

Cultural Critique: Textual Allusions to Dream of the Red Chamber

Among Taiwan's Modernists, Pai's appropriation of Western concepts is most obviously mixed with traditional elements. Along with the humanist assertion of the private self and the celebration of the libido, Pai has specially stressed the sentimental aspect of human emotion, clearly echoing his favorite classical Chinese novel, *Dream of the Red Chamber*.

Their possession of a high degree of sentimentality is what distinguishes people of New Park from the outside world. In a passage of book 2 that immediately follows the passage quoted above, the narrator employs an emotion-tinged tone to continue his description of the "kingdom": "This hidden, unlawful, tiny site of ours has been the scene of a history so *tragic* yet so hidden to the outside world that *tears* are inadequate to describe it" (italics mine). The few white-haired old-timers in the park further predict that members of their kingdom will be forever attached: "After an absence of five to ten or even fifteen or twenty years, [they] would suddenly show up on a moonless night beside the lotus pond to pay a return visit to the dark kingdom of their youth. They would stroll anxiously around the pond, as though looking for the soul they'd left behind."

In the same passage, the narrator mentions the beautiful water lilies that were in the lotus pond before being pulled out by men sent by the municipal government. The red water lilies stand for the more passionate form of ch'ing: they are compared to fire and "bright red lanterns" and are mentioned when Dragon Prince kills Phoenix Boy. Such violent passion is a natural desire, just as the lilies are part of the natural landscape. Significantly, the symbol of private emotion is eradicated by the public law enforcers, to be replaced by an artificial cultural emblem, the octagonal pavilion that is intensely hated by everyone in the private "kingdom."

In *Dream of the Red Chamber*, Ts'ao Hsüeh-ch'in extensively employs Taoist and Buddhist ideas, the traditional countercultural trend to the dominant Confucian tradition. In Pai's novel, references to such a religious frame of thought are also unmistakable. Most notably, as the lotus flower is the seat of the Buddha, the lily could also be seen as symbolizing the state of enlightenment, or nirvana, and the transcendence of passion and desire. In particular, since in Chinese the word "lily" is a homophone of the word for pity or compassion (lien), it is being used as a pun, just as Ts'ao Hsüeh-ch'in uses it in the name of Ying-lien (should be pitied), a symbolic character that appears in the preface to *Dream*. The look of wisdom and pity of the old-timers in the park when telling stories to newcomers—"The oldtimers would nod their heads and lower their eyelids slightly, looks of pity on their faces. Knowingly and in voices filled with emotion, they would put the scene in front of them into perspective."—apparently recalls the complexion of the merciful Buddha, who looks at human sufferings with compassion and understanding (18).

The preface to *Dream of the Red Chamber* claims that the novel is based on a story inscribed on a magical stone under the Greensickness Peak in the immortal realm, copied and circulated by a certain Monk Vanitas. The inscription relates the origin of the stone. When the goddess Nü-wa molds a large quantity of blocks of stone to repair the sky, she leaves a single odd block unused. This block of stone, possessing magic powers, is then taken by a Buddhist and a Taoist monk to the world of mortals to live out the life of a man "before finally attaining nirvana and returning to the other shore" (Hawkes 49). The story in *Dream of the Red Chamber* is a detailed record of the human life lived by the incarnated stone, Pao-yü, literally "precious jade." Born into a wealthy gentry family of the Chia clan, Pao-yü, to the annoyance of his father, shows no enthusiasm to follow what has been prescribed for young gentlemen of his social status, namely to study the Confucian classics in preparation for the civil service examinations and a career in officialdom. Instead, he whiles away his days in the family's luxurious park, the Prospect Garden, frequenting parties and poetry clubs and engaging in all sorts of elegant pastimes with a dozen beautiful and talented female cousins and bondmaids.

One prominent feature of *Crystal Boys* clearly alluding to *Dream* is the microcosm device. Like the Prospect Garden, both New Park and Cozy Nest are utopian kingdoms within the boundary of which the value of the hegemonic culture is reversed and the value of the private self, here *ch'ing*, or sentimentality, is elevated. The father figure in Pai's novel also unmistakably represents the authority of the public, outside world. One apparent message of *Crystal Boys* is that the culturally determined parental expectations for male offspring of a gentry family in a Confucian society, always involving public service to the state, seriously represses natural, personal feelings, often resulting in a love-hate relationship between father and son. The name of Dragon Prince is part of the set phrase *wang-tzu ch'eng-lung*, literally "to expect one's son to become a dragon." Yet the fact that Dragon Prince is obsessed with love and passion stands in the way of his performing the prescribed duty of a son. Both Fu Wei and A-qing have disappointed their fathers because their "immoral behavior" has caused them to be rejected by such social institutions as the school and the army, preventing them from becoming "useful" members of society. The protest against paternal authority can thus be understood as a criticism of residual social norms handed down from the feudal system. The intricate entanglement of the relationship between father and son and the individual's responsibility to the public is rooted in Confucian ethics: because society and nation are regarded as extensions of the family, loyalty to country (*chung*) and filial piety (*hsiao*) are two sides of the same coin. Just as Pao-yü's father is a Confucian scholar-official, the three fathers in *Crystal Boys* are all unconditionally loyal to the state. The father of A-qing, an expelled brigade commander, for example, though humiliated by being unfairly discharged as a traitor, dreams about sending his son to military school. The father of Dragon Prince, a successful statesman, and Papa Fu, a retired general, are both gravely injured by their sons' homosexuality, which prevents them from serving the country (Papa Fu's son, in particular, is a promising young lieutenant in the army). The father's renunciation of the son is therefore more than a family affair, as it is done on behalf of the society and the state. The unfaithful son, therefore, is also considered a disloyal citizen.

As Pao-yü indulges in playing with girls, the "work ethic," or conformity to the pragmatism of the society at large, is also downplayed in Pai's work, probably a reflection of the antiestablishment "hippie" mentality. Although the boys in New Park are from disadvantaged social backgrounds and lack opportunities for social advancement, they also frequently reject offers to better their lives in exchange for hard work. A-qing's refusal to work in the Cafe Silver Chariot and Little Jade's giving up the job at the drugstore as soon as he realizes that it will not further his dream of going to Japan to search for his father in a way parallel Pao-yü's resentment of studying for the civil service examinations. Furthermore, the fact that the most important scenes in *Crystal Boys* revolve around social gatherings, festive banquets, and carnivalesque parties may be seen as the influence of a common structural feature of traditional Chinese novels of the Ming and Ch'ing dynasties; it at the same time, however, implies a criticism of the society's pragmatism and its repression of the instinctual body, physical gratification, enjoyment of food, sex, play, and communal fellowship.

In *Dream*, Ts'ao Hsüeh-ch'in has effectively used femininity to suggest a set of alternative values—the private and sentimental, as opposed to the public and pragmatic—to undermine masculinity, the patriarchal cultural order, and the law of the father. Beginning in the preface, he has emphatically ranked the talents of the female characters over those of the males and has accentuated this unorthodox view through a famous remark made by Pao-yü: "Girls are made of water and boys are made of mud. When I am with girls, I feel fresh and clean, but when I am with boys I feel stupid and nasty" (76). In its resistant function, Pai's use of homosexuality in *Crystal Boys* is similar to Ts'ao's elevation of femininity—the boys in New Park are extremely affectionate and sensitive. At the same time, both authors have apparently participated in a countercultural movement of their times. Ts'ao, by building his glorification of the feminine quality on the long-standing association between femininity and refined elitist culture in traditional Chinese society—a phenomenon described by the author of a recent article as "the feminization of culture" (Wang Yuejin)[12]—has offered an effective new variant to strategies commonly employed in vernacular fiction, notably elevating its level to the realm of high culture. By drawing on the activist equal rights movement, with which the gay movement is closely associated, and by focusing on homosexual prostitutes, a doubly oppressed minority in society, Pai protests two different forms of oppression in modern society: discrimination on the bases of sexual preference and poverty.

Despite these similarities, *Crystal Boys* departs from its classical model in some significant respects. In *Dream*, there is another opposition besides that between public and private. That the stone and its incarnation Pao-yü are alternately described as *wan* (recalcitrant or stubborn) or *ling* (spiritual and enlightened or enlightenable) reflects contradictory perceptions from two different standpoints. From the Confucian perspective, Pao-yü's temperament and his obstinate refusal to submit to orthodox views reflect a foolish stubbornness, a leftover trait of the "useless block" rejected for the lofty cause of repairing the sky. From the Taoist-Buddhist perspective, however, Pao-yü possesses a spiritual, miraculous quality that enables him finally to transcend love and passion and to attain enlightenment.

The ultimate message Ts'ao Hsüeh-ch'in intends to convey is the Buddhist conception of disenchantment from the world of form and illusions necessary for the attainment of nirvana.[13] Pai Hsien-yung, with all his allusions to Buddhist imagery, has never gone so far as to advocate such a religious transcendance; the theme of *Crystal Boys* is still essentially embedded in the liberal humanist tradition. This thematic difference may be illuminated by a discussion of the central image of the heart, or *hsin*, in Pai's novel, which is roughly a counterpart of the extremely complex, ultimately ambiguous image of the stone in *Dream*.

As the Chinese do not have a clear-cut heart-mind dichotomy, *hsin* is a faculty that has the function of both. It is both intention and feeling, sense and sensibility, emotion and practical reason. It is something that hosts *ch'ing*, but at the same time harnesses it, checking its overflow. In *Crystal Boys*, *hsin* is the site of both passion and compassion, two dominant functions also represented by the image of the red lotus (the heart and the lily actually seem to accompany each other, as in the scene in which Phoenix Boy is murdered). This symbol provides the key to understanding the meaning of the fated love between Dragon Prince and Phoenix Boy.

The dragon-phoenix pair is apparently modeled on the stone-plant connection between Pao-yü and Tai-yü in *Dream*, which is a relationship predestined in their former life. The inscription on the stone tells the reader that, when the spirit of the stone finds himself unworthy to be used in repairing the sky, he wanders about with feelings of shame and resentment and chances upon a beautiful crimson pearl flower on the bank of the Magic River. He waters the flower with dew, finally causing it "to shed her vegetable shape and assume the form of a girl." This fairy girl, grateful to the stone for giving her life, thinks to herself that, since she does not have the sweet dew, the only way in which she can repay the stone-celestial "would be with the tears shed during the whole of a mortal lifetime if he and I were ever to be reborn as humans in the world below" (53). The incarnation of this fairy is apparently Pao-yü's delicate and sensitive cousin and lover, Tai-yü, whose most prominent trait is a habit of easily breaking into tears.

The relationship between Dragon Prince and Phoenix Boy also seems to be one that involves the giving and the repayment of a life-giving favor. When Dragon Prince stabs Phoenix Boy in the chest, he claims that he has previously given the latter his heart and is now taking it back. Phoenix Boy, who from childhood has shown an unusually violent temper, easily loses his senses and cries excessively, repeating that he has never possessed a heart. When stabbed, he does not show hatred or grievance but only sadness, as if he owes his life to Dragon Prince. This "life" is apparently a most intimate love, something that Phoenix Boy has missed in the orphanage.

The function of the heart in *Crystal Boys*, like the stone, holds the key to personal salvation. When Dragon Prince kills his lover, he is demonstrating an excessive passion, a form of ch'ing that is destructive. Although hsin is the source of ch'ing, because of the dominance of the latter, the proper function of hsin to regulate, control, and balance emotion is apparently obfuscated. Then, like Pao-yü who temporarily loses his jade, Dragon Prince, during the first six months of his exile in New York, is also said to have lost all human feeling. He only comes back to his senses and repossesses a heart when, one day, he saves a Puerto Rican boy and sees on his chest a red scar that is shaped exactly like the human heart. If the miraculous stone in *Dream* is what finally enables Pao-yü to see through the "red dust" and the illusory world and to reach enlightenment, the heart in *Crystal Boy* is also the instrument to achieve forgiveness and compassion. The regained heart of Dragon Prince is what enables him to commiserate with the homeless boys in New York and later leads him to atone for his past. The similarity, however, seems to end here.

The highest value honored by the unusually stubborn, brilliant, and mischievous Pao-yü seems to be the more delicate part of ch'ing, not excessive passion. Pao-yü is said to possess extremely sensitive feelings and to be emotionally dedicated not only to his playmates—his cousins and bondmaids, who in the stone inscription are described as a batch of lovesick souls incarnated in human bodies—but also to his parents and other family members. As Ts'ao Hsüeh-ch'in puts it, the significant condition of enlightenment is to see through and transcend ch'ing, the emotional attachment to other people, which is the strongest human bondage for Pao-yü. On his decision to become a monk at the end of the novel, Pao-yü even discards the stone that he has possessed since birth, which is the tool by which he attains enlightenment.

Pai Hsien-yung's emphasis on the more radical manifestation of ch'ing as passion appears to indicate a Western influence. As both Dream and Pai's work are in a sense embedded in and provide a parody of popular fiction of their times, the amorous ch'ing in the "talents and beauties" (ts'ai-tzu chia-jen) stories of Ts'ao's time and the melodramatic passion in modern-day romance may have found their way into their particular conceptions of ch'ing. But the more significant difference is that Pai has never advised the total transcendence of ch'ing as Ts'ao Hsüeh-ch'in does. He seems to perceive the narrowly conceived ch'ing, in either the destructive passion between lovers or the love-hatred between estranged father and son, as a distorted, unenlightened form of emotion, which should be transformed into understanding, tolerance, and indiscriminate compassion.

After all, humanism, rather than Taoist or Buddhist religious beliefs, is the major import of Pai's work. Unlike the Nativist writers in Taiwan who are his contemporaries, Pai does not give a sociological view of the social problems with which he is deeply concerned. As a liberal humanist, he tends to emphasize the importance of the individual's capacity to understand and to sympathize. The kind of compassion proposed in the novel is particularly representative of the liberal ideal familiar in the United States, as it rejects all forms of discrimination and oppression in modern society, including those resulting from class and ethnic distinctions. Dragon Prince comes from an upper-class background, but he comes to associate with boys of New Park, most of whom were raised in the slums. During his exile in the United States, he met numerous homeless boys of different ethnicities—blacks, Puerto Ricans, Jews, Italians—wandering the streets of New York. In a sense, it is *ch'ing*, broadly conceived as the basic human emotion, that has formed an invisible tie among them all.

To Dissolve the Nieh: Protest and Reconciliation

Whereas C. T. Hsia insightfully observes Pai's unusual sensitivity to the relationship between the sexes, which is partially attributable to his homosexuality,[14] Ou-yang Tzu makes a contribution by pointing out Pai's fondness for the uncanny. She observes that in a number of the stories in *Tales*, Pai alludes to the concept of *yüan-nieh*, a popular Chinese view of retribution derived from the Buddhist belief that human suffering is caused by wrongdoings committed in one's previous life or by one's ancestors.[15] This view is most explicitly expressed in a story in *Tales*, "Ku-lien hua" [Lone flower] (1970).

In "Lone Flower," the middle-aged madam of a night club, apparently a lesbian, has been involved with two other prostitutes, one fifteen years ago on the mainland and one in Taiwan. Both of them, Wu-pao and Chüan-chüan, have passively submitted to brutal sexual abuse from their patrons. Whereas Wu-pao commits suicide, Chüan-chüan, who in a mysterious sense is cast as the reincarnation of Wu-pao, finally has her revenge by striking her man, the rascal K'o Lao-liu, to death with an iron.

Ou-yang sees that Pai's conception of this story has a superstitious dimension, inimical to rational explanation (153). She suggests that, while K'o Lao-liu represents the bestial side of human beings, Chüan-chüan, who has a masochistic tendency, also participates in the sins of the flesh (160). Thus, both Wu-pao and Chüan-chüan seem to be victims not only of visible eternal evil imposed on them by others, but also of their own *nieh*, which is hereditary. In the case of Chüan-chüan, the seeds of the evil *nieh* were planted by her parents: by her insane mother, who once almost bit her to death, and by her father, who raped her at the age of fifteen. That Chüan-chüan should become peaceful and even happy in the insane asylum after murdering K'o Lao-liu and becoming insane herself ironically marks the end of the vicious cycle of *nieh*.

This relatively marginal theme of *Tales* comes to assume a primary significance in the thematic structure of *Crystal Boys* and becomes pivotal to Pai's moral vision. In the novel's focus on the notion of *ch'ing*, which takes *yü* as its excessive form, spiritual love and libidinal desire become mutually implicating, rather than ontologically opposing each other. The author apparently sympathizes not only with those possessing ch'ing, but also with those helplessly tormented by yü, and places the most serious blame on those characters who refuse to understand the sensitive, tormented souls. This sympathy is justified by Pai's interpretation of the source of ch'ing and yü as hereditary. One may therefore understand the nieh in the title of the book Nieh-tzu to stand for yüan-nieh, in addition to the common interpretation of the title as referring to the rebellious son as a curse on his parents. The new interpretation would suggest that the sons themselves are burdened by a curse, condemned with predestined sufferings,[16] and that the prototype of this suffering is the biologically determined sexual preference. As one gets his body from his parent, arguably the parent is at least partially responsible for having transmitted the seeds of suffering to the son. Thus, when the father, representing the laws of the society, regards homosexuality as a debased form of lust—sinful, subhuman, bestial, and immoral—it is an injustice with an ironic implication of self-accusation.

Consistent with his habit of universalizing, Pai apparently uses homosexuality to symbolize a permanent human condition. As the popularized Buddhist belief has it, the ultimate cause of suffering is the possession of a body, a vessel capable of decay. When A-qing waits on Papa Fu at his deathbed, he has to assist the old man with his bowel movements. A-qing's mention of the bad smell of the stool calls special attention to the material basis of human existence, the trap of the flesh, which makes humans vulnerable to the four unavoidable calamities of life: birth, aging, illness, and death. That Pai is deliberately making the point that it is unjust to discriminate against homosexuality, in his view an inherited physiological condition, is evident in the character Heavensent Fu. A boy from the orphanage, born without limbs but possessing an unusually delicate sensitivity, Heavensent Fu (an ironic name given by his adoptive father, Papa Fu) represents the extreme form of innocent human suffering, which may be considered a nieh and must be traced to one's parent or former life.

Although the austere father, by refusing to understand his son's suffering, is violating basic humanity, Pai Hsien-yung seems to envision the possibility of reconciliation. This message is clearly inscribed in two episodes toward the end of the novel.

In the aforementioned death scene of Papa Fu, A-qing's service recalls the traditional Chinese anecdote in which the filial son, in order to determine the seriousness of his father's illness, offers to taste the latter's stool. By performing the traditional duty of a son, A-qing seems to be ritualistically "adopted" by Papa Fu. It is with reference to the natural life cycle, the four calamities that everyone must go through, that the father-son relationship is most meaningful. Since Papa Fu is the only father among the three in the book who has repented his harshness to his son and, by offering help to homosexual boys, has indicated a willingness to understand the real nature of his son's behavior, this new relationship between A-qing and Papa Fu may be taken as a symbolic reconciliation between father and son, the authority and the outcast, the oppressor and the oppressed.

The other episode indicating a reconciliation is the final episode of the novel. After Papa Fu's death and the folding of the Cozy Nest, A-qing and his friends seem to have been reincorporated into society, mostly working as waiters. On New Year's Eve, out of nostalgia, A-qing revisits the lotus pond at New Park and once again meets Dragon Prince there. The latter, after adopting a crippled boy from the Park and helping him through an operation, seems to have partially amended the *nieh* he has committed and thus enjoys more peace. The two have a conversation that rehearses once more and finally concludes the Dragon-Phoenix legend. On leaving, A-qing discovers in the octagonal pavilion an alarmed teenage boy shivering with cold and fear. Full of empathy, A-qing invites the homeless boy, Luo Ping (Lo P'ing), to take shelter in his apartment. The ending passage of the book thus reads:

> Luo Ping and I ran side by side down deserted Loyalty West Road. I was reminded of my school days, when I was a platoon leader during military drills, responsible for calling the cadence as we ran laps around the athletic field. Luo Ping and I, accompanied by the sound of exploding firecrackers and met by a chilling headwind, ran down [the extremely long] Loyalty West Road, with me calling out the cadence:
>
>   Left right
>   Left right
>   Left right
>   Left right (328)

In a literal translation, the name of the road on which they run is the "West Boulevard of Loyalty and Filial Piety." In the vertically printed Chinese text, the cadence appears as an ascending shape on the page. One may interpret this final scene as a gesture of compromise. The son, by pleading with the father for understanding and forgiveness, seeks to be reintegrated into the dominant social order, the traditional social edifice that is bastioned by "loyalty and filial piety." As a moderate, Pai issues his protests not to deny authority, but rather to register grievance and express his hope for a more understanding, tolerant society.

Wang Wen-hsing's two novels *Family Crisis* and *Backed Against the Sea* are significant milestones in Modernist Chinese fiction. In both thematic content and stylistic practice, Wang's work attains a high degree of success in the appropriation of the modernist ideology and aesthetic. These two books' critical reception by a domestic audience, however, has differed drastically. Whereas *Family Crisis* created an immediate stir, followed by intermittent, energized discussions, *Backed Against the Sea* has been largely neglected since its publication. Accordingly, the approach to be taken in the following discussion will also vary. The discussion of *Family Crisis* will be prefaced by a critical survey of existing critical views on the work, as some of these views closely reflect the changing intellectual climate in Taiwan over the last two decades. The section on *Backed Against the Sea*, in contrast, will be devoted mainly to analyzing the work itself, for the simple reason that few extensive, in-depth analyses of the novel currently exist.

Family Crisis

At the most superficial level, *Family Crisis* is a bildungsroman, the psychological journey of the hero Fan Yeh from early childhood to young adulthood in a poor lower-middle-class mainlander family. Fan Yeh's childhood affection for his parents, lovingly depicted in lyrical passages in the early part of the novel, gradually changes into a love-hatred of the most tormenting kind as he grows older. In the latter part of the book, the ultrasensitive young hero develops an intense aversion to his parents' vulgarity and petty-mindedness—a result of meager education, weak personalities, and the family's stringent financial condition—and is at the same time deeply troubled by shame and self-blame. At times, the would-be young intellectual Fan Yeh turns his anger to the Chinese family system and concept of filial piety, only to become more deeply aware of his own entrapment by their invisible bonds. Toward the end of the book, when Fan Yeh has taken over the role of the breadwinner after his father's retirement, his fury caused by his father's senility breaks out more frequently and takes more violent forms. Besides frequent scolding, he at one point even forbids his father to finish his birthday meal as punishment for some trivial offense. Finding all this maltreatment unbearable, the father suddenly disappears from the house one day and never returns in spite of the son's extended search.

A Critical Survey

If Pai Hsien-yung's protest on behalf of the socially ostracized son in *Crystal Boys* reflects a discontent with certain repressive elements of Chinese culture, the very fact that he envisions a possible reconciliation between authority and the outcast makes his challenge of the existing value system less than radical. The unusual subversiveness of *Family Crisis*, then, rests in the fact that it is not the son, but the father, who is banished from the family, a serious anomaly in a society where paternal authority is traditionally considered sacrosanct and filial piety is the model for all ethical relationships. That the book portrays Fan Yeh's "unfilial" behavior without explicit authorial condemnation is easily taken as a threat to the moral order of the society. In the first few years after the novel's publication in 1973, the country's cultural policy makers treated it with great suspicion, even placing restrictions on public discussions of the book. Considering the dominance of the neo-traditionalist discourse in Taiwan, to which the book represents an open defiance, the government's reaction and the indignation, expressed by some conservatives, at its moral ambivalence are all quite natural. However, the provocative impact of the novel is not confined by sociopolitical boundaries. At least one critic in the People's Republic of China, where feudalistic ideology is not officially sanctioned, has expressed heartfelt disapproval of Wang's defilement of the family relationship.[17] And it is perhaps Joseph Lau, an overseas Chinese scholar, who has most eloquently articulated the novel's deeply disturbing effect on the Chinese consciousness: "The 'truth' [presented in *Family Crisis*] is something that we, as people in a society that still pays lip service to traditional morality, dare not, and do not have the heart, to face" (Lau, "Shih-nien-lai" 11).

If Wang's courage in exposing a hidden complex in the modern Chinese psyche touches a deep chord in his targeted readers, it is his technical sophistication that transforms such soul-rending self-examination into a gratifying artistic experience that earned him the highest compliments from Taiwan's mainstream formalist critics immediately after the book appeared. Leading critics of the time, such as Yen Yüan-shu and Ou-yang Tzu, ardently praised the compelling immediacy and superior "psychological realism" of the novel; the excellence of their critical presentations has solidly established the novel's canonical status.

The only area—and a crucial one—that receives less than satisfactory treatment from this group of critics is Wang's radical language experiment. Both Ou-yang Tzu and Chang Han-liang have provided meticulous descriptions of Wang's innovative language use, classifying it into such categories as repetition, distortion of syntax, graphical alteration of ideograms, use of sound symbols or onomatopoeic words, and coinage of new word combinations. But they have not, strictly speaking, gone far enough in their exploration of the possible aesthetic presuppositions that would adequately account for Wang's unusually painstaking "battle" with the language (Wang claims that he can only write—actually, rewrite, since the draft of the whole story is already completed—seventy characters per day). With their essentially formalist training, these critics have basically taken Wang's linguistic manipulations as devices aimed to defamiliarize or deautomatize the reader's habitual response to conventional language. A facile association between the awkward, bizarre language style and the troubled mental state of the tormented hero, an interpretation supported by Wang himself, is therefore frequently taken to be the final answer, and the thornier issue of aesthetic assumptions left unaddressed.

As long as deviant language use is seen as a technical device conceived primarily to enhance a work's aesthetic effect, the accomplishment of Wang's language experiment must remain at best dubious. Ou-yang Tzu, for one, concedes, with her usual candor, that certain oddities of the language in *Family Crisis* seem excessive and suggests that they are perhaps involuntary results of the author's stylistic changes over the long process of the novel's composition ("Lun Chia-pien" 318). Her view is echoed by another discerning critic of the novel, James C. T. Shu, who further proposes a theory to explain the inevitable imperfection of Wang's linguistic experiment, suggesting that, because today's written vernacular Chinese is still in the process of evolution, it cannot provide Wang a well-established stylistic norm from which to deviate (190–191). The significant limitations of the norm-deviation model, with its presupposed conception of "intrinsic literary effect" as having been fully exposed by speech act theory in the 1960s and 1970s, makes the formalist approach insufficient to deal with Wang Wen-hsing's language.

When the intensity of Taiwan's oppositional Nativist cultural discourse increased in the 1970s, Family Crisis became a central target of ever more malicious attacks. The populist Nativist critics blamed Wang for "brutalizing the standard Chinese language." Wang's intellectual elitism and the deliberate obscurity of the novel were interpreted as an arrogant rejection of common readers.

The Nativist position against the novel still informed Lü Cheng-hui's "Wang Wen-hsing te pei-chü" [The tragedy of Wang Wen-hsing], written as late as 1986. In this essay, Lü first identifies Wang as a member of Taiwan's most Westernized generation of the 1960s, who willingly submitted to cultural imperialism from the West—a political product of the Nationalist government's postwar diplomatic policies. He then continues to assert that Wang's self-imposed alienation from Taiwan society is a consequence of his elitist self-perception as a "progressive," Westernized intellectual in a third-world milieu, an alienation that is qualitatively different from that of the Western modernists who are self-exiled artists in highly materialistic capitalist societies. Therefore, he argues, Fan Yeh's rebellion is not a symptom of a universal father-son conflict, as Wang may think it is, but is rather caused by Fan's subscription to Western bourgeois individualism, which creates an unbridgeable gap between him and Chinese society and its special cultural fabric. Since Fan sees no purpose for his life in a society that he rejects, he is ultimately an "absurd" rebellious hero, who wastes his energy in aimless, self-consuming rebellions.

This explicitly polemical essay interrupted the predominantly ahistorical critical discourse thus far surrounding Family Crisis by focusing on the historical specificity of the book's ideological position, explaining the work with reference to the intellectual climate of the 1960s. Drawing strength from the most positive contribution of Nativist criticism, it correctly identifies the novel's major import as the confrontation between Chinese and Western, feudalistic and modern ideology. At the same time, its insistent conviction that Taiwan's Modernist literature is imitative of the literary modernism of Western capitalist society perpetuates the nationalistic and socialist preoccupations of the Nativist critics.

Unlike the Nativist activists, who, with an explicit political agenda, publicly denounce modernism and express nostalgia for precapitalist cultural forms, Lü, as an academic critic writing in the 1980s, felt obliged to provide theoretical justification for his condemnation of literary modernism. On the one hand, he echoes Lukacs, a Western critic Lü admired, in seeing literary modernism as formalist distraction from real sociopolitical issues ("because of Wang's incorrect aesthetic conviction, he created an enigmatic literary style, which concealed the social reality of Taiwan that he might have acutely observed as an artist") (113). On the other hand, while implicitly acknowledging literary modernism's philosophical roots and critical potential in capitalist Western societies, following Frankfurt school critical theory, he nevertheless insists on denying its place in Taiwan's social context, supporting his argument with the highly essentialist notion of the cultural uniqueness of the Chinese tradition. Lü fails to see that the already full-blown capitalist Taiwan society—especially in the urban areas—and the particular logic of the market system is certainly capable of generating a "modernist" consciousness in its own writers and that Family Crisis's iconoclastic attitude toward the traditional Chinese family system represents precisely a complex reaction to the intensified disintegration of older sociocultural formations in Taiwan today.

Largely treating the same issues as Lü, but within a different intellectual context, another critic, James C. T. Shu, includes in his consideration the objective historical precondition of Fan Yeh's rebellion: the "philistine" spirit in contemporary Taiwan society. He calls Fan Yeh "a potential artist brought up in a society entrenched in materialism" (184),[18] who essentially represents the author's own self-projection. Shu also tries to compare and contrast the novel with earlier monuments in modern Chinese literary history. The crucial difference between Family Crisis and the anti-Confucianist works of Lu Hsün and Pa Chin, Shu argues, is that authors of the latter works could "diagnose a diseased society" in sociopolitical terms by identifying feudal ideology as the arch villain in early twentieth-century China, whereas Wang is helplessly caught up in a much more debilitating situation and can no longer effectively pin down the disease inflicting him and his contemporaries. It may be argued that this powerlessness is a combined result of new social conditions related to capitalist development in Taiwan and of a special mode of perception, an individualistic cognitive mode attributable to the influence of Taiwan's Modernist literary movement of the sixties. Because Fan is an alienated artist, Shu says, Fan Yeh's "insights about values are subjectively and intuitively derived," and his "holistic mode of perceiving things . . . collapse the moral and the aesthetic into an undifferentiated whole" (188).

An important contribution of Shu's article is that he has elaborated on the link between Fan Yeh's radical revolt against the Chinese family system and a larger and more persistent *episteme* in modern Chinese cultural history—an iconoclasm at the most comprehensive level, which was initiated by the May Fourth intellectuals, who were the first to take the Chinese family system as the epitome of the repressive old social order. Given that Taiwan's Chinese-Western cultural debate of the 1960s, of which the novel is a legitimate product, is essentially a restaging of the May Fourth Chinese intellectuals' painful struggle to reassess their own cultural heritage, this argument is certainly tenable. In an apparent attempt to reconcile the two significant themes—the newly introduced, Western, modernist, individualist vision of reality, and the older, but also foreign-inspired, May Fourth antitraditionalism—Shu concludes his essay with this pronouncement: "Inside the 'unfilial' son is an artist at odds with bourgeois society and a 'mad' rebel against the establishment" (192).

Valid and insightful as Shu's argument is, I would nevertheless contend that, although iconoclasm is a significant feature of the novel, it can only be seen as a pretext for several other more sophisticated themes that are substantially informed by modernist ideology and that can only be illuminated when the novel's form is given sufficiently serious consideration. Edward Gunn is right in observing that "what has proved elusive in the commentary on Wang's fiction is a theory which accounts for the particular nature of Wang's formal experiments as an integral part of the significance of his portraits" ("Process" 29). As a work written in the period of late modernism, the novel presupposes a history of formal evolution of modern fiction that occurred before the time of its own composition. It thus has an exceptionally self-conscious, carefully engineered formal structure,[19] in which the thematic messages are intricately encoded. This assumption will be the point of departure of the following discussion of Family Crisis.

In a sense, the primary goals of Family Crisis are to subject traditional Chinese family ethics to radical revision and to demystify the concept of filial piety on the grounds of Enlightenment ideas of rationality. Chinese parents are seen to be coercing children to accept filial duties (for instance, in chapter 9, Fan Yeh's father predicts that the young child is bound to be unfilial after growing up, creating in him an intense feeling of guilt and resentment) mainly for the sake of self-preservation, to oblige the children to support them in their old age. The sense of responsibility thus instilled in the child is inherently precarious. Since emotional attachment to one's parent is part of one's appreciation for the care parents provide, once the material basis for love is removed, some other factor, such as personality conflict, easily turns the parent-child relationship into a bitter love-hate relationship. With both the emotional bondage and the ethical prescriptions firmly in place, the child is doubly trapped.

It is only natural that such messages, harmless as they seem as theory, have proven to be difficult for Chinese readers to accept emotionally as a principle of praxis; and they undoubtedly are extremely disconcerting to the author himself. However, seriously subscribing to the modernist ideology, Wang has treated creative writing as a process through which the most intense inner battles are fought, and the various modernist aesthetic strategies have allowed him simultaneously to demystify the concept of filial piety and to register faithfully the horrendous emotional impact of this action on his own psyche. In a personal interview in 1982, Wang made a crucial statement about the novel, calling it "a private memoir, written by Wang Wen-hsing on Wang Wen-hsing." Most significantly, Wang also told how he deliberately concealed his identity in the novel "because some of the memories are still too painful." Pressed regarding the difference between the author's experiential self and the "implied author" of the novel, Wang reformulated the statement and said that the narrator of the novel is actually the "fictitious author" (implied author), who, in writing his private memoir, tries to hide his own identity by speaking in another's voice. One is immediately reminded of Fredric Jameson's discussion of the modernist aesthetic in The

Political Unconscious (228). The special kind of "memoir" Wang writes seems to be a creative encounter of the author with his own past, a process in which he "rewrites" his personal history with the conscious goal of transforming the painful reality into style.

The work is therefore not an autobiographical novel in the ordinary sense. It is rather a conscious attempt to transform some intensely disturbing experience into art. Deeply aware of the scandalous nature of this experience, Wang is determined to present it in a form that goes beyond the model of the psychological novel, with ordinary notions of motivation and behavioral patterns. The artistic form that he employs allows one to project the private, intimate experience onto larger intellectual frameworks—a universalizing strategy—and to preserve the radical contradictions, inconsistencies, and schizophrenic personal traits, that are found in the real experience. The remaining part of this discussion will comment on some of the more important textual strategies Wang employs in Family Crisis.

Artistic Patterning as a Means of Relativizing Subjective Experience

In this novel, immensely complex psychological experience is rendered through meticulous textual patterning. The book has a carefully engineered framework that divides it into 172 semiautonomous minichapters—some of them containing only one line and the longest running for several pages—revolving around two intersecting narrative lines. The primary narrative line is biographical, recording Fan Yeh's life since early childhood, in 157 chapters, each designated by an Arabic numeral. The development of this story is interrupted intermittently by another narrative line, containing fifteen chapters labeled by letters of the Roman alphabet, which follows Fan Yeh's search for his father after the latter's mysterious departure.

Within this structure, there is an obvious tension between fragmentation and order. The segmentation of the story into short chapters naturally cuts the narrative flow and creates a sense of discontinuity; its alienation effect, self-referential quality, and undermining of the realistic illusion have been frequently observed (Chang Sung-sheng, "Ts'ung Chia-pien"; Gunn, "Process" 33). The novel's fragmented structure is further an effect of the juxtaposition of disparate literary modes: the dramatic mode, in which social scenes are presented, and the lyrical mode, which poetically registers the hero's sensory experiences. The story is also interspersed with lengthy interior monologues and a number of well-developed episodes, which are virtually miniature short stories. Shifts and inconsistencies in the narrative point of view, results of intentional authorial manipulation, are another cause for the impression of incoherence (Chang Sung-sheng, "Language").

The centrifugal forces thus produced, however, are effectively countered by the structural unity generated by well-wrought, close-knit textual patterns. Episodes in the primary narrative line are organized around thematic kernels and a number of recurring motifs—prominent among them are the Oedipus complex motif, the death motif, and the initiation motif. Other patterns are formed by the periodic recurrence of specific settings, such as typhoon scenes and an airplane passing overhead, which appears at the beginning of each large part indicating a new stage of the hero's growth. On the whole, the effect is like that of symphonic movements, composed with the cadence of repetitions and variations.

The simulated musical pattern is even more conspicuous in the other narrative line that follows Fan Yeh's search for his father. The intermittent appearance of slightly varied newspaper notices summoning the runaway father rhythmically punctuates the progression of the primary narrative line and evokes unpleasant—criminal or scandalous—associations. The repetitiveness of Fan Yeh's search soon gives the impression of circularity—he is constantly riding in the train, on the streets of a strange city, or in another monastery or church where runaways may take refuge, but the trips always take him back to where he began, his home. The book also symbolically ends with the chapter designated by the letter O—which is a sign of completion, returning to the starting point of "zero," fulfillment of a cyclical process, as well as the equivalent of the Greek omega, the end—in which the two narrative lines finally converge.

Such deliberate formal arrangements based on the more abstract form of the purer arts, music and poetry, may be viewed, together with Wang's highly aesthetic use of language discussed in the previous chapter, as the author's self-conscious efforts toward stylization, as textual strategies to recode his personal history in artistic terms.[20] Furthermore, the particular formal features that depart from the conventional models of realistic narrative—first breaking the temporal continuum and then subsuming the episodes under arbitrary sequence—must also be seen as more than a demonstration of Wang's postrealist consciousness of form. They in fact perform a significant thematic function by relativizing values honored at any particular moment.

In the chronologically arranged, semiautonomous chapters depicting slices of the hero's life, Wang strenuously adheres to the Jamesian point-of-view technique so that a high degree of verisimilitude is achieved, and each chapter features a fully activated subjectivity (for the most part the subjectivity of the hero, Fan Yeh). However, thoughts and emotions expressed in each chapter are immediately undercut by the fragmented structure of the novel. It is by repeatedly relativizing the subjective experience of the hero that the author can remain faithful to individual moments of "truth" in the agonizing history of his painful relationship with his father. To borrow from Fredric Jameson's idea of the containment strategy of modernism, that of "canceled realism" (Political Unconscious 266), Wang seems to be first evoking the realistic experience in order in another moment to "suppress it," to recontain the agitated emotions thus aroused in a rationalistic, artificial frame.

The philosophical perception of temporality and subjective experience seems to be part of the existentialist metaphysic that had a deep impact on Taiwan's Modernists of the 1960s. For Wang, the phenomenological insight about subjectivity seems to have served as a rational basis for his precarious detachment from both the "self" and the troubling experiences of the past. As a matter of fact, another structural feature of the novel reveals, perhaps more directly, Wang's intention to recast his personal experience using a model that is governed by the purer logic of reason.

Although few critics have commented on it, the overall plot structure of Family Crisis is ostensibly modeled on that of a detective story, showing the author's explicit intention to program the reading process according to what Barthes calls in S/Z "the hermeneutic code." The disappearance of the father at the beginning of the book is presented as a "mystery"; even though the answer to the mystery is partially hinted at, both narrative lines are progressing toward a final discovery. As the central event (the father's departure) is focused on twice, once at the beginning and once at the end, the reader is forced to notice how his or her perception has been modified through the course of reading, so that two important points may be driven home. First, Fan Yeh's prediction at the beginning of the story that his father's escape from the house is bound to become an embarrassing social scandal that "shakes the whole island" does not materialize. Instead, the reader learns that there are many other homeless old men who take refuge in monasteries and churches, places where Fan Yeh searches in vain for his own father. The tragedy of the Fan family is in fact a pervasive one in this morally callous society. Second, by giving the reader an inside view of the "history" of the son's banishment of his father, the scandalous incident is in a sense being "explained" and the mystery being accounted for. Thus the letter O heading the closing chapter may stand for the exclamatory utterance of discovery "Oh!"

Western Intellectual Trends as "New Myths"

Similar to Pai Hsien-yung's elaborate textual allusions, which work symbolically in Crystal Boys, Wang's skillful ordering of events under several rubrics of significance forms an internal thematic structure that effectively engages the reader in symbolic readings. Although the conceptual frameworks within which Wang's symbolism operates are those familiar from the early days of the Modernist literary movement, namely, Freudianism, existentialist metaphysics, and Jungian mythology, Wang has invested much more energy in Family Crisis than people like Ch'i-teng Sheng and Shih Shu-ch'ing have in their works. His accomplishment is naturally greater than theirs.

Certain important thematic cores in the primary narrative line, such as the Oedipus complex and the death theme, have been frequently discussed in criticism of the novel. I will therefore focus mainly on the thematic encodings in the narrative line ordered by letters of the Roman alphabet.

Wang Wen-hsing has apparently used this narrative line to project the story into abstract systems of meaning. It takes Fan Yeh out of his immediate social context and onto a "journey." What he encounters in the journey constantly forces him to reflect upon his life and put into perspective his relationship with his father. The visions he thus acquires are often richly symbolic and serve the purpose of universalizing the private experience depicted in the primary narrative line. Of central importance is the father-quest theme that makes references to currently popular myth theories.

The quest for the father (the two characters hsün-fu, literally father-search, appear from time to time in the notices that Fan Yeh puts out in newspapers summoning his father) is both the nominal purpose of Fan Yeh's journey and the cause of his deep-seated psychological complex. It starts early in the book in the dream scene of chapter B. The pleasant, young, handsomely dressed father who returns in Fan Yeh's dream right after his father leaves is the image that Fan Yeh has subconsciously retained since childhood, which in many ways sharply contradicts his feelings about his rapidly aging father. In chapter F, Fan Yeh runs into an elderly man on the train whose fatherly air immediately reminds him not of his real father but of the image of the ideal father that he once projected onto a neighbor. Then, in chapter M, Fan Yeh is inspired to make an eloquent speech—to himself—about "fatherly love." He praises the paternal sacrifices made by ordinary people such as the clerk he reads about in the newspaper who took bribes to support his family, the middle-aged men he sees who illegally sell blood in front of the public hospital, and the coolies and peddlers in the market who "exhausted their wits and strength," supposedly to keep their children from starvation (187).

Thus, from an individually idealized father-image, Fan Yeh seems to have proceeded to a sense of "community" with other suffering human beings. He seems deeply touched by the universal humanity manifested in those men who consume themselves, who "sell their blood, bodies, and labor," in order to preserve the human race. At this point of his spiritual journey, a climax, he attains the maturity of manhood and becomes ready to participate in the natural course of preserving the life cycle. In one sense, the journey is purgatory for Fan Yeh, in that he has found a philosophical truth. In another sense, it conveys an ironic message about Fan Yeh's actual plight: just as prescribed by the myths, the sin of murdering one's father is only atoned for by one's taking over the father's role. By invoking the notion of the biological life cycle and by suggesting that father-banishment and father-killing are dictated by natural forces, Wang is not far from making the statement that Chinese family ethics were also created to facilitate the perpetuation of the collective life of the human race. Thus with the "new myths" about the meaning of life, he seems to have come to terms with the older metaphysics that are apparently a source of genuine conflict in his life.

Another influence many critics have mentioned is existentialism. Instead of repeating the argument, I will point out a few examples of Wang's skillful creation of an existentialist setting. In a practical sense, Fan Yeh's father-quest is both aimless and absurd, given the population of Taiwan and the fact that he has not a single clue as to the father's whereabouts. So the reader more than once encounters the lonely hero in the streets of a strange city. Often the heat of the scorching sun has scared everyone else away. Sometimes he appears in a crowd of strangers, such as a traffic jam caused when a madman tries to direct traffic (chapter L). He constantly carries a newspaper (indicating mediated contact with the world) and is kept at a distance from people by his large, dark sunglasses. He is often surrounded by empty religious symbols. The monastery rooms are almost always empty. Churches and temples do not respond to people's needs. The following passage is vividly reminiscent of Albert Camus' *The Stranger*:

> He was walking in the middle of a street, under the scorching sun at high noon. Because of the severe heat, the street was empty, devoid of any human figure. The street was flanked on both sides by square concrete structures, their lower portions submerged in dark shades. He walked forward: in his hand he was holding a rolled newspaper; he had just visited a church, again, in vain. He proceeded forward, behind him fell a dwarfed shadow. At his back in the sky was the cross. (44)

The cross in the empty sky, while giving the picture a surreal cast, completes the image of Fan Yeh as an alienated existentialist hero inflicted with metaphysical agony. Guilt-ridden with a cross at his "back," Fan Yeh is now transformed into a Christ figure who must be crucified for the sin of having usurped his father's position.

Therefore, one significant function of this narrative line is to place Fan Yeh's life in the larger context of the universal history of humankind. This higher level of meaning complements, qualifies, negates, and problematizes the private, experiential "truth" that is powerfully asserted by the primary narrative line through highly successful realistic representation of concrete events of everyday life.

In a sense, the generation of Wang Wen-hsing was caught in a "desacralization" process in which the dominant ideological coding of the precapitalist, feudalist sociocultural formations were replaced by new myths about the "meaning" of life at a moment when the Chinese society of Taiwan was passing through the modernization threshold. Just as their counterparts in prewar Japan and the contemporary People's Republic of China have done, the Modernists found new Western metaphysics, such as existentialism, Freudian psychoanalysis, and Jungian myth, powerful weapons to deconstruct the remnant feudal ideologies—"family ethics" in Wang's case—and to resist their psychological control. Thus James Shu was right in connecting Fan Yeh's sensational criticism of the family system with May Fourth iconoclasm, for it is arguable that modern Chinese intellectuals' attempt to "decode" feudalism has been an ongoing process since the early twentieth century and is still very much an incomplete project. Lü Cheng-hui is also partly right about Wang's treating Western-style bourgeois individualism as an alternative to feudalistic family ethics. By linking the ideological views of Fan Yeh and Wang Wen-hsing too closely, however, Lü neglects the fact that the mode of Western thinking most elevated by such Modernists as Wang Wen-hsing and Ou-yang Tzu is Enlightenment rationalism rather than bourgeois individualism. It is precisely the rationalistic habit of thinking that has enabled Wang to put his own radical opinions into perspective. The way Wang presents Fan Yeh's burgeoning rationality during different phases of his development (including his apparently flawed reasoning about the Chinese family system) sufficiently demonstrates his awareness of the frenzy that typically accompanies rationality.[21]

Much as he values human rationality, Wang's higher goal as a modernist artist is to watch himself acting. Most critics have considered certain distinctive features of Wang's work, such as the element of the antinovel, the highly aesthetic style, and the incoherent narrative perspective, as ingenious technical innovations. The above discussion is meant to prove—along the lines of Fredric Jameson's argument about narrative as a socially symbolic act (Political Unconscious 225)—that they are also textual strategies employed to resolve symbolically, on the aesthetic or imaginary level, an overwhelmingly contradictory situation in the author's life.

Backed Against the Sea

The social contradictions expressed in Family Crisis are not limited to the family. The book also includes, for example, perhaps the best treatment of parochialism, class snobbery, and the financial stringency of the dislocated middle-level mainlander gentry family in post-1949 Taiwan literature. However, many of these social references are subordinate to the main themes and cannot be easily reduced to clear positions. Much more elaborate, thought-provoking commentaries on social and cultural issues are found in Wang's ambitious second novel, *Backed Against the Sea*.

It appears indisputable that both the philosophical import and the presentational manner of this novel are heavily indebted to the Western literary tradition. Wang apparently intends to suggest to the reader the intellectual scope of the novel with the four books the narrator takes with him into exile, Tolstoy's *Resurrection*, Nietzsche's *Thus Spake Zarathustra*, Dostoyevsky's *Notes from the Underground*, and Gide's *The Fruits of the Earth*, all modern Western classics that deal with such topics as civilization, values, rationality, alienation, and moral responsibility.[22] Also, according to Wang himself, in this work he deliberately tries to appropriate the "seriocomic" mode, as well as the techniques of parody and black humor, all of which are modeled on modern Western literature.[23] The Western influence certainly diminishes its claim to originality. As Leo Lee perceptively points out, the novel contains visible textual affinities with such contemporary Western literary works as Philip Roth's *Portnoy's Complaint* and Joyce's *Ulysses*, and even with the Hollywood movie *Candy* ("Beyond Realism" 75–76). One may also add that traces of Samuel Beckett's later novels, such as *Molloy*,[24] are obvious both in the novel's theme of existentialist absurdity and in the antihero's racy narrative style.

It may not be too farfetched to argue that this indebtedness to, or "derivativeness" from, the Western literary tradition is a logical consequence of a basic assumption of Taiwan's Modernists, an assumption that Wang Wen-hsing has taken more seriously than others and has substantiated with more solid efforts than any other writer. That is, the Modernists believed from the beginning that the Western modernist tradition could provide them with the necessary intellectual frames and technical means to examine in depth important issues about life that the native Chinese narrative tradition failed to offer.[25] *Backed Against the Sea*, then, is a remarkable attempt to explore certain issues about the meaning of life and to communicate them through artistically sophisticated presentational modes that are deemed endemic to Western literary modernism. In this study I will specially call attention to two thematic aspects of the work. First, since the local sociocultural settings inevitably serve as the object of Wang's philosophical contemplation, he has offered some thought-provoking insights about contemporary Taiwan society as well as about humanity. Second, as the Modernists consciously take literary writing as an "intellectual project," it is natural that their philosophical inquiries are often deeply meshed with personal preoccupations. In Wang's case, such inquiries are inseparable from his genuine subscription to Enlightenment rationality and from his persistent interest in interpersonal communication and the workings of "fate" (in both the metaphysical and practical senses). Because of the extreme complexity of the work, my explication will be supported with extensive textual references.[26]

The narrator of *Backed Against the Sea* is a Beckett-style antihero, a middle-aged, retired military man of doubtful moral reputation who addresses himself as *yeh*, a slang form of self-address connoting arrogance (literally, *yeh* means "father" or "your father"; when used in conversation, it implies an insult to the partner in conversation). Once again Wang adopts a setting familiar from existentialist literature. The narrator has recently fled from the center of Taiwan's modern civilization, Taipei, to an impoverished fishing village on the island's coastline, Shen-k'eng ao (Deep Pit Harbor), in order to escape the adverse consequences of his embezzling and gambling. Whereas Fan Yeh in *Family Crisis* is overburdened by kinship relations and conventional ethics, the narrator of this novel is a loner free from familial and social obligations, and his sole purpose in life is to fulfill two sets of basic needs, those of a physical nature (food and sex), and those springing from his exceptionally lively, though somewhat uncultured, power of intellect. Realizing after his arrival at the harbor that there are no fish to catch during this season, he is forced to operate a fortune-telling stand to maintain minimal subsistence. The peculiar nature of this profession and the great amount of leisure it provides unexpectedly lead him to an uncanny spiritual quest, unleashing contemplations about important issues in life that are luxuries denied to modern individuals caught up in normal, civilized lives.

On the discursive level, the whole novel is made up of the antihero's extended monologue, on a sleepless night, which willfully mixes insight with heresy, rational thought with pure nonsense. The first hundred pages, approximately one-half of the book, forms a large unit consisting primarily of the narrator's pseudophilosophical reflections on things near and far, ranging from food prices in local restaurants to ideas about freedom and democracy. Even the episode in which the narrator relates his fortune-telling experience contains more speculation than action. The second half of the book, however, mainly comprises a recounting of incidents that have occurred during the first ten days of the narrator's stay at the harbor. Though antisocial by temperament, he makes some contacts with local residents, such as the clerks in a certain Dialect Research Bureau—he boards there for cheap meals—and girls in local brothels and teahouses.

Modern Civilization and Its Discontent

The anti-hero's seemingly nonsensical remarks are disguised critique of Taiwan at a time when an export economy and industrialization have initiated in its society a structural transformation. The location where the story takes place, Deep Pit Harbor, a half-deserted fishing harbor only miles away from Taipei, is a symbol of all the ills brought about by this process. As an exile of the modern metropolis Taipei and a newcomer to the fishing village, the narrator is psychologically situated halfway between the two extremes of modern civilization. He has therefore gained a unique vantage point from which to observe and comment on both the universal condition of social progress and the particular cultural ideology that has dominated post-1949 Taiwan society.

Contrary to the socialist realism advocated by the Nativists, Wang's critique is offered not through direct thematic formulations, but rather obliquely through the special dynamics of narrative discourse. The middle-aged veteran represents a special socioideological group—middle- and lower-class mainlander émigrés—and his coarse vitality, piquant wit, and childlike fascination with the signifying process of language become crucially instrumental in the author's attempt to unravel the unexamined assumptions underlying popular opinions shared by the same speech community. While the narrator tries to amuse himself by thinking through words, words are also thinking through him. At the same time he derives pleasure from distorting set phrases, twisting popular idioms, poking fun with maxims, and naming and deliberately misnaming situations, his discourse becomes a parody of the very act of conceptualizing things in language. As Bakhtin says, "the ideological becoming of a human being . . . is the process of selectively assimilating the words of others" (341). In this book, many of the words that appear underlined, in parentheses, or cast in bold print may be read as marks of public "myths" prevalent in post-1949 Taiwan. The narrator's conscious or unconscious distortion of them calls attention to the ideological basis of this particular culture.

The date of the story, specifically identified by the author as 1962, is significant in that the sixties marked Taiwan's economic takeoff. While the country marched full-speed toward industrialization and capitalism, discrepancies between urban and rural modes of living rapidly increased. Taipei at this time was already a modern metropolis in its embryonic form, considerably more prosperous than other parts of the island, whereas Deep Pit Harbor, separated from Taipei by only four hours' train ride, represented the island's numerous backward regions whose "blood" was being sucked by the unremitting process of urban expansion. Yet, unlike the Nativists who have treated the city-village hostility solely from the standpoint of the often idealized rural people, Wang sees the city and the rural regions as belonging to the same economic chain. Thus the disappointed narrator complains that "everything good has been exported to Taipei"—choice fruit, meat, and even good-looking girls (15–16). Deep Pit Harbor is not depicted as a precapitalist pastoral haven—in fact the narrator considers "pastoral" to be a mere euphemism for primitive poverty and ordinary people's romantic imagination about the countryside to result from sheer ignorance (19)—but as a mirror image and a parody of the city, where everything is stripped bare or driven to its extreme so that the absurdity inherent in this civilization is bluntly exposed. For example, the prominent presence of foreign religion in Taiwan is symbolized by the Catholic church, the only specimen of modern architecture in the village, standing aloof on the hill in sharp contrast with the town's shabby cottages made of wood and straw. The impoverished residents of the fishing village use the pawn shop as a local bank, whose financial strategy is described as "cutting off the flesh in one part of the body to fill the wound in another part" (18). Sex, food, and religion are the important trades that prosper in this place despite, or as a consequence of, the general poverty—probably because the enjoyment of food and sex are the only rights that the poor and the rich share (17–18).

In the first quarter of the book, the narrator's thoughts mostly revolve around the absurdities of "civilized" life in a more universal sense. For example, in his typical aphoristic manner, the narrator contemplates the nature of the memoir as a literary genre. In order to write a memoir, one must first be a celebrity (as if only celebrities have memory). Therefore, the memoir is a literary genre the value of which does not come from the efforts one makes while writing but solely from the efforts made before one picks up the pen—somewhat like the one-time collection of life insurance benefits (2). Or, recalling the troubles he has gone through to obtain medical proof of his ulcer—which caused massive bleeding for many years—in order to be discharged from military service, the narrator jeers at the unreasonable requirement for such a proof with an absurd analogy: as if a newborn baby must hold in its little fist a "birth certificate" to prove that it has actually been born (11). The person who helped the narrator get the certificate acts as if he has done him a great favor; in fact, he has usurped the "ownership" of the ulcer while the narrator bled for it (11–12). Or, once he asks in puzzlement, why is it that all the people in society must have a "profession," as if this were the only "sign of existence." He asks, is it possible for a person without a profession to show "signs of existence" (54–55)? This remark is one of many with obvious existentialist overtones.

The narrator's deliberation on food prices offers an interesting comment on the intriguing phenomenon of customer psychology. He first suggests that "seasonal price" ought to be added as the fifth idol to Francis Bacon's list, since every customer seems to be in awe of it, intimidated by its underlying arbitrariness. Theoretically speaking, however, the seasonal price does not have to be expensive—it might even be relatively cheap, if a price had dropped. He thus decides to try to order such a forbidding dish. It turns out, however, that none of the dishes marked with "seasonal price" is even available. In fact, many of the shabby-looking local food stands have colorful posters advertising fancy dishes for decorative purposes only. The real food they sell, all unappetizing snacks, are "one price for all," two NT each regardless of what you get. The narrator sarcastically remarks that this is an "epoch-making" innovation: instead of prices being set according to the value of commodities, commodities are regulated by their prices (20–22). The parodic use of economic terms throughout the book is a means of expressing Wang's observation that contemporary Taiwan society was going through an important transition. The abstraction of experience, the arbitrariness of value under the market system, and the phenomenon of fetishization are manifestations of the logic of capitalism.

Such intellectual reflections on "modern" experiences are not merely "ideological distraction" or a way "of displacing the reader's attention from history and society to . . . experiences of the individual monad," but undoubtedly have a realistic import, albeit in a modernist sense as Fredric Jameson suggests.[27] The novel's references to the social setting of Taiwan in the 1960s and early 1970s probably show more originality and perceptiveness than any other literary representation of the period. For example, by frequent parodic use of urban jargon in reference to local phenomena in Deep Pit Harbor—such as saying that the local clinic has adopted the latest in "open-style" management by treating patients right in front of people passing through—the narrator sarcastically measures the backward fishery town against the standards of modern civilization embodied by the city of Taipei, calling attention to an immense disparity (17). Or, the narrator's own story may be taken as an epitome of the chaotic social conditions of Taiwan in the years following the Retreat. Because he is a veteran, the narrator's only social connections in Taiwan are with people from his home province on the mainland, especially those of the same clan. He relied on one of them to help him leave the army and find a job, while repaying him by running errands in an illegal business in which the latter was involved. Recently, however, his embezzlement of a small office fund was discovered, and his patron has refused to continue supporting him. Infuriated by this "betrayal," the narrator complains with indignation: "Treating me this way, do they possess any human feelings (ch'ing) and sense of justice (i) at all?" (7–8). It is of course preposterous for the narrator to invoke such outdated codes of honor as ch'ing and i, which governed interpersonal relationships in the old social formations, while he himself follows a more utilitarian, predatory kind of rule. Yet this very self-contradiction and confusion of values nicely offer a glimpse of the way residue from the feudalist past, on the one hand, and modern utilitarianism, or pure lawless exploitation, on the other, dominated post-1949 Taiwan society before greater order was reestablished.

The most intricate social critique, however, rests in the author's comment on the dominant cultural ideology. An excellent example is the narrator's deliberation on materialism. In a didactic mood, the narrator begins by preaching against the "American lifestyle" he has seen in Hollywood movies. He disapproves of the Americans' excessive material comfort and their dedicating a whole lifetime to work in order to possess all kinds of machines—televisions, videotape recorders, washers, mowers, and fancy cars. He regrets that in their materialistic culture, no one understands the "true meaning of life." The speech is concluded with a profound-sounding dictum that turns out to be the narrator's own invention: "Life is not to be used, but to be cherished, to be appreciated with leisure. . . . In any case, one should try to be a person, instead of being occupied with work—as I, *yeh* himself, have always said." No sooner than this is proudly pronounced, he senses something wrong with this line of thought:

> Hey, wait a second, wait a second, wait a second, to put it this way seems, it seems, a little weird. It sounds as if I am the kind of person who is "content with poverty and finds happiness in the Way" and, "being content, is always happy"; that I all year long only need two or three sweaters and one single pair of shoes to live on, doesn't it? Of course not—of course, of course not. Yeh naturally wants to chase after wealth and fame, and beautiful women to embrace. Yeh thus is a person full of contradiction, knowing, clearly knowing that wealth and glory are not worth anything, and from the beginning there is not an iota of need to aspire for it, yet *yeh* just, in spite of everything, wants it "*badly*," "*cannot*" do without it.—Contradiction!—Contradiction!—Yeh as a person is an ennn-or-mous *contradiction*!—Yeh is "contradiction." (30–31)

The denunciation of "Western materialism" on moral grounds nicely manifests the narrator's false consciousness, conditioned by the prevailing neotraditionalist, conservative cultural discourse. The narrator belongs to a socioideological, sociolinguistic group that upholds this moralistic stance, and, as a language user, he unconsciously participates in the mythifying function of words. The tour de force of the novel, however, rests in its persistent disruption of the socially constructed moral consciousness. Though unwittingly reiterating the language of his community, the narrator, being an original thinker of sorts, refuses to submit to its categories and thus is not constrained by its logic. The powerful weapon to which he repeatedly resorts in order to resist the tyrannous control of language is arbitrariness. Like any other language user, he cannot attain a transcendental standpoint; he can only rebel against language by bluntly declaring that he chooses to honor the logic of "contradiction" and by arbitrarily reversing his position when it suits his whim.

Thus, through exposing the logical fallacies, paradoxes, and deceptive nature of common discourse, the author has engaged in a process of "ironic demythification" whereby his own critique of the society's moralistic neo-traditionalism is refracted, if not directly reflected. Whereas there has never been a shortage of cultural criticism in modern Chinese literature, this novel is a rare sample of the "writerly text" that offers a forceful criticism of the dominant cultural discourse.

Poverty and Human Capacity for Compassion

Many elements in this novel combine to paint a realistic picture of some peculiar phenomena in post-1949 Taiwan society. To name just a few, the narrator's use of all sorts of military metaphors in his account of sexual experiences reminds readers not only of his own background as a soldier, but also of the prominent military presence in post-1949 Taiwan society as a whole. The narrator's diagnosis of the problem with contemporary Taiwan literature—that it has created too many poets but little good poetry and that it is too easy to get literary fame, partly because writing is non-lucrative and therefore irrelevant in this materialistic society—reflects an insight that many people have come to concur with. Above all, the most important matrix of themes in this novel involves poverty, the poverty of the socially disadvantaged—in this case mainland or settlers—within a thriving economy.

As material scarcity was a prevalent social phenomenon in the years following the Retreat, both Modernists and the Nativists who launched their careers in the late 1950s and early 1960s were preoccupied with the theme of poverty. There was a marked difference in their approaches, however. Whereas the Nativists celebrated the human potential for dignity in the face of a humiliating environment, the Modernists showed more concern with the individual's capacity for compassion in the face of other people's suffering. The Nativists privileged Taiwan's rural inhabitants; the Modernists dealt more with the urban underclass. The Nativists showed a tendency to romanticize, and the Modernists strived to attain an unsentimental realism.

Poverty in *Backed Against the Sea* is first of all treated in its personal, psychological dimension. Having run out of luck and full of resentment, the narrator is ready to blame anyone but himself—thus the outburst of a string of profanities that opens the book. The condition of impoverishment generates not only anger and discontentment but also a struggle to survive. The narrator's resourcefulness in obtaining the basic necessities, in making everything *wan-neng* (multifunctional), such as the all-purpose bathtub converted into a bed and a desk, even earns from himself a congrautaltory grin. Such a robust and defiant victim of poverty evokes little sympathy, even if he is not responsible for his predicament. A mainlander veteran without valuable social connections, the narrator was indeed a member of one of the most disadvantaged social groups at the time.

The hero's wretched condition is not only treated without sentimentality, but it plays a significant role in the novel's special text-reader dynamic. As his external possessions are reduced to the very minimum, his apathetic contemplation of other people's problems and his disinterested, perversely witty observations about the sheer destitution of Deep Pit Harbor are free from ordinary moral implications—for he is someone who possesses even less—and work with a Brechtian alienating effect. One example is his "original" discovery about human eating habits—working-class people love sweet things because they need more calories; those who know the art of using salt have a higher degree of civilization (22). Or, noticing that before the fish come to the harbor, the local people have nothing to do but loaf around all day, the narrator questions why God should have given brains to these people. All they do is take the brains to fill up parts of their lower body (57). The dehumanizing quality of poverty is no place else expressed in modern Chinese literature in such a caustic manner.

The work not only plumbs the "depth" of Taiwan's contemporary civilization where poverty resides, as symbolically conveyed by the name "Deep Pit Harbor," but also tries to probe the deep recesses of individual moral capacity. Since such early stories as "Wan-chu shou-ch'iang" [The toy pistol] (1960) and "Hei-i" [Black coat] (1964), Wang Wen-hsing has been questioning the possibility of meaningful interpersonal relationships and the innate perversity of human nature. Such questions are pressed more compellingly in the second half of this novel, in which the narrator comes into contact with members of the "Dialect Research Bureau" and local prostitutes.

Although the narrator can rationally philosophize about the poverty he sees in his surroundings, "misfortune" appears to be a more purely subjective experience. Wang Wen-hsing seems to have serious doubts about ordinary people's ability genuinely to empathize with the misfortune of others.

The incidents to be discussed shortly, in most of which the narrator fails to respond with moral propriety to other people's misfortunes, may serve to bring out one central theme of the novel, the inherent limits of the human capacity for compassion.

The first incident comes at the end of the fortune-telling episode. When the narrator discovers that the young seaman who has lost his life in the storm is the eldest son of the captain with whom he is presently having a conversation, he is truly taken by surprise; he is so surprised that he utters some extremely insensitive words despite himself: "'Is that true—'? The tone expressed in my phrase made it sound as if I was saying, 'Oh! So it's you—and that's who it is!—who has won the 200,000 NT state lottery, is that true?'" (78). Although his immediate response is not in compliance with civilized behavioral codes, the narrator is not necessarily untouched by the miserable situation. The next day, after learning that the unlucky captain is going to set out fishing again in spite of the tragedy, the narrator makes a euphemistic speech, calling the captain someone who "bravely shoulders the cross of fate," who nobly engages himself in "the eternal struggle between human will and the cruelty of nature"—he has already predicted that the captain is destined to die eventually on the high seas (85–86). The apparent hollowness of the affected, high-flown style of the narrator's speech is deliberately parodical; together with the narrator's callous response on the previous day, it testifies to the fundamental inadequacy of any social discourse to properly respond to the bleak reality of daily human existence.

The next few examples involve the narrator's association with members of the "Dialect Research Bureau," who are a host of incompetent or physically or mentally ill civil service staff expelled by Taipei's central bureaucracy in the name of "dispersion" (for theoretically the Taiwan government was in a state of war with the mainland and had to "disperse" its offices and staff to different regions).[28] With biting sarcasm, the narrator remarks that these people are trying so desperately to cling to their jobs that they take any work they can find, including the compilation of the history of the bureau itself. The even more chilling message the author conveys, however, is that although these people's plight truly deserves sympathy, they are so utterly despicable as to incite more contempt than commiseration. For example, the bureau office routinely turns into a madhouse toward the end of the day, when the staff members exchange obnoxious, childish personal assaults and even get into physical fights like primary school brats. Though equally unfortunate and belonging to the same social class, the narrator is nevertheless superior to these people in terms of intelligence and sanity. He watches such farcical spectacles with an aloofness mixed with amusement and disdain.

It is only when one looks into their personal histories, when one learns that almost every one of these people suffers from some kind of chronic disease (some have real mental problems) that these people become sympathetic in a sociological sense. One bureau member, Yü Shih-liang, is a perfect example of a passive victim whose life story contains mishaps not uncommon among mainlander émigrés. Yü's wife has been insane for many years, and recently, after a still-born fifth child—the Catholic church has not granted his wife permission to have an abortion—she has been institutionalized, leaving four young children in different orphanages. As Yü tells the narrator, it all started with a piece of bad luck: "Originally, I had three girls to choose from. For who knows what reason, I have picked this one." Here Yü refers to a common match-making situation through which many mainlander men arranged their marriages with local Taiwanese girls, typically much younger, by paying the girl's family a large sum of betrothal money, frequently the total of their life savings.

More decent than most other bureau members, Yü is nevertheless despicable in his own way; his weakness, reminiscent of that of Fan Yeh's father in *Family Crisis*, is an utter lack of willpower. Overwhelmed by misfortune, he deals with everything with spineless submission. When the quick-tempered doctor urges him to get money to purchase blood in order to save his wife, he follows the order even though he sees no point in saving her. At the end of the day, in total exhaustion, Yü submissively follows a neighbor who invites him to a mah-jong game and almost loses all the borrowed money.

For the narrator to treat such unworthy, pathetic figures that he chances upon in life with apathy is, realistically speaking, all too human. Yet the author seems to be preoccupied with the deep moral implications of such human behavior, and, by relentlessly focusing on the narrator's "natural" apathy in the following incident, he presents the reader with a more complicated philosophical issue. Once, in a casual before-supper chat, Yü Shih-liang tells the narrator of an incident in his family. His lunatic wife once took a kitchen knife and pulled over her third child, claiming that she was going to butcher the child "to make some sausages for the New Year." The tragedy was barely prevented by the eldest son, who offered to be killed in place of his younger brother and thus somehow brought his mother back to her senses. Yü, after finishing the story, inappropriately remarks that his third son is in fact the most plump of all his children (137). Hearing this, the narrator promptly breaks into laughter, right in Yü's face, despite the apparent pathos of the story.

This laughter—just like the reader's laughter elicited by the fighting scenes in the bureau office—is what Bakhtin calls "ambivalent laughter," as it at once betrays an instinctive mischief and a subconscious uneasiness about one's own moral indecency. The fact that the author depicts the disagreeable, absurd, and miserable facts of life with deliberate jocularity, or "black humor," is therefore intended to create the essential psychological frame necessary for the reader to grasp the "real" essence of these people's misfortune.

Another obstacle to realistic comprehension of human misery is, from the modernist point of view, sentimental romanticization. The following episode exposes the self-deceiving quality of humanitarianism with cutting humor.

In the last part of the novel, the narrator recounts one of his recent visits to the local teahouse. The girl he gets that day is extremely unresponsive and somnolent. She reminds him of another teahouse girl in Taipei with whom he thought he was in love. He goes on to recall that he even offered to give the girl 30,000 NT for her ransom, with no conditions attached. The next evening, instead of delivering the money as he had promised, he wandered listlessly for a long time on the dreamy streets of the city, and finally entered another teahouse.

This story is an apparent parody of a popular plot, and it may be worth pointing out for the sake of contrast that the same plot is used in a celebrated short story, "Chiang-chün tsu" [A family of generals] (1964), by Ch'en Ying-chen, a leading Nativist. In Ch'en's rewriting of the plot, the mainlander veteran's generous donation of his retirement pension to save a Taiwanese girl from being sold into prostitution for a second time does not achieve the intended goal, but the action itself touchingly affirms the possibility of selfless altruism, especially among poor and socially exploited people. Wang Wen-hsing is apparently extremely cynical about such altruistic sentiment. His skepticism, directed at the widely abused terms of humanitarianism, is satirically expressed with comical deflation in a passage that describes the narrator's first meeting with the teahouse girl to whom he later offered the ransom:

> I was extremely moved. At that dark, extremely small seat, I thought about such profound questions as I had never thought about in my life: for example, life, human life. What is its meaning? Why is it that such a nice woman must suffer from torments like this—when confronted with other people's suffering, what can you *do*? In what way can you possibly be of any *help*? In this world, there are numerous women like her—Pretty Pearl—that was probably her name, too. In what way can we free all of them, every single one of them, from such a miserable life? I exhausted my brain searching for methods—but couldn't find any—in the end, it occurred to me, the only remedy was perhaps that, when one has sex with them, one must do it well—at least this way they would be rewarded with something, maybe. The teahouse is in fact an excellent place for educational purposes: In a short period of time, it teaches you many many things about life and about society. "Teahouses are classrooms"—those who frequent them are in fact more thoroughgoing "humanitarians" than anyone else you can think of. (172–173)

With its outlandish irreverent humor and underlying seriousness—the question "what can you do?" seems seriously to be directed at the inflated goals of self-styled humanitarians—the passage is exemplary of the "seriocomic" mode that Wang intentionally appropriates in this novel. Wang's employment of this particular mode offers an effective modernist antidote to the romantic vision of life that has prevailed in serious modern Chinese literature ever since the May Fourth era.

The incident that immediately follows the narrator's recollection of the Taipei teahouse girl forcefully bears out the theme of "moral failure," as the narrator demonstrates how instinctive feelings of compassion are no match for petty self-interest (175–176). The narrator suddenly notices on the girl's sleeve a white woolen ball that, according to local custom, suggests that one of her family members just passed away. The narrator is stunned "as if bitten by a snake" and immediately feels a powerful sense of shame. "Which one in your family?" he naturally inquires. The question immediately triggers a heartbroken cry, which "transforms the girl's face into an ugly mask." When the crying continues for a long time with no sign of stopping, the narrator becomes anxious; he is worried that his paid visit will be wasted on the girl's tears. So he finally decides "shamelessly"—but also practically—to use her hand on himself. Whereas the improper responses to the sad stories of the captain and Yü Shih-liang are so spontaneous that they are almost involuntary, this time there is a conscious betrayal of one's moral instinct. Yet the reader may not find himself or herself necessarily superior to the narrator, simply because his moral failures are still quite human. The question pressed by the author is therefore one that pertains to the basic limits of humanity in the most practical sense.

A Rationalist's Religious Quest

The third incident to be discussed here is at once the most difficult to theorize and the most fundamental to Wang's literary project. In the fortune-telling episode, through the narrator's attempts to explore the mysterious realm of the preternatural, Wang seems to be carrying on a personal quest that has motivated several of his earlier works, in which he pursued the subject of fate with a typically equivocal mode of thinking. This equivocalness, it seems, reflects both Wang's allegiance to and his distrust of rationalism, an important new idol for Taiwan's intellectuals of Wang's generation. Although subscription to Enlightenment rationality has been at the heart of the Chinese intellectuals' antitraditionalism since the May Fourth period, a philosophical contemplation on the justifications and limitations of the "rationalist" mode of thinking, as found in *Backed Against the Sea*, is rarely seen.

Among Wang's early stories with the manifest theme of existential absurdity, such as "The Ma-tsu Festival by the Sea," "Dragon Tower," "Cold Current," "Calendar," and "Happiness Supreme," "Ming-yün te chi-hsien" [Line of fate] (1963) most directly confronts the issue of fate. In this story, the young hero slashes his own palm in order to create a simulated "line of fate." The thematic implication of this act is brilliantly summed up in Edward Gunn's article "The Process of Wang Wen-hsing's Art":

> The story . . . presents a boy who, after being advised that the short life-line on his palm predicts premature death, extends his life-line by slashing his palm down to the wrist, where he narrowly avoids fatally opening an artery. A concept of fate as a pre-ordained process has left no

room for choice and hence no moral context for action. By defying this the boy has, through his choice, attempted to create a moral context in which his act is to be judged life-giving. On the other hand, the boy's parents insist that his life-line means nothing, that it is merely an insignificant sign of chance. This the boy cannot accept, since it consigns his sense of being to contingency. Hence the boy has defied both necessity and contingency, the one robbing him of choice, the other robbing him of the significance of choice, and thus together of any moral order. Yet his act of freeing himself from pre-ordained order and imposing pattern on contingency has led to the brink of self-destruction: the scar on his palm remains a symbol of a will to meaning and destruction. (31)

The drastic measure taken by the boy to test the actual dominance of fate in human life is transformed into more symbolic gestures of challenge in the fortune-telling episode that I will discuss shortly. For the moment, I would like to call special attention to the exceptionally rationalistic mode of thinking that Wang's characters have adopted when they reason about human mortality. Before cutting his palm, the boy has carefully gathered evidence about the lifespans of his grandparents in order to draw inferences about the meaning of his own life line. In another story, "Calendar," the healthy and happy seventeen-year-old boy is also struck with alarm and sadness at the sudden realization of his own mortality. His epiphanic discovery comes about through a mathematical calculation: as he amuses himself by drawing calendars on blank sheets of paper, he finds out that all the years he will live can at best fill up very few sheets. In "Happiness Supreme," the young man commits suicide after his first sexual experience, based on the logic or pseudologic that "if *this* is what people call the happiest thing in life, *then*, life is really not worth living" (italics mine). Although the traumatic initiation into death is a most common motif in literature, Wang's stories are distinguished by the characters' obstinate reliance on reason and logic in their attempts to comprehend experienced reality.

In *Family Crisis*, traces of the hero's burgeoning rationality are found in many incidents from Fan Yeh's childhood. He once abstractly contemplates the value of a new pen:

Two weeks ago he got a new pen. He often has a strong desire to use it, yet for fear of spoiling it, he suppresses his desire and feels greatly tormented. Later on it suddenly dawns on him, if he "wants" to use it now he should "use" it, it cannot be called "wasteful." Quite the opposite, it gives the pen an additional function—giving him pleasure. Whereas if he does not use it, he not only cannot have the pleasure, but on the contrary will inflict a pain on himself. In another few days, he will use the pen naturally without any feeling, as the desire will be gone, then he would have lost (for no good reason) the pleasure that he could have gotten. Thus he has learned a lesson from this experience, and from his previous experience with holding a piece of melting ice—that is, one should enjoy the happiness the present moment has to offer. He was eleven years old that year."[29] (110–112)

The precocious boy's philosophical contemplation on the nature of pleasure and his attempt to modify his behavior according to logical reasoning are remarkable. That Wang registers this experience with the detail of the boy's age, furthermore, shows his consciousness of the development of rationality. It is this self-consciousness that is most intriguing and deserves careful analysis.

James Shu has observed that Fan Yeh is "a potential artist brought up in a society entrenched in materialism" and that "he himself inevitably absorbs some of the [society's] philistine values" (184). That Fan Yeh's rational habit of thinking fundamentally distinguishes his materialism from that of his society is easily overlooked. Ironically, Shu observes that Fan Yeh's revolt against the family system does not have the "logical vigor" of that of the May Fourth iconoclasts, overlooking the possibility that this revolt is used by Wang to illustrate precisely the kind of fanatical behavior generated by ardent, excessive devotion to rationalism. The father-son relationship in nineteenth-century European society that Fan Yeh admired may not be historically accurate, but as twenty-three-year-old Fan Yeh sees it, it represents "enlightened" human relationships, relationships that conform to reason. Wang is not merely depicting a Chinese youth's struggle to shed the shackles of feudalistic ideology, as the May Fourth writers were; he is dealing with a special case in which excessive zeal for a new "metaphysics," that of Enlightenment rationality, is the motivation for the antitraditionalism. That Fan Yeh's radical argument against the Chinese family system is presented with obvious fallacies and in an unmistakably "immature" tone (Wang could certainly have come up with a better mouthpiece if he had wanted to) betrays the author's deep awareness of the problematic nature of the situation, even though he is himself deeply entrenched in the rationalist frenzy.

It may not be farfetched to regard Fan Yeh as a victim of "rational" reasoning and to see his sufferings as results of the limitations and sterility of rationality, which fails to assist him in coping with the complex reality of his life. The fanatical potential of rationalism is well demonstrated by Wang on other occasions. Several times when Fan Yeh exercises his reason with youthful ardor, his lively imagination interferes and carries him away to some groundless conjecture or pure paranoia. To cite only one example, once when Fan Yeh tries to find "logical" reasons to reject his childhood adoration of his parents, he suddenly begins to suspect his parents' loyalty to each other: "Why should he trust his father? Almost every father in other families has extramarital affairs, why should his father be an exception?" In a short while, however, he realizes his own absurdity and "suddenly became tired, and feels deeply ashamed of himself" (157).

In *Backed Against the Sea*, Wang's exploration of the efficacy and limitation of rational reasoning takes a more complex form, partly through the narrator's half-jesting manner of speech and partly through the presence of more paradoxes and fake signs. The narrator's puzzled responses to the equivocal quality of the sign is elaborately dealt with in the fortune-telling episode, an episode that Wang himself considers most difficult to read.

Although the narrator has been forced into fortune-telling as a means of survival, the peculiar nature of this vocation has so kindled his curiosity that he has launched an elaborate search for some "metaphysical truth." Rationalistically inclined, he is eager to condemn any form of "superstition" but must confess a secret, indeed compelling, yearning for evidence that would either prove or deny the existence of a preordained fate. He therefore decides to conduct an experiment: he privately memorizes all the external signs that, according to the fortune-telling manual, are good or bad omens and then waits to see if his own predictions are fulfilled. The results are enigmatic and puzzling. The weather turns out to be precisely the opposite of his forecast. Out of the five predictions he makes for a fishing boat and four fishermen on that boat, only one is clearly fulfilled—the tragedy that kills three crew members on the boat supports the hero's warning against the trip. The first fisherman, whose features portend death by fire within three days, ends up dying in the storm; the captain has survived, but it is uncertain whether he will eventually die on the open sea as indicated by the lines on his palm. The death of the captain's son completely invalidates the narrator's prediction. The case of the fourth fisherman, who is also killed, is even more baffling, since the narrator, out of impatience, has capriciously pronounced his impending death without even consulting the manual.

On the surface, his test yields no conclusions, and the hero's quasi-religious quest proves inconsequential. The psychology involved in this quest, however, yields a great amount of paradoxical truth. The quest of the narrator is accompanied by meticulous measuring in the determination of positive or negative evidence, through a manner of reasoning that is rigorously logical. Therefore, under the guise of playfulness, the approach the narrator adopts here to test the truth of a transcendental presence echoes that of the boy in "Line of Fate," a scientific deductive method based on limited available evidence.

The narrator's hypothetical description of the mystery of the universe is still rather rationalistic, presuming a higher order of intelligence than that possessed by human beings. He envisions a mystical power that "determines" everything, a "master scheme" or "design," and a "blueprint" behind the cosmic order. When it comes to the channels through which human beings may have a glimpse of this mystery, he posits two possibilities: either through the fortune-telling manual (the written text, the scripture, what has been institutionalized) or through a mystical power that humans themselves would not be able to explain (the superhuman, the miracle, the spirit) (48–49). Both channels still need the mediation of human intelligence—humanity holds the key to its own understanding of the mystery through the interpretation of external signs.

There are two kinds of signs present in this episode. Authentic signs are such features as lines on a person's palm, moles on one's body, the color of one's complexion. The narrator complains that the instructions provided by the manual for interpreting these physical signs are often arbitrary. They are arbitrary first in that they lack statistical support and, second, in that they are based on equivocal evidence (44–45). Surely this can hardly be considered a new discovery. The second type of sign, the fake sign, is much more interesting. The first fake sign is introduced shortly before the fortune-telling episode.

While washing his face, the hero studies his own features with childlike interest: "Long, white eyebrows are a sign of longevity," so the fortune-telling manual says. His eyebrows are quite long—and they are even white! But it is the color of the soap bubbles. Then the hero, somewhat surprisingly, wonders whether this coincidental sign would have virtually the same effect as a real sign. The incident ends on a humorous note with the hero commenting on the fortune-telling manual's cunning reversal of causality—one could naturally tell a person's longevity if his eyebrows had already turned white. The apparent absurdity of this incident, however, is not to be taken at face value. The author has just prepared the reader for a more dubious and sinister view of fake signs.

There are at least three more instances in which the same kind of coincidental signs are presented (the yellowish hue on a client's forehead is suspected to be a symptom of hepatitis, the bright color of the clothing worn by the captain's son is taken as auspicious, and dirt on the palm of the surviving fisherman, if real, would coincide beautifully with the manual's description). These signs are ostensibly arbitrary because their presence in the environment is purely coincidental. However, the fact that they are on the surface merely deceptive can also be interpreted in another manner. Could it be that this deception is in effect purposeful? Is it, by any chance, part of a larger device, a plot designed by fate to entrap us? If it were, we would be doubly tricked. The problem of the ultimate equivocality of signs has been thrown back at us with greater intensity.

The significance of this treatment of signs is a vivid portrayal of a dark corner of the human psyche, a fear of the uncanny, of the irony of life, of being outwitted and duped by fate. Ancient Greek and Shakespearean tragedy both dealt with the same kind of sinister feelings by turning human wisdom against human beings themselves, making humans the unwitting instrument of fate in fulfilling its scheme. Another contemporary Chinese writer, Huang Ch'un-ming, explores the same theme in his story "Lo" [The gong] (1969). After knocking on an empty coffin three times with a broom, the superstitious hero fears that he may have caused the death of Master Yang. He cannot fall asleep until he finally has convinced himself otherwise with an interpretation of another ambiguous sign. It is the same uncanny feeling that haunts the narrator of Wang's novel, except that Wang's hero is more uncompromising and intellectually more aggressive. By deciding to test the truth, he has virtually initiated a dialogue with the unknown, just as the boy in "Line of Fate," by sheer willpower (and luck) might have created a real life line for himself.

Wang Wen-hsing has indicated that in *Backed Against the Sea* he tried to present a fundamentally atheistic view of religion. Paradoxically, however, the highly rational search narrated in this book has confirmed a provisionality that anticipates a later religious quest by the author. When the narrator logically, if not all that scientifically, tests his hypothesis, the procedure has been so artfully devised that the very signs that suggest the improbability of the hypothesis also serve as evidence of undeniability. Since the narrator has conceived the rules for this quest in intellectual terms, the quest must remain open-ended if one cannot rule out the possibility of a positive answer.

Wang's formal conversion to Catholicism in 1986 may indicate acceptance of this provisionality. Before his conversion, Wang made an uncharacteristically direct statement about his religious quest in a note published in a magazine ("Shou-chi" 98). The author of the note, watching a bird pecking on its own image reflected in a mirror, feels sorry for the bird in its futile quest for self-knowledge. The knowledge that we human beings possess about the plight of the bird, the author reasons, is by definition inaccessible to the bird, since it requires a perspective only human beings can have. The apparently metaphorical situation in this note echoes the hypothesis verbalized by the narrator in *Backed Against the Sea* about a higher order of intelligence, a transcendental existence with superior knowledge about human beings. The message is this: Human beings should acknowledge the limitation of their knowledge; any denial of the possibility of a universal hierarchy is only presumptuous. Again, most rationalistically, the author has reached a conclusion negatively, based on a rational choice to honor the hypothetical.

As an avowed modernist writer, Wang seems to have derived a peculiar dynamism from his enthusiasm for determinacy that paradoxically enables him to describe a quest that leads to inevitable undecidability. The following description of a modernist in a lecture by Douwe Fokkema seems to characterize him well. In contrast to the realist who "creates an epic world, by means of a comprehensive, encircling and inclusive narrative . . . [the] Modernist does not try to be complete and lacks the certainty that would make him attempt to discover the laws governing human existence . . . however, he is an intellectual who never gives up thinking, even if he knows that the results of his deliberations can be only provisional. Therefore, he often presents them as hypotheses." (13–14). The fortune-telling episode in *Backed Against the Sea*, it seems, epitomizes the process by which Wang Wen-hsing, a latter-day modernist, searches for "determinacy" with a negative assurance, having already taken into account its hypothetical nature.

"Crude Experience" and Art

Wang's religious quest, it seems, continues. Upon completion of *Backed Against the Sea*, Wang became particularly interested in the religious fables written by Tolstoy in old age, and he has apparently remained critical of Christianity even since his conversion to Catholicism. In recent years, Wang has developed a strong interest in Buddhist scriptures. Although Wang has never openly discussed the parallelism between his religious and artistic quests, they undoubtedly share the same dynamics and influence each other. Although a more elaborate study of this parallelism must await the completion of Wang's next book, the sequel to *Backed Against the Sea*, which Wang has been working on for ten years, I would like to make some preliminary observations about Wang's views of art based on the novel *Backed Against the Sea*.

Generally speaking, it seems that Wang has begun to reject the dominance of the more sterile form of rationality that his previous work *Family Crisis* in many ways represents. If rational comprehension of "reality" and "experience" systematically distorts and if logical reasoning only leads to provisional conclusions, then perhaps more value ought to be assigned to experience itself in its more pristine, crude form. The new stress on crude, nonintellectual experience in *Backed Against the Sea* seems to serve as an antidote to the rationalistic frenzy of Fan Yeh. The nonsensical sophistry and intricate paradox of the narrative discourse of *Backed Against the Sea* may be taken as parodies of Fan Yeh's serious-minded, rationalistic, or sometimes pseudorationalistic reasoning. The ribald and jocular middle-aged veteran is in fact deliberately conceived as a foil to the ultrasensitive, moody, and scrupulously upright young intellectual in *Family Crisis*.[30] The earthy, childlike happiness of the prostitute the narrator meets toward the end of the novel, a character surrounded with symbols suggestive of spiritual salvation, for instance, seems to flow naturally from her physical health, magnanimity, endless energy, and appetite for simple pleasure—even the most trivial details of life are for her sources of joy. In a certain sense, even the boisterous, distasteful wrestling scenes in the Dialect Research Bureau office are rendered with such liveliness that they exude the hilarious gaiety of carnivalesque revelry.

In *Backed Against the Sea*, Wang seems especially to stress that art, like sex, must preserve the original substance of raw and crude "experience." Art is repeatedly associated with physiological drives and libidinal gratification. At the beginning of the novel, after letting out a string of profanities, the narrator says that his verbal articulation—which is the virtual content of the novel—is motivated by an animalistic need for expression, just like the howling of a dog (1–2). In fact, the narrator repeatedly stresses that the creative process ought to be physically motivated and generate the same kind of gratification as sexual pleasure (94–99); he even poses an analogy between unproductive sexual positions and fancy artistic experiments that are complex and elaborate in appearance but sterile in content (158–159).

That Wang constantly applies the same imagery to art and sex in this novel fully indicates that he perceives an intricate relationship between the two. As Wang has frequently described his own writing as an "everlasting battle," the novel's sex scenes are also full of military metaphors. More thematically revealing, however, is Wang's use of the Zen metaphor for both art and sex. The narrator says that the best traditional Chinese poem ever written is the Bohdi poem written by the Sixth Patriarch of the Ch'an [Zen] Buddhist sect (93–95). The imagery used in a key passage on sexual desire also unmistakably alludes to Zen. The effort to fulfill the insatiable physical desire for sex is compared to a man's foolish attempt to catch the image of the moon reflected in a ditch by jumping in and out of the dirty water, which not only exhausts him, but also makes him filthy and foul-smelling all over (162). Since the metaphysical school of traditional Chinese poetics, heavily influenced by Zen thought, frequently compares poetry (or the aesthetic experience of poetry) to a "flower in the mirror" or the "moon in the water" (J. Liu), it seems that Wang is also linking art and sex, seeing both as physically motivated struggles to attain an ultimately elusive object—the experience of fulfillment. Due to limits inherent in the existential condition of humankind, such efforts often yield imperfect results: the narrator's sexual experiences are invariably frustrating, and the experience of artistic creation is so unbearably painful that the narrator deems it unworthy of his dedication. Nonetheless, as the Bohdi poem greatly admired by the narrator may finally suggest, Wang's attitude toward art is after all positive:

> Bodhi originally has no tree,
> The mirror also has no stand.
> From the beginning not a thing is,
> Where is there room for dust?[31]
> Sixth Patriarch of Ch'an Buddhism

Although the poem ostensibly suggests the illusory nature of reality, including art, the fact that the poem itself is preserved and admired as great art may attest to the true value of art—it both exposes the illusory nature of experience and preserves the illusion as an aesthetic experience. Together with the theme of temporality in Family Crisis, this notion of the relationship between art and reality echoes the widely held modernist view that art wrests experience from the flux of time and preserves it outside of history as an aesthetic experience. For Wang, the imaginary absoluteness of art may serve to compensate for the ultimate indeterminacy of religious truth. Moreover, as the creative process is seen by Wang as a daily struggle, a physical acting-out of the "quest,"[32] it becomes a "substitute gratification" for his more rationalistic intellectual quest.

CHAPTER FIVE

The Nativist Resistance to Modernism

In the late 1960s and early 1970s, as the Modernist fiction writers began to mature artistically, the resistance to modernism's dominance of Taiwan's literary scene also began. The precursor to a large-scale denunciation of the Modernist literary movement was the 1972 New Poetry debate, which involved a number of academic critics and Modernist poets who discussed specific Western-influenced features in contemporary Taiwan poetry. The consensus reached in this debate seemed to be that, despite its other merits, the currently practiced New Poetry suffered from such unhealthy qualities as semantic obscurity, excessive use of foreign imagery and Europeanized syntax, and evasion of contemporary social reality. These features, furthermore, were considered symptomatic of the faulty style generally promoted in Taiwan's Modernist literary movement.

Even though it may not be unusual in literary history for critics and writers periodically to reexamine and revolt against the current dominant style, the New Poetry debate bore a special social implication in that it was closely tied to Taiwan intellectuals' growing consciousness of their endangered Chinese cultural identity. In what was later known as the *hui-kuei hsiang-t'u* (return to the native) trend around the turn of the 1970s, progressive intellectuals criticized the blind admiration and slavish imitation of Western cultural models, and exhorted their compatriots to show more respect for their indigenous cultural heritage as well as greater concern for domestic social issues. Many liberal scholars, especially returnees from the United States, played important roles in igniting this new current, which at first revolved around several universities and intellectual magazines.[1]

This nationalist concern is manifest in arguments presented in the article that triggered the New Poetry debate, "Modernism and Tradition in Some Recent Chinese Verse" (Kwan-Terry). According to the diagnosis of the author of this article, John Kwan-Terry, an overseas Chinese professor of English literature, the epidemic poetic disease was rooted in a "cultural crisis" and in Chinese writers' lack of awareness of the pitfalls of the Modernist literary project:

> Our complacent possession of a few borrowed facts, or satisfaction with the mere working of a borrowed, mechanical civilization cover a terror at our contemplation of our true selves. Modern poetry, like our common language, no longer seeks moral truths and attitudes to life as a natural habit, and this loss of vitality reflects the crisis in our culture. What modern poetry needs is not just a linguistic, but also a spiritual revolution in which literature will, as in the past centuries, enrich the potentialities of the language heritage in terms of a liberation and communion of feeling.[2] (197)

By equating stylistic fashion-seeking and lack of moral interest and by calling for a "spiritual revolution," Kwan-Terry strikes a moralistic note. Indeed, a similar nationalistic-moralistic tenor has persisted in Taiwan's Nativist literary discourse, which developed right after the New Poetry debate.

The Nativist Literary Debate and Its Aftermath

The Modernist-Nativist Contention

From the early to mid-1970s, a group of critics began to renounce publicly the foreign-influenced Modernist work and to advocate a nativist, socially responsible literature. This trend reached its apex with the outbreak of a virulent Nativist literary debate in 1977 and 1978 and suddenly declined when, in 1979, several key figures of the Nativist camp exited from the literary scene and became directly involved in politcal protests. Nativist literature as a creative genre—the main features of which are use of the Taiwanese dialect, depiction of the plight of country folks or small-town dwellers in economic difficulty, and resistance of the imperialist presence in Taiwan—can be traced back to a patriotic literary trend under the Japanese occupation (J. Wang). While inheriting the dominant nationalist spirit from this earlier trend, the Nativist literature champions of the 1970s had their own political agenda as well.

Viewed retrospectively, the Nativist camp was the first oppositional formation at a critical juncture in Taiwan's post-1949 history. After two decades of political stability and steady economic growth, the country suffered a series of diplomatic setbacks at the turn of the decade—beginning with its expulsion from the United Nations in 1971, followed by Richard Nixon's visit to the People's Republic of China and the termination of the country's diplomatic relations with Japan in 1972—that caused not only international isolation, but also a confidence crisis among intellectuals. The crevice thus created in the Nationalist government's state control provided an opportunity for frustrated native intellectuals to vent discontent that had been building for years: anxiety over the country's future, which had frequently been glossed over by the *fan-kung ta-lu* (regain the mainland) slogan; indignation about political persecutions of dissidents; and many other grievances against the authoritarian regime. What made the government particularly uneasy, however, was the Nativists' advocacy for a noncapitalist socioeconomic system.

As the problems accompanying the country's accelerated development grew, long-repressed socialist ideas began to resurface. Unlike the majority of the country's liberal intellectuals who demanded political democratization but supported capitalist-style economic modernization, the Nativists believed that the socioeconomic system of Taiwan must be changed. They launched fierce attacks on the government's economic dependence on Western countries (especially the United States), which allowed the "decadent" capitalist culture to infiltrate the life of Taiwan's people; feeling indignant on behalf of Taiwan's farmers and workers who paid a high price in the process of urban expansion, they also attempted to draw public attention to adverse effects of the country's economic development as a whole.

Such oppositional voices posed a threat to the Nationalist government, which was convinced that the logical consequence of the upsurge of socialist ideology would be a Communist insurgency backed by the Chinese government on the mainland. In addition, the regionalist sentiment implied in the Nativist project immediately touched on an extremely sensitive issue, the "provincial identity problem" (*sheng-chi wen-t'i*). Not only had tensions between native Taiwanese and mainlanders always been a source of disquieting feelings, but the unbalanced distribution of political power was an epicenter on the verge of eruption.³ As a consequence, even though some of the leading Nativist critics were socialists or nationalists rather than separatists who promoted Taiwan independence (Ch'en Ying-chen, for example, has always been a staunch advocate of future reunification with China), the Nativist critical discourse as a whole could not but be deeply entrenched in the ongoing political strife between the native Taiwanese and the mainlander-controlled Nationalist government.

It is therefore undeniable that literary nativism was used by a special group of people at a particular historical moment to challenge the existing sociopolitical order. However, it appears that ideological debates in modern Chinese society inevitably generate widespread polemics around literature, as evidenced by numerous such disputes in the May Fourth period, in the thirties, and during the entire Communist reign on the mainland. The traditional Chinese pragmatic view of literature and the legacy of a gentry ideology, which assigns to intellectuals, especially writers, lofty social missions, have combined to make literary discourse a genuine political space. As a result, the attacks launched by the Nativists on the Modernist writers, whose literary ideology is a conspicuously apolitical one, have largely centered on the latter's default of their social responsibilities as members of the intelligentsia.

The home base for the anti-Modernist critics was the journal *Wen-chi* [Literary quarterly], founded in 1966. With Yü T'ien-ts'ung as the central mover, the journal's founding members included several writers already known for their Modernist work, such as Ch'en Ying-chen, Liu Ta-jen, Shih Shu-ch'ing, and Ch'i-teng Sheng. The journal had, furthermore, discovered two important writers, Huang Ch'un-ming and Wang Chen-ho, whose fiction significantly departed from the current Modernist fads and depicted rural life with unaffected realism. Although both writers refused to label their works "Nativist," the literary reformers on the journal's editorial board were ready to use them as weapons in their fight against the Modernist hegemony.

In 1973, T'ang Wen-piao, a visiting math professor at National Cheng-chih University closely associated with *Literary Quarterly*, fired criticism at the Modernists' elitist tendency and neglect of the masses.⁴ The straightforward accusations so startled liberal critics that Yen Yüan-shu referred to this critical attack as the "T'ang Wen-piao Incident." However, even more vehement militancy was to be seen when the Nativist critics chose individual writers as targets. Almost concurrent with the T'ang Wen-piao Incident, Literary Quarterly organized a series of seminars to examine the thematic implications of Ou-yang Tzu's fiction and branded it corrupt and immoral (Ho Hsin; T'ang Chi-sung). A combatant spirit was aroused, and, by the mid-1970s, writers in Taiwan's literary circle were already deeply split into opposing groups.[5]

The literary climate in this decade became truly unpleasant with the increasing politicization of critical discourse. With the founding of a radical magazine Hsia-ch'ao [Summer tide] in 1976 and its provocative use of such taboo terms as "proletarian literature" (literally, literature of workers, peasants, and soldiers) and "class consciousness," the deep-seated anti-Communist sentiments of the liberals were incited. In the summer of 1977, the country's leading Modernist poet Yü Kuang-chung wrote a short essay titled "Lang-lai le" [The wolf is here] openly accusing the Nativists of being leftists. This fatal charge ignited highly emotional responses and retaliations from all sides, and polemical writings about literature and politics began to flood the country's newspapers and literary magazines. This so-called Nativist literary debate came to an end only in the middle of 1978 as a result of threatened government interference.[6]

During the debate, intellectuals of different ideological persuasions formed two temporary coalitions. On the one hand, to resist the Nativists' leftist dogmatism, the liberal Modernists sided with progovernment writers and literary bureaucrats. On the other hand, such older, established literary figures as Hsü Fu-kuan and Hu Ch'iu-yüan allied with the Nativists and defended the intellectual's right of political intervention.[7] New and existing magazines and newspapers also established distinct partisan alliances. Sandwiched between government supporters and various oppositional factions, the less politically minded Modernist writers soon found themselves forced into roles imposed on them by others.

The impact of the Nativist literary debate was largely emotional. As the debate involved numerous exchanges of personal insults, it created a schism between the Modernists and the Nativists that was to take a long time to heal. While conservative attacks on Nativist literature often carried with them potential political threats, many self-styled Nativist critics were overly adamant in their attempts to impose ideological guidelines on creative writers. Some even resorted to distasteful name calling,[8] which only made it doubly clear that the Modernists had been used as scapegoats for an unbridled outburst of antigovernment sentiment.[9] Liberal academic critics played ambivalent roles in this dispute. For instance, such respected critics as Yen Yüan-shu and Ch'i I-shou endorsed the Nativists' nationalist stance and the notion of socially responsible literature, but they were at the same time disturbed by the confusion of art and politics. Their largely rational, well-informed views on artistic matters, however, fell largely on deaf ears.

Although the Nativists took the offensive position in most of the feud, some serious Nativist thinkers also found the debate profoundly disappointing. Ch'en Ying-chen, for example, regretted that the discussion was never elevated to a higher theoretical level, never became a "neo-Enlightenment" intellectual movement (6: 102). Such activists as Yang Ch'ing-ch'u and Wang T'o, who had intended to use literature as an ideological weapon, also seemed to have experienced tremendous frustration, which eventually led them to pursue political goals through more direct channels.

Misconceptions About the Modernist-Nativist Polarization

Joseph Lau once wrote: "While it is true that what distinguishes the hsiang-t'u writer is his engaged spirit, one is disturbed by his intolerance for another kind of writer who wants to retain, in Virginia Woolf's apt phrase, 'A Room of One's Own'" ("Echoes" 148). The Nativists' exclusiveness may be rooted in their tendency to think along the axis of polar opposition—modernism versus nativism, avant-garde experiment versus realistic writing, and urban, capitalist economy versus the agrarian mode of production in rural areas[10]—privileging one term of the opposition over the other. This binary mode of thinking has caused many people to perceive writers of the sixties and seventies as two antagonistic groups, a perception that must be held largely responsible for some serious misconceptions about the real nature and scope of the Modernist literary movement. My discussion of Huang Ch'un-ming, widely recognized as the best Nativist writer, is aimed to redress some of these misconceptions.

In the wake of the Nativist literary debate, many critics eagerly tried to argue that innate "nativist" qualities in the work of such writers as Huang

Ch'un-ming and Wang Chen-ho had enabled them to be largely exempt from the corrupt Modernist influence almost from the very beginning, even though they launched their careers during the Modernist literary movement. Whereas the later development of Wang Chen-ho seems blatantly to belie this benign attempt to excuse him from modernism, Huang Ch'un-ming has been elevated to the status of a Nativist cultural hero. This idealization of Huang's nativist essence underlies the otherwise excellent study of Huang by Liu Ch'un-ch'eng, *Huang Ch'un-ming ch'ien-chuan* [A prebiography of Huang Ch'un-ming] (1987), which contends that Huang Ch'un-ming "almost immediately" rejected the modernistic indulgence in nihilism and self-pity, something that would have led him to self-destruction (221).

As one of the most talented fiction writers and original observers of social reality in Taiwan's post-1949 era, Huang deserves many of the compliments that have been showered upon him in the last two decades. Disturbing, however, are the assumptions about Modernism behind this image of an idealized Nativist immune to contamination. To use Liu Ch'un-ch'eng's work as an example again, Liu has followed many others before him in branding the Modernist literary movement "anemic," "nihilistic," and a "dead-end" literary project (218–219, 230), and in suggesting that the Nativist stories published in *Literary Quarterly* during the late 1960s heralded the demise of the Modernist literary movement.[11]

Moralistic interpretation of literary features of the earliest phase of the Modernist literary movement and total neglect of any evolution of the Modernists since the rise of Nativist literature have, in fact, been characteristic of widely accepted critical views during the last decade. Such misconceptions reflect a confusion between the "Modernist fad," a version of Taiwan's post-1949 youth culture amidst which the Modernist literary movement was born, and the Modernist literary movement itself, a viable literary movement not confined to such ephemeral cultural trends. Such a narrow definition of the movement could hardly account for the mature Modernist works discussed in Chapter 4. Moreover, emphasis on such negatively conceived Modernist characteristics as nihilism tends to obscure the more quintessential features of Modernist work, such as universalism and a humanist concern with individual experience. These features, as will be demonstrated, are prominent in Huang Ch'un-ming's stories of the late sixties and early seventies, before he began to write more consciously about topical issues relevant to the collective fate of residents in Taiwan.[12]

As many critics have pointed out, in most of Huang's stories of the late 1960s, the central theme is the individual's struggle against the inevitable disintegration of an older agrarian community. Negative images of modern technology are presented as encroaching on the pastoral rural lifestyle—or on the characters' nostalgic vision of it. In "Lo" [The Gong] (1969), the loudspeaker carried by a tricycle that has replaced the more primitive gong beating as a way to disseminate local news to the villagers not only has caused the gong beater Kam Kim-ah to become unemployed, but also threatens to bring down a "tradition." In "Ni-ssu i-chih lao-mao" [The drowning of an old cat] (1967), the swimming pool built on the Dragon's Eye spring, which was first objected to and then accepted by the villagers, represents the erosive power of corrupt city life. The local government's use of democratic procedures to enforce its decision to build the pool, which is designed to be a summer resort for people from a neighboring town, furthermore, takes advantage of the villagers' ignorance of modern society and, in the author's view, must be considered a malicious offense against the "noble savage."

Such treatment, rather than being "realistic," as most critics of Huang perceive it to be, reflects a preconceived disillusionment with modernity, which is, contrary to what the Nativists seem to believe, not an exclusively Nativist characteristic, but a central position of the Modernists as well (as evidenced by the case of Wang Wen-hsing). The most important point, however, is that instead of communicating a socialist message, these stories are primarily humanist, for they treat modern civilization, including technology and democracy, as a potential threat to basic human values. In contrast to such ideological writings of the seventies—such as those by Yang Ch'ing-ch'u, Wang T'o, and Huang's own stories since 1972—Huang's early stories contain an elaborate and highly sensitive treatment of the inner experiences of the individual and frequently employ the romantic notion of tragic transcendence as a means to ultimately affirm humanity.

Modernist thematic conventions have apparently left explicit imprints on "Erh-tzu te ta wan-ou" [His son's big doll] (1968), one of Huang's best-loved stories. Although the story deals with an uneducated small-town young man, whose disadvantaged position is a direct consequence of poverty-induced illiteracy, stressed throughout the work is not the debilitating social environment, but the protagonist's endangered sense of self. In his job as a costumed advertisement, Ch'un-shu suffers most harshly not only from a sense of humiliation, which is a result of his sensitive personality, but also from something more ineffable, the existentialist fear of loss of identity. Indeed, significant echoes of popular existentialist motifs abound in this story. Roaming from street to street under the scorching sun, Ch'un-shu is constantly attacked by a threatening dizziness: "In the heat, the glare of the asphalt road ahead made it impossible for him to see anything. Off in the distance everything was shrouded in a bile-colored haze, which he dared not even try to look through" (Goldblatt, *Drowning* 38). While fear of physical failure is realistic, it also suggests a fear of loss of self. The sense of absurdity and alienation is suggested vividly by the anachronistic costume of a nineteenth-century European general. "Looking in the mirror with only half of his face painted, he would smile sorrowfully as waves of vague emptiness surged through his mind" (41). The famous ending of the story, in which the hero puts on his make-up so that his son can recognize him, accentuates the theme of the existentialist quest for identity.

That the individual experience is often described for its own sake is further witnessed by Uncle Ah-sheng's temporary rise to a sagelike personality in "The Drowning of an Old Cat." When he persuades the villagers to resist the local government, Uncle Ah-sheng allegedly experiences a miraculous transformation that gives him "the appearance of a religious soul completely at peace with himself" (30). "The extraordinary mystery of faithful devotion to a belief can cause a man to approach godlike sublimity. This was probably the case with Uncle Ah-sheng—he had already begun the process leading to that plateau where man and God exist together as an apostle" (31). Such elevated feelings, lasting only for a short while, are subjective private experiences meaningful only to the individual. By suggesting that Uncle Ah-sheng's heroism constitutes a futile act of social resistance and is trampled in the course of social progress, the author is trying to affirm humanity, even in its moments of failure.

In the equally dramatic ending of "The Gong," the gong beater Kam Kim-ah is even more unmistakably cast as a tragic hero. It is through a presumptuous attempt to impress his employer, while being ignorant of the bureaucratic rules of civilized society, that Kam Kim-ah brings about his own downfall, but his final gong beating is a fantastic success—if seen as a dramatic performance. Kam Kim-ah's unusual sense of pride, his desire to be "a man of society," is the cause of his downfall, as it first alienates him from the funeral helpers and then deprives him of the job opportunity he desperately needs, but it is also what affirms his personal worth and distinguishes him from Lu Hsün's despicable image of the Chinese peasant, Ah Q.

The dilemma encountered by Chiang Ah-fa, the head of a worker's family in "Hsien" [Ringworms] (1968), has more comic undertones. Ah-fa cannot tell the difference between letting the town's doctor (a childhood pal of his) insert an IUD in his wife's uterus and allowing his wife to take a lover. His poverty, however, makes him wish that his wife would go ahead and have the IUD inserted without informing him. The problem is that, as a faithful wife, she won't take the initiative. Although Huang is passing judgment on society when he uses ringworms as a symbol for the characters' failure to face reality—"If you don't mention it, it won't bother you"—what is really at stake here is still Ah-fa's sense of pride. In the end, no prospect of improvement in the family's financial condition is in sight, but Ah-fa's pride has been kept intact.[13]

It is only in the later stories of Huang, such as "P'ing-kuo te tzu-wei" [The taste of apples] (1972), that the poor are no longer able to sustain their pride. The wife of a worker whose leg is crushed by a car driven by an American colonel cries loudly on purpose to earn sympathy from the foreigners. The husband, at first angry with the colonel, turns around to thank him and even apologizes for his anger. The loss of self-respect as a result of overpowering external conditions—the American and Japanese imperialist presence—undoubtedly indicates a shift of the author's attention from the individual to the environment, to the collective fate of the group as united by class or nation.

Another feature, seldom noticed by critics, that underlines Huang's change in artistic orientation since 1972 is his abandonment of aesthetic appreciation as a salvational or at least spiritually elevating experience. In his earlier stories, Huang on many occasions showed a fascination with odd external forms and colors. In one of his prefaces he describes how he was struck by the image of a boy he encountered in the village, a boy who paints the fingers of his deformed hand in five different colors and continuously shakes them back and forth. Then, in the lyrical piece "Yü" [Fish] (1968), the "engraved design of a fish shape," which is Ah-ts'ang's painfully lost fish crushed by a truck into the muddy surface of the road, offers another instance of the strange mixture of beauty and cruelty. The truck that crushed the boy's bonito fish and changed it into a bizarre graphic image on the muddy mountain path is an emblem of the industrial age, but the fact that it changes the use value of the fish into an aesthetic one, incomprehensible to the boy who has just lost his token of trust, conveys a characteristically "modernist" irony. The ending of the story "Fish," moreover, has a resonance that extends beyond the story's ostensible sphere. Because Grandpa is so enraged by Ah-ts'ang's stubborn insistence that he has brought back a fish, a fight breaks out. Their quarrel, however, brings an unexpected echo from the valley: ". . . did bring the fish back!" As this phrase reaches their ears from afar, both are startled. The distant echo seems to have served as testimony to the boy's words—as if a third party, here a responsive nature, suddenly decides to participate in the little drama between the boy and his grandpa, momentarily lifting them from their petty but genuine miseries.

In his later stories, Huang still uses grotesque images, such as the ugly but innocent smile of the mute girl in "The Taste of Apples" and the horrifying sight of the colored skull under the cap of a beautiful angelic girl in "Hsiao Ch'i te nei i-ting mao-tzu" [The cap of little Angela] (1974). The function of this technique, however, is now drastically different from that in the earlier stories. It is meant to elicit humanitarian sympathy, not simply fascination. Thus, when the American colonel in "The Taste of Apples" is taken aback by the sight of the mute girl and exclaims, "Oh, my God," his first-world humanitarianism and altruistic attempt to help the family are portrayed ironically. Furthermore, whereas the richly suggestive images in Huang's earlier stories offer glimpses into a mysterious realm that evades reasonable analysis, the precise symbolic implications of the apple, "sour and pulpy . . . frothy and not quite real" (Goldblatt, Drowning 184), which suggests Taiwanese people's feelings about American aid in the postwar years, apparently better serves the purpose of conveying an ideological message.

The Rise of Ideological Writings

Placed within a larger historical context, the Modernist-Nativist split is part of the continual struggle in modern Chinese history between liberal and radical intellectuals with different reform programs and different views of literature's social function. The new paradigm of ideological writing established in the mid-1970s moved in a direction diametrically opposed to that of the introspective, humanist, and universalist approach of the Modernists and deliberately focused on the historical specificity of contemporary Taiwan society. In addition to later works by Huang Ch'un-ming on imperialism, such writers as Yang Ch'ing-ch'u and Wang T'o explored capitalist exploitation as it affected urban factory workers and fishermen. These literary efforts were also backed by some serious theoretical thinking, although most of the Nativist literary debate itself was virtually divorced from contemporary literary practice.

Wang T'o's 1977 essay "Shih 'Hsien-shih chu-i' wen hsüeh, pu shih 'hsiang-t'u wen-hsüeh' " [It's "literature of the present reality," not "nativism"] stood out among numerous polemical writings precisely because of its accurate representation of the reality of recent literary practice. The main argument Wang proposes in this essay is that, instead of writing about rural regions and country people, Nativist literature is concerned with the "here and now" of Taiwan society, which embraces a wide range of social environments and people. Nativist literature thus should be defined as a literature rooted in the land of Taiwan, one that reflects the social reality and the material and psychological aspirations of its people. By using the term *hsien-shih* (contemporary reality, the "here and now") rather than *hsieh-shih* (realism) and by enlarging the scope of Nativist literature to include all levels of social reality in Taiwan, Wang has disentangled the confused debate over the Western-imported literary term "realism" and has foregrounded the Nativists' ideological position by stressing high-priority issues. The essay, therefore, represents an important step in the Nativists' self-definition.

The critical evaluation of Nativist work produced in the 1970s, however, is in general not very positive. Although the change in thematic conventions since the seventies met the approval of most critics, excessive ideological concern is considered an impediment to Nativist literary achievement. Even though Huang Ch'un-ming is often regarded as an exception, many have felt that his art, too, deteriorates in direct proportion to the increase in social commentary in his later works.

However, just as Modernist literature continued to evolve after the rise of Nativist literature, the practice of Nativist literature did not come to an end even though the Nativist literary debate folded toward the end of the 1970s. In the continuing efforts made by such Nativist ideological writers as Ch'en Ying-chen, Sung Tse-lai, Li Ch'iao, and Wu Chin-fa in the 1980s, one can discern a sharp increase in formal consciousness, which has led to some genuinely innovative techniques. Although a detailed discussion of all these writers is beyond the scope of this study, I will consider some of the artistic endeavors of Ch'en Ying-chen, the most important Nativist critic and writer.

Ch'en Ying-chen's Departure from Modernism

Ch'en Ying-chen started to publish fiction in 1959 after graduation from college, in a style characteristic of the early phase of the Modernist literary movement. However, by the time he joined Literary Quarterly in 1966, he seemed to be disenchanted with modernism. He was imprisoned shortly afterward for participating in a Marxist reading group, and his literary career was virtually interrupted for seven years. When he was released in 1975, he promptly rejoined Yü T'ien-ts'ung and soon became the leading champion of Nativist literature. His criticism of Taiwan's Modernist literary movement, more thoughtful than anyone else's, was largely endorsed by Nativist supporters.

Literary and Cultural Criticism

Ch'en Ying-chen's general view of literature before the 1980s was largely dominated by the simple "reflection theory," with decisively socialist and moralistic overtones. Although these qualities frequently degenerated into crude dogmatism in the hands of lesser Nativist critics, Ch'en, as a practicing writer, has shown great awareness of complexities and has continually refined and modified his views.[14] Ch'en's most important contribution, however, is that he has established himself as the most persistent and powerful opposition to the liberal-humanist literary discourse popular in

Taiwan since the 1960s. Ch'en's comments on contemporary Taiwan literature, though scarce and skimpy, are extremely important as they depart from the formalist New Critical approach and exhibit a strong historical consciousness.[15] Since his 1983 trip to the United States as a guest of the International Writers' Workshop at the University of Iowa and subsequent tours of Taiwan's Asian neighbors, such as Japan, Korea, the Philippines, and Indonesia, he has further shifted his attention to the global aspect of the spread of modernism in this century as part of the expansion of capitalism. This new awareness has led him to align Taiwan's Nativist literary movement with similar nationalist struggles against Western literary influences in other third-world countries as a unique postcolonial phenomenon.

Despite Ch'en's laudable contributions, his criticism of Taiwan's Modernist literary movement has some major flaws from a strictly scholarly point of view. First, as is evident from his writings over the last twenty years, Ch'en has consistently confused modernism with avant-garde antirepresentationalism. Although he slightly modified his negative judgment of the Modernists in an interview of 1987 (6: 87–89), the grounds for Ch'en's objection to Taiwan writers' excessive zeal for effete modernist innovations have never changed. For example, in the same 1987 interview, he argues that "the path of modernism can be only traveled once; it is meaningless to imitate someone who draws three noses on a human face" (6: 88), a statement that nicely sums up the well-sketched-out arguments in two essays written before his imprisonment—"Hsien-tai chu-i te tsai k'ai-fa" [Toward a new departure of modernism] (1967) (8: 1–15) and "Chih-shih jen te p'ien-chih" [The intellectual's prejudice] (1968) (8: 16–21).[16] Although these early essays offered a remarkably sensible response to a literary phenomenon of the 1950s and 1960s, the reiteration of the same points in the late 1980s shows that Ch'en has hardly updated his knowledge of more recent Modernist works.

Second, Ch'en's more specific criticism of Modernist style reflects (or may have initiated) a prominent tendency among critics of the Modernists to focus on obscurantism, the "illogical quality of language," and the excessive attention given to form rather than content ("Ssu-shih nien" 17, 23), which, though aptly characterizing the earlier Modernist fiction and New Poetry, does not address the specific problems of recent Modernist fiction. In fact, Ch'en once said, "The New Poetry debate of 1972 was fundamentally anti-imperialist and anti-West. This focus was very important, and the Nativist literary debate several years later was merely an extension of the New Poetry debate" (6: 99–100). It seems fair to assume that Ch'en's overriding ideological concerns have made the finer distinctions between the more avant-garde poetry and prose of the 1950s and 1960s and the largely more formalist, realistic works of such Modernist fiction writers as Wang Wen-hsing, Pai Hsien-yung, and Wang Chen-ho rather insignificant to his literary criticism.

All such premature judgments of Taiwan's Modernist literature have been rooted in Ch'en's identification of the 1960s as a period in which "Taiwan's Modernist literature and art reached their climax and overmaturity" ("Ssu-shih nien" 23). Although, as previously argued, this method of periodization ignores the historical fact of Modernist development, the gap in Ch'en's knowledge of contemporary Modernist literature is understandable. In his postimprisonment years, Ch'en has been more interested in political and cultural than artistic matters. Furthermore, the rivalry between the Nativists and the Modernists in the 1970s has deprived him of the distance necessary for impartial evaluation of Modernist works. Nonetheless, Ch'en's verdict on the Modernists has become hegemonic in the years since the Nativist literary debate; they are not only voiced by Nativist partisans, but have influenced more independent critics of a younger generation as well. A good example is the 1987 special issue on the Nativist literary debate put out by *Nan-fang* [The south] magazine.[17]

Although this special issue offered a perceptive reinterpretation of the Modernist-Nativist strife with the aid of a theoretical framework derived from Frankfurt school critical theory, when it came to evaluating Taiwan's Modernists, it simply re-presented Ch'en's flawed perception with a characteristic Nativist militance, as shown in the following passage: "The Modernist literature in Taiwan completely denied the function of literature for social critique (*whereas Western modernism did not*); although it made considerable accomplishments in experimenting with literary techniques, it was eventually rejected by everyone because its understanding of the modern condition was out of pace with the social reality of Taiwan" (my italics) (T'ung Wan-tou 11).[18] It is regrettable that these otherwise excellent reassessments of the Nativist literary debate have resorted to awkwardly differentiating between Western modernism and Modernist literature in Taiwan, rather than offering an original critique of the latter, simply to perpetuate a dogma established during that debate.

The bias against the Modernists, in its more prevalent form, has a distinctive moralistic import, of which Kwan-Terry's article still provides the most lucid presentation, as it sees in the Modernists a "spiritual hollowness," a "pathological tendency to personal and social disintegration, and a consequent inadequacy to face essential reality in life, love, and death and birth" (197). If Ch'en should not be held solely responsible for this moralistic attitude, he is at least one of its preeminent spokesmen. The blind spot in such a moralistic position is its overlooking the most valuable contribution of the Modernists: their appropriation of the modernist ideology and aesthetic as a means to reexamine their own culture. While Ch'en and other Nativist and neo-Marxist critics in the 1980s have voiced harsh criticism of Taiwan's increasingly commercialized cultural environment, few have acknowledged that modernist elitism was often the last resort for Taiwan's serious artists in their resistance of the dominant culture's commodification of literature and the pulp sentimentalism it has nourished. In this respect, one may concur with Joseph Lau's remark that "although the *hsiang-t'u* (Nativist) theoreticians invoke the laws of socio-historical determinism to explain the rise of recent *hsiang-t'u* fiction, no equal time has been given to consider the sociohistorical circumstances under which the modernist group of writers came into being" ("Echoes" 148).

In all fairness, Ch'en Ying-chen's role as an intellectual dissident and a cultural critic may well surpass his significance as a literary critic. In the last decade, as political control has relaxed considerably (especially since 1983) and as he has matured as a thinker, Ch'en has spoken powerfully on several important sociopolitical issues. Ch'en was the first to chastise multinational capitalism for encroaching on the personal and national identity of residents of Taiwan, and his fiction about the transnational corporation has created a popular subgenre. As Taiwan's changed relationship with the People's Republic of China triggered a series of debates on unification versus separation, Ch'en fought wholeheartedly against the separatists, who denied the Taiwanese people's Chinese identity, making public an earlier "split" within the Nativist camp.[19] Then, more recently, amidst much vocal criticism of the Nationalist white terror during the earlier postwar decades,

Ch'en reexamined this issue against such historical events as the Chinese Communist Revolution, the Korean War, and the U.S. cold war policy, and proposed the theory that the persecution of leftist intellectuals in the 1950s had left society with an "intellectual poverty" syndrome.

While Ch'en is different from most of Taiwan's political activists who as a rule care little about theory, he has also directly participated in many political events. He supported the first labor party in Taiwan, marched against the decision to import American agricultural products, wrote anti-Japanese political essays, visited the People's Republic of China, and founded the magazine *Jen-chien* [Human world] (1985–1989) to explore such social problems as prostitution, aboriginal minorities, and environmental pollution. The combination of political activism with a serious intellectual quest has reminded many people of China's most revered modern intellectual, Lu Hsün.[20] Indeed, Ch'en's trenchant criticism of "intellectual poverty" and bourgeois complacency (*hsing-fu i-shih*, literally happiness [false-]consciousness) in contemporary Taiwan society is very much in line with Lu Hsün's famous criticism of such aspects of Chinese "national character" as a slave mentality and political apathy. In addition to the May Fourth legacy, Ch'en also consciously tries to link himself with the idealistic patriotism of progressive Taiwanese intellectuals, a tradition that can be traced back to the Japanese occupation, to the postwar years between 1945 and the Retreat, and to the 1950s.[21] Finally, personal traits from a Protestant background—strong sense of mission, humanitarian compassion, and religiously conceived moralism—heavily underscore Ch'en's literary project, making Ch'en a unique figure in post-1949 Taiwan's literary scene.

A Battle for Representation

One crucial difference between Ch'en and the Modernists is their views of the literary representation of history. It seems that during his early contact with the modernist aesthetic, Ch'en was already deeply bothered by the notion that modernism is a form of "ideological distraction," a way of displacing "attention from history and society to pure form, metaphysics, and experiences of the individual monad" (Jameson, *Political Unconscious* 266). Therefore, after their initial orientation to literary modernism, whereas Wang Wen-hsing launched ambitious programs to perfect the modernist code—Wang's unique language experiement is said to have started in "Dragon Tower," written during 1964 and 1965—Ch'en's work of the same period, between 1963 and 1965, exhibited a thematic and formal ambivalence that pointed to a discontent with the artistic mode itself. Such discontent eventually led to Ch'en's well-known renunciation of his own earlier works in a 1975 essay, "Shih lun Ch'en Ying-chen" [Preliminary remarks on Ch'en Ying-chen], written after his release from prison (9: 3–13). The following discussion is aimed to demonstrate that the ostensible modernist characteristics of Ch'en's early fiction frequently concealed his repressed "political impulses" and his deep-seated desires to come to terms with contemporary history.

In Ch'en's early fiction, existentialist and historical themes often converge in a veteran character afflicted by the traumatic experience of war. As war represents the ultimate nihilistic fear, it also points to a taboo subject in those years, modern Chinese history. It is true that spiritual impotence is most frequently presented as the result of moral failure, such as in the case of the character K'ang-hsiung in "Wo te ti-ti K'ang-hsiung" [My brother K'ang-hsiung] (1960) and the elder brother in "Ku-hsiang" [Hometown] (1960), but history is undoubtedly a hidden cause of the mental sufferings of some of Ch'en's most memorable characters, such as Wu Chin-hsiang in "Hsiang-ts'un te chiao-shih" [Country teacher] (1960), the son-in-law in "Mao t'a-men te tsu-mu" [Cats and their grandma] (1961), and most notably the protagonist in "Wen-shu" [Documents] (1963). The typical agony that these characters apparently suffer from is, on the one hand, "existentialist," resulting from a failure to comprehend and cope with the pressures of crude reality, and, on the other hand, historical, as the psychological disease is a trace left by history. The bleak atmosphere of these stories therefore indirectly reflects their author's repressed feelings about the political taboo.

During the Nativist literary debate, critics often compared Ch'en's treatment of the mainlander émigrés with that of Pai Hsien-yung and perceived the difference to be between the progressive and the reactionary political stance. The drastic differences between their literary treatments of history are in fact probably rooted in personal biography. As a mainlander and the son of a general in the Sino-Japanese War, Pai had the advantage of "witnessing history," even if somewhat vicariously. History then becomes for him an object of nostalgia, something in the past tense or embodied in the vicissitudes of life; for him history is nicely universalized with the aid of the modernist aesthetic. Someone like Ch'en, however, would have been largely deprived of knowledge of this history, for it was systematically distorted, concealed from the public; ironically it thus became a source of great fascination. In his fiction, Ch'en has constantly resorted to the literary imagination to rediscover or re-create history, often by projecting himself onto a mainlander character (so that his mainlander characters, unlike those in Pai's *Tales of Taipei Characters*, are frequently younger males of Ch'en's own age). The imaginary landscape of mainland China depicted in such stories as "Country Teacher" is remarkably appealing with a touch of romantic melancholy; the incredible cruelty of Chinese warlords is recreated with macabre bleakness in "Documents"; and the image of the wandering young pessimist, burdened with both metaphysical and historical agony made its last appearances in "Tsui-hou te hsia-jih" [The last summer days] (1966) and "Ti i-chien ch'ai-shih" [My first case] (1967).

Ch'en employed trendy "modernist" devices to deal with his central concern in works, such as "Documents," published in *Modern Literature* between 1963 and 1965. "Documents" is about a middle-aged mainlander from a warlord family, who, though prosperously settled in Taiwan, is haunted by nightmares about brutal killings in the war and is thus unable to lead a normal life. Driven crazy by the sinister intuition that a cat, which has mysteriously appeared, is the incarnation of a young Taiwanese prisoner he once executed (it turns out to be none other than his wife's brother), he shoots his wife while hallucinating. The contrived, melodramatic story about abnormal psychology, typical of Modernist work of this time, inevitably weakens the serious theme the author intends to explore—the psychological wound left on the individual consciousness by the history of war-ridden China.

Ch'en's attention shifted to contemporary history in another Modernist story, "Ch'i-ts'an te wu-yen te tsui" [The poor, poor dumb mouths] (1964). The cause of the mental illness of the protagonist, a former art student, seems to be nothing other than the stagnant, claustrophobic sociopolitical atmosphere of the 1960s—isolation from the outside world, the monopoly of American cultural influence, and the brain-drain phenomenon that brought many college graduates to North America. Here Ch'en is playing with the paradoxical meaning of sanity just as Lu Hsün did in "K'uang-jen jih-chi" [The madman's diary]. The patient's vision of a dark room filled with poisonous insects, leeches, toads, and bats is a madman's insight into a reality that evades comprehension by normal people.

An even more important dimension of this story, however, is its implicit comment on Ch'en's own quandary, for he was simultaneously attracted to and dissatisfied with what modernism stood for at the time. The alienated protagonist is deeply bothered, but also bound, by the habit of conceiving the world in aesthetic terms. One day while on a stroll, he sees some workers on the roadside and observes that their legs have such beautiful muscles that they may serve as excellent models for art class. Right after this, on his way back to the mental institution, he meets a crowd of spectators watching the police inspecting the body of a young prostitute who has just been murdered. The student's reaction to this sight is a mixture of pity and a sensational pleasure, and this, as the protagonist seems to have sensed, is his real disease, an involuntary impotence in the face of the cruelty and suffering of the common people.

At the time when Ch'en presented this subtle theme in this story, he was deeply entrenched in the modernist aesthetic, which supposedly "defuses" and "prepares substitute gratifications" for social, historical, and political consciousness. The use of Shakespearean lines to describe the wounds on the woman's corpse in order to achieve a sensational effect is characteristic of this aesthetic mode. The dark room envisioned by the protagonist, while reminiscent of Lu Hsün's "iron house" in the preface to *Na-han* [Outcry], is more picturesquely depicted, with apparent traces of the Modernist fondness for exotic imagery. (The brave man who finally breaks the darkness with a sword and lets in the sunlight is even a "Roman" warrior.) And the story is inevitably a story of self-denial. The protagonist predicts that, when the sunlight shines into the dark room, everything that is weak and ugly shall wither and perish, including himself, a prediction that seems to suggest that Ch'en was conscious of his weakness for the Modernist aesthetic displacement of moral action. Several other Ch'en's stories of this period, such as "I lü-se chih hou-niao" [One stray green bird] (1964) and "Wu-tzu chao-yao che te t'ai-yang" [The lonely sunshine] (1965), are all characterized by restlessness and self-doubt, which are turned into repulsive self-indulgence and narcissism in the tediously lengthy story "Lieh-jen chih ssu" [The death of a hunter] (1965).

Between 1966 and 1968, as is often observed by critics and as Ch'en has observed himself, Ch'en made substantial progress in broadening the horizon of his observations as well as commenting on contemporary history in a more direct, critical, and objective manner. Whereas "T'ang Ch'ien te hsi-chü" [The comedy of T'ang] is an explicit satire of the intellectual craze for Western thought, such as existentialism and neopositivism, "My First Case" is probably the best work of this period. The story is built on the dual theme of existentialist agony and historical trauma. The mysterious suicide of the middle-aged mainlander Hu Hsin-pao, who has experienced a "sudden loss of the sense of purpose in life," is presented as a courageous choice of death upon the discovery of the "meaninglessness" of his life as a rootless, dislocated mainlander. The mainlander-Taiwanese difference is nicely presented by the image of the tree. The narrator, a young policeman assigned to look into the case, is a native Taiwanese securely rooted in this land, like a tree. The mainlanders are compared to branches cut off from the tree, which, though able to sustain life for a period of time, are eventually destined to dry up. Hu's sensibility about the "meaning" of life and his refusal to prolong his life among the "living dead" (like the physical education teacher and his wife) cast him in the image of an existentialist hero.[22]

The most commendable feature of this story is Ch'en's skillful interweaving of several realistic themes into the plot with unprecedented pointedness. The policeman-narrator repeats the sentence "There must be a reason [for the suicide]," but ironically this very reason has consistently eluded his comprehension. His inability to understand Hu's suicide is explained by his differences from the latter in regional background, education, and class. Like the lower-class Taiwanese working women in two other stories, "Na-mo shuai-lao te yen-lei" [The old and weak tears] (1961) and "One Stray Green Bird," who symbolize Mother Earth and an instinctive life force, the policeman is a less privileged Taiwanese who always feels a twinge of humiliation at the presence of college graduates. His lower social status, Taiwanese ethnicity, and inferior intellectual ability are in some sense a blessing, as he is the only "happy" person among all the characters. He has a nice wife and a hot supper waiting for him after work. To some extent, he also represents the "intellectual poverty" Taiwan's rigid formal education system has produced. The phony suicide report he writes at the end of the story is an apparent pastiche of lectures he attended at the police academy, lectures that masqueraded as orthodoxy within Taiwan's hegemonic culture. By portraying a sympathetic character like the policeman as an unself conscious victim of ideological indoctrination, Ch'en has made his first sharp criticism of Taiwan's dominant culture.

In his 1975 preface, Ch'en Ying-chen remarked that his fiction had shifted from the subjective, individualistic, and romantic to the objective, rational, and critical during the last two years of his preimprisonment period, 1966 and 1967 (9: 3–13). Interestingly, the Modernists also seemed to be undergoing similar transitions. C. T. Hsia, for example, has pointed out that a change from the subjective to the objective approach also occurred in Pai Hsien-yung's stories after 1964. Both Pai Hsien-yung's and Wang Wen-hsing's more mature works, *Tales of Taipei Characters* (1965–1971) and *Family Crisis* (1965–1972), were under way in this period. Writers who launched their careers during the Modernist literary movement, it seems, had just completed a stage of technical apprenticeship and were ready to explore material from their own lives in their work.[23] The difference between Ch'en and the other two writers was one of artistic approach. Even though the Modernists also turned to contemporary history for subject matter, as, for example, Pai Hsien-yung in *Tales of Taipei Characters* and Wang Wen-hsing in *Family Crisis*, they were more interested in using textual strategies and symbolic systems to render particular instances of universal human history. After this transitional period, therefore, the Modernists and Ch'en took divergent paths: whereas the former continued to pursue modernism, Ch'en was on the verge of denouncing his past and searching for new forms of expression.

The nature of Ch'en's search may be aptly characterized as what Jonathan Arac calls a "battle for representation" in his reexamination of the dispute between modernism and realism in the twentieth century in *Critical Genealogy* (294–305).[24] As noted by Arac, "the power of representation is something sought, indeed passionately struggled for, by groups that consider themselves dominated by alien and alienating representations" (295). Ch'en's concern with historical representation had much to do with the Nativists' use of "realism" as a political weapon. Although the term "realism" was never clearly defined in the Nativist literary debate, it apparently served an essential political function—because "realism" was seen to be the opposite of "modernism," and, because antimodernism was equated with anti-West and anti-imperialism, it was adopted by Ch'en's cohort of Nativists as their own artistic idiom.

Two stories, "Yung-heng te ta-ti" [The eternal land] (1970) and "Mou i-ko jih-wu" [One afternoon] (1973), written and published under pseudonyms during Ch'en's imprisonment, may not be interesting as literature, but they represent straightforward, albeit crude, attempts in his battle for representation. Here Ch'en has allowed his repressed political impulses to dominate by making explicit allusions to Taiwan's current political situation in the form of political allegory.

In "The Eternal Land," the terminally ill father (representing the older Nationalists) has lost the family wealth (the mainland) but insists on passing the guilt on to his son. Bedridden upstairs, he still keeps his son under tight surveillance while waiting impatiently for a "ship" that will supposedly take them back home. The son has inherited, without fully understanding it, a sense of guilt, and he seems aware that the days for him and his father as masters of this land are numbered. Out of loyalty, however, he constantly lies to his father about the weather, his father's health, and the prospect of returning home. The daughter-in-law, ransomed from another master— the Taiwanese from the hands of the Japanese—is exploited and treated as an inferior member of the house. She constantly dreams about escaping to a foreign country and has conceived a child by someone from her native countryside. The son in the other story, "One Afternoon," commits suicide after discovering that his cowardly, impotent personality was a result of the way his despotic father raised him. One day before his suicide, he finds a secretly guarded package, containing records of his father's youth— in the May Fourth period—and is deeply shocked by the degree to which his father's generation has degenerated since their younger days. After his suicide, his Taiwanese girlfriend, who was formerly a house maid and has conceived a child by him, rejects the father's hypocritical, condescending offer of help and decides to take care of the child herself.

The spiteful, subversive political messages of these stories—resulting from the author's anger in prison—nonetheless contain some thematic threads traceable to Ch'en's early stories. Although the relationship between mainlanders and Taiwanese is never, in the early stories, portrayed as one between oppressor and oppressed, conqueror and conquered, it is always taken as symbolically representing actual forms of domination and power distribution in Taiwan society. The contrast of strong, natural, lower-class women with impotent, intellectual male characters is also common.

The only new element, it seems, is the identification of the authoritarian father, who is the hidden source of oppression and apparently the object of Ch'en's lifelong resistance efforts. More interesting for the present study are the implications of the new formal features. The self-sufficient symbolic framework is constructed to encode historical interpretations without the guise of a morbid subjectivity that permeates most of Ch'en's early stories. It seems that the harsh lessons taught by new events in Ch'en's life had forced him out of his quandary. No longer wavering between the modernist aesthetic and realistic representation, he was ready to use literature as a means of historical interpretation.

In Ch'en's postimprisonment works, the historical vision is always formulated in terms as definite as allowed by circumstances. As a result, he has increasingly approached the ideal of "critical realism." Such stories as those in the Washington Tower series and the novella *Chao Nan-tung* [Chao Nan-tung] (1987) have explored, with reasonably successful realism, the various forms of ideological domination in contemporary Taiwan society.[25] One may disagree with Ch'en's moralistic condemnation of multinational capitalism—for example, as Thomas Gold's *State and Society in Taiwan* has demonstrated, the economic prosperity of Taiwan today is enviable from the point of view of Brazil and other Latin American or African countries. Or, one may follow Jefferey Kinkley's argument and perceive these works as having undercut some of the very premises on which Ch'en based his ideological criticism of transnational corporations. Nevertheless, what Ch'en has accomplished in analyzing and diagnosing contemporary social problems has no match in post-1949 Taiwan history. Stories such as "Wan-shang ti-chün" [Emperor of all trades] (1982) and *Chao Nan-tung* are reminiscent of the longer novels of Mao Tun and Ting Ling in their attempts to encompass a wide range of social phenomena while testing specific ideological prescriptions. It is these works that have solidly established Ch'en as a prominent heir to the "realist" tradition of China's pre-Revolution period.[26]

Romantic and Moralistic Literary Treatment

Whereas the Modernists considered sentimentalism the worst symptom of modern Chinese literature and thus reacted against a prominent "legacy" of May Fourth romanticism, Ch'en Ying-chen deliberately appropriated the romantic style of the pre-Revolution periods of modern Chinese literature to emulate its humanitarian ethos. Whereas the liberal Modernists of the 1960s adopted a relativist attitude toward morality and were interested in reexamining conventional ethical norms, Ch'en held on to a more conservative moralist stance, as suggested by the negative image he paints of modern humanity in his 1967 essay "Toward a New Departure of Modernism," an image of "degeneration, immorality, fear, licentiousness, disorder, nihilism, anemia, absurdity, defeat, violence, alienation, despair, anger, and ennui" (8: 1). However, Ch'en's romantic, moralistic vision is essentially different from Ch'i-teng Sheng's aggrandizement of the ego and occidental exoticism; it has a spiritual dimension that must be rooted in Ch'en's Protestant background. The following discussion will explore these characteristics of Ch'en's earlier work, with the purpose of elucidating their intricate relationship with Ch'en's political project.

One way to highlight Ch'en's romantic, moralistic approach is to focus on his treatment of poverty—the most prevalent social ill of Taiwan during the two postwar decades—which developed in several phases. In the first couple of years of his career, the prominent theme of poverty receives an unquestionably subjective treatment. Poverty is only vaguely identified as a consequence of social exploitation; it is more often romanticized as possessing a nostalgic, sorrowful beauty, most notably in "Tsu-fu ho shan" [Grandpa and his umbrella] (1960) and "Apple Tree." In "Country Teacher" and "Ssu che" [The dying man] (1960), this "beauty" is even part of the emotional appeal of the imaginary motherland, China. At the same time, poverty serves an important function as an "objective correlative" of the author's humanitarian sentiments. The heroes of these stories, mostly melancholy youths, bitterly resent the unfairness that the poor must endure; the idealists among them, such as Wu Chin-hsiang in "Country Teacher" and the elder brother in "Hometown," therefore make futile attempts to play the role of savior of the poor.

Although the Modernists may have a weakness for the uncanny, they are so rationalistically predisposed to stay away from mysticism. Spiritual transcendence, however, is frequently used by Ch'en as a form of resistance. From the star that appears in the sick boy's dream in "The Noodle Stall" to the apple tree that embodies everyone's private aspirations defined against individually experienced oppression, the "dream" is presented as the poor's only way of resisting the harsh reality of their lives. To be sure, in "Apple Tree," the cynical ending acknowledges the power of reality over imagination—after the young art student and the carpenter's crazy wife have a glimpse of celestial bliss, the woman dies and the young man is arrested. However, Ch'en has established a link between death and spiritual transcendence. Before the death of the mad woman in "Apple Tree," she shows an indescribable beauty; the grandmother in "Cats and Their Grandma" passes away in a sitting posture, which seems strangely to correspond with her wish to be incarnated as Buddha; and the gorgeous coffin the dying man builds for himself in "The Dying Man" and his fantasy about the boat trip suggest a mysterious grandeur associated with the experience of death, with biblical allusions.

Finally, whereas the Modernists are most concerned with repressive human rules, Ch'en has persistently struggled with spiritual degeneration, frequently in Christian terms. His early story "My Brother K'ang-hsiung" has received much critical attention precisely because it has, in a discursive manner, dramatized this struggle. Both the narrator and her idealistic brother are repelled by the hypocrisy of the rich; yet, in the end, both of them fail. The feeling of impotence even leads the young rebel K'ang-hsiung to pronounce, with indignant cynicism: "Poverty is sin." Both brother and sister have in their own ways deceived themselves. The brother resorts to imaginary humanitarian deeds—he has "built many schools and hospitals for the poor in his utopia"—and the sister, having married into a wealthy Christian family and thus become a member of the class she defies, treats her self-abandonment and her secret determination to stay free from its values as a furtive gesture of rebellion. The brother finally commits suicide after an illicit relationship with an older woman, and the sister, while facing the image of Jesus on the cross at church services, is overwhelmed by a sense of fear, shame, guilt, and betrayal. Her confusion of her brother's naked body, which impressed her when she was helping clean the corpse, with that of Christ can be taken as an affirmation that the higher moral order embodied in Christ's self-sacrifice is precisely what has claimed her brother's life. Therefore, both young people in the end lose their battle not to the values of the mundane world they challenged with youthful passion, but to a truer, more powerful Christian moralism that makes "nihilism and anarchism" childish and fake.

The Convergence of Personal and Political Themes

Although the themes of romantic idealism, Christian moralism, and spiritual transcendence seemed to be submerged under various others in stories written after 1963, they reappeared in the early 1980s, effectively demonstrating that, even in his more ideological writings, Ch'en's approach is considerably different from that of such younger Nativists as Wang T'o, Yang Ch'ing-ch'u, and Sung Tse-lai, who are primarily concerned with socioeconomic exploitation and poverty in a collective sense. After two decades, Ch'en reinserted these themes in the context of his lifelong obsession with history and politics. The messages conveyed are therefore extremely complex. The following is an attempt to interpret these messages by examining the story "Shan-lu" [Mountain path] (1984).

"Mountain Path" deals with the subject of political prisoners of the 1950s through a woman's confessional recollection of her life and those of her friends who made sacrifices for leftist political ideals; it ends with her death in profound disillusionment and remorse. Aside from being one of the first daring treatments of the leftist idealists persecuted in the 1950s,[27] "Mountain Path" features another theme that has been a central concern of Ch'en for some time: the rampant materialism in Taiwan's affluent society of the 1980s, which, as he sees it, impedes the cultivation of spiritual values and corrupts basic humanity.

The heroine in "Mountain Path," Ts'ai Ch'ien-hui, has devoted her life to the upbringing of the younger brother of her fiancé's good friend Li Kuo-k'un, whom she secretly admired and who was executed as a Communist in the 1950s, leaving his family in dire poverty and helplessness. Since her own fiancé was also sentenced to life imprisonment, she conveniently pretended that she had been married to Li and was therefore accepted as a member of the family. The story begins twenty-five years later, with Ts'ai living a comfortable life with the family of Li's brother, Kuo-mu, now a successful professional operating his own accounting firm. One day she suddenly reads in the newspaper that her fiancé is going to be released. This news shocks her in the painful realization that the material comfort she now takes for granted and the way she has taught Li's brother to avoid politics have ironically betrayed the ideals for which Li and her fiancé sacrificed. Losing the will to live, she becomes sick and dies, leaving a beautifully written letter, in Japanese, to her fiancé.

The frame story about Ts'ai's hospitalization and subsequent death is given in a naturalistic mode.[28] Although the doctor cannot provide a scientific explanation for Ts'ai's death—indeed she dies of the same despair that kills Wu Chin-hsiang in "Country Teacher"—the narrative discourse nevertheless presents the diagnostic procedure with scientific precision, furnishing the reader with details, such as blood pressure records, prescriptions, and so on. In contrast to this "objective" mode, Ts'ai's letter is rendered in an elegant Japanese feminine style, which aptly expresses the highly subjective nature of Ts'ai's encounter with history as a romantic idealist. The juxtaposition of the two contrasting narrative modes in this story is thematically effective. On the one hand, the painful awareness that the individual's vision of history is frequently limited seems to be conveyed by the deliberate use of subjective lyricism in Ts'ai Ch'ien-hui's letter. The naturalistic factual descriptions, on the other hand, put into perspective or even offer a critique of the sentimental story of Ts'ai's life.

Ts'ai is perhaps the purist idealist among Ch'en's characters. The moral principles that she asserts and carries out with remarkable strength have been unsuccessfully pursued by K'ang-hsiung, Wu Chin-hsiang, and the elder brother in "Hometown." Most intriguing, however, is that her idealism is realized through an indirect channel. She has not directly participated in social reform or political action; in fact, her sacrifice has no public consequence at all. The motivation for her heroic self-sacrifice for the Li family is a highly personal, romantic sentiment—her secret admiration for Li Kuo-k'un's revolutionary passion. Thus the meaning of her sacrifice is contingent first on the reader's recognition of the value of a youthful passion and second on what her sacrifice supposedly means to young Li, namely the value of family kinship.

Ts'ai's sacrifice has another motivation, a moral one, as she suspects that her own brother betrayed the young revolutionaries by giving the authorities a list of their names. Thus Ts'ai has vowed to atone for her brother's sin. The notion of crime and punishment, and the idea that one person's sin can be atoned by another carry Christian overtones, especially as Ts'ai seems to believe firmly in a material-spiritual, flesh-soul opposition. One passage in the story describes the sense of pleasure she derives from watching her own flowerlike young flesh toughen under the labor of helping the Li family. The same material-spiritual opposition, it seems, makes Ts'ai ashamed about her material comfort when the news about the political prisoners arrives. Although the hatred of the comforts of modern life echoes Frankfurt school critical theory, to which Ch'en frequently makes reference in his essays,[29] the context in which this condemnation is made has an implication more moralistic than sociological.

The all-important context of romantic idealism and Christian moralism is, to be sure, a political one and one with a unique allusion to the common existentialist theme of betrayal. Ts'ai's brother is the first person who betrays, supposedly out of cowardice. In the end, Ts'ai sees herself as betraying her friends by failing to carry on their humanitarian ideals; her betrayal is thus caused by a moral failure (this indictment, of course, is directed toward the majority of middle-class Taiwan residents who pursue material success at the expense of political involvement). Yet the greatest betrayal is not by an individual, but by history itself. As Ts'ai's letter reveals, her greatest puzzlement is that, over the last twenty-five years, history has shown that the communist ideals for which patriotic leftist intellectuals gave their lives and bet the future of their country have also failed. This discovery seems to be the most devastating, for it renders everyone's sacrifice wasted.

It is true that one may read the death of Ts'ai Ch'ien-hui as another act of atonement—this time for her own rather than her brother's mistake—and thus ultimately an affirmation of her and the author's own faith in spiritual values. In this sense, Ch'en has again used death as a means for the helpless to resist the harsh realities of life and to attain a moral victory. However, one cannot but feel that the ultimate message conveyed in this story is rather gloomy, as "history," the lifelong obsession of Ch'en, is presented as a real culprit, as the history of modern China has subjected idealism, patriotism, and ideological conviction to nothing but mockery.[30] Although Ts'ai's death may be taken as a gesture of protest, there is a greater sense of irony and failure than of spiritual transcendence.

CHAPTER SIX

Conclusion: Entering a New Era

In a sense, the articulation of dissident views during the Nativist literary debate forced the government to exercise greater tolerance and thus paved the way for more intense struggles toward political democratization, which have rapidly gained momentum since the early 1980s. Eventually, with the formation in 1987 of an oppositional party, the Democratic Progressive party, literature was largely relieved of its function as a pretext for political contestation. It became, however, even more inextricably involved in the country's booming mass media. Most notably, the two competing media giants, the *United Daily News* and *China Times*, each claiming the loyalty of a group of writers, invested heavily in their literary pages for marketing purposes. The annual fiction contests they sponsored between the mid-1970s and the mid-1980s gave creative writing a solid boost—an overwhelming majority of the writers of the baby-boom generation rose to literary prominence by winning these contests.

The Nativist theorists may have felt at once frustrated and vindicated in the 1980s, as the "spiritual corruption" of capitalist society, which they had predicted, became unmistakable with the ascendance of mammonism and a sharp rise in the crime rate. The overall cultural environment also became heavily consumer-oriented. Not without a touch of irony, even Nativist literature itself was largely coopted by the cultural establishment, especially between the late 1970s and early 1980s. Newspaper supplements and literary magazines were inundated by pseudo-Nativist works, which displayed Taiwanese local color but contained little ideological content.[1]

As public fervor for both the Modernist and the Nativist causes subsided, the literary scene of the 1980s was largely dominated by the baby-boom generation, whose vocational visions were drastically different from those of their predecessors. Rather than treating creative writing as an intellectual project or a political quest, they were more concerned with popularity and with various problems affecting Taiwan's middle-class urbanites, especially the new social affluence and the relaxation of moral standards. Some writers, such as Huang Fan and Li Ang, with a cynical intellectual pose, offered critiques of materialism and the cultural impoverishment it caused; others, such as Hsiao Sa and Liao Hui-ying, with down-to-earth pragmatism, examined the new social factors that had changed ordinary people's way of life, showing particular interest in liberated sexual views and the problem of extramarital relationships; still others, such as Yüan Ch'iung-ch'iung and Chu T'ien-wen, falling back on the sentimental-lyrical tradition, focused their attention on subjective, private sentiment with a posture of complacency in regard to sociopolitical issues. Whether progressively or conservatively inclined, the new generation of writers seemed to share a common response to the emergence of new political situations. As knowledge about the Chinese on the other side of the Taiwan Strait suddenly became available and with the public debate over unification and independence intensifying on a daily basis, many of the writers of the baby-boom generation tended to deliberately stress their unique cultural identity, rooted in the specific sociohistorical realities of Taiwan's post-1949 era.

Writers' approaches to literature in this decade were certainly pluralist. While writers of the Modernist generation published their more mature works during this decade, literary products of the younger generation were marked by a rich diversity—chüan-ts'un literature,[2] works about life in business corporations, political fiction, neo-Nativist literature, resistance literature,[3] feminist works, and science fiction—the orchestration of a multitude of discordant "voices," is the characterization suggested by the title of one critic's collection of essays, Tsung-sheng hsüan-hua [Polyphonic clamor] (D. Wang). A comprehensive examination of this literature no doubt requires a new analytical scheme. Some strands of the literary development of the 1980s, however, were connected clearly to what has been discussed so far in the present study.

Westernization Discourse Revisited

The broadly defined "return to the native" trend carried over into the early 1980s beyond the Modernist-Nativist contention. After the Nativist literary debate, new interest in an indigenous literary heritage fostered a trend that may be described as manifesting a "cultural nostalgia." Several former Modernist writers made notable contributions to this trend. Shih Shu-ch'ing and Li Ang, for example, turned consciously to folk traditions and native subject matter in their writing. Lin Huai-min, a former Modernist writer who studied under Martha Graham while in the United States, founded the first Chinese modern dance troupe and produced the well-received *Yün-men wu-chi* [Cloud gate dance series] and incorporated both classical Chinese and folk Taiwanese elements in his choreography. Their accomplishments set an important tenor for creative endeavors of the new decade, even while encouraging commercial exploitation of traditional and native cultural signs.

As the indigenous replaced the foreign, becoming the primary source of exotic imagination, and a Chinese/Taiwanese cultural identity came to occupy a prominent place in the public consciousness, the coming into vogue of a "postmodern" trend since the mid-1980s reopened the Pandora's box and once again raised issues about Western influences on contemporary Chinese literature. In a pattern closely resembling that by which such earlier Western literary trends as romanticism, realism, and modernism were appropriated by Chinese writers, the postmodern mode of writing has become a new fad and its surface markers, such as double endings, juxtaposition of the factual and the fictional, and the technique of pastiche, among others, have appeared profusely in works by both greater and lesser writers. Such imitative literary products cannot but recall works written during the earliest phase of the Modernist literary movement and not surprisingly were considered of dubious value by such a veteran Modernist writer as Wang Wen-hsing.[4]

As a matter of fact, one discerns not a little similarity between writers of the "postmodern" trend and the Modernists, especially in terms of their intellectual predisposition. At a recent seminar sponsored by *Free China Review*, the twenty-nine-year-old writer Lin Yao-te thus asserts: "Whether a novel will become a good novel does not depend on the subject. It depends on the technique" (23). The comment of another writer, Chang Ta-ch'un (whose recent work *Ta shuo-huang chia* [The big liar] has been regarded as a "postmodern" work par excellence), also recalls immediately the Modernists' strong awareness of the marginal role consigned to literature in contemporary society: "Twenty or perhaps even fifty years ago, people put great importance on the strong influence that literature and society exerted on each other. But today, literature no longer plays the leading role that it did in traditional Chinese society. Writers were considered intellectuals endowed with the heavy responsibility of writing with great concern for the world. But contemporary writers do not have this commitment, and are therefore much more limited in their scope" (21).

Although the younger writers consciously subscribe to a more cynical, "postmodern" ideology—as evidenced by their emphasis on difference, tolerance of pluralistic coexistence of the incommensurable, and, above all, their "appetite" for indeterminacy[5]—which is uncongenial to the Modernist temperament, there are unmistakable similarities between the two generations of writers: their philosophical pose, their globalism, and the way they look toward the West—or Western-influenced literary traditions such as those of Eastern Europe and Latin America—for literary models. As prescribed by "postmodern" ideology, however, the younger writers are more keenly aware of the self-other dichotomy and thus do not endorse universalism as the Modernists did.

Strictly speaking, a majority of the writers of the Modernist generation were never as fully committed to the modernist ideology and aesthetic as the few Modernists singled out for discussion in this study. Although they did not concur with the Nativists' pejorative view of the Modernist literary project as reflecting a "compradore" mentality, they were nonetheless bothered by its derivative, "unauthentic" nature. This uneasiness is indicative of an inherent dilemma faced by modern Chinese writers as a whole and will be briefly explored with the example of Li Ang, a writer belonging to both the Modernist and the baby-boom generations.

Howard Goldblatt has observed that Li Ang must be considered "the most consistent, successful, and influential writer of sexual fiction in Chinese" ("Sex and Society" 150). While dedicated to the theme of female sexuality, Li has never been fully committed to any particular artistic approach and has made several notable shifts between more modernist and more realistic techniques. There is no doubt that her appropriation of the Modernist technique is unusually impressive; her quasi-avant-gardist work of the late 1960s successfully employs a "dream aesthetic" in dealing with a young woman's sexual fantasies, and her best-known novella, The Butcher's Wife (1985), shows the influence of the modernist aesthetic in its highly sensational treatment of such primitive instincts as hunger and lust. Nevertheless, unlike Wang Wen-hsing or Li Yung-p'ing, Li Ang has never pledged her faith in aesthetic modernism but instead has claimed that she writes "to reflect the times and to explore problems" (Nien-hua xi).

Like most of the Modernists, Li is a member of the intellectual elite; she has a master's degree from a U.S. school and is on the faculty at the College of Chinese Culture. Over the years, Li has consistently followed highbrow intellectual discourse, from existentialism to poststructuralist cultural theory. Nevertheless, she seems to have at the same time kept a measured distance from such imported frames of thought and, consciously or unconsciously, has exhibited a halfhearted skepticism. Such an ambiguous attitude may be discerned even in her first story, "Hua-chi" [Flower season] (1967), written at the age of sixteen.

The instant fame won by "Flower Season" upon publication may be largely attributed to the treatment of a sensational topic by a precocious young woman writer. On a sunny winter day, a school girl cuts class to go on a bicycle trip with a florist to pick up a Christmas tree. While sitting on the back seat of the bike, the girl fantasizes about her chances of being suddenly attacked and raped by the middle-aged florist; the potentially boring trip to the nursery is thus transformed into an imaginary adventure. The literary merit of the story rests largely in the author's skillful presentation of the girl's playful awareness that her apprehensions are probably groundless, something wrought by an overly potent imagination.

Although Li Ang's daring exposure of the teen-age girl's sexual fantasy shows the influence of the liberal atmosphere of the 1960s, a real note of sophistication appears in the narrator's cynical observation that, after all, the girl's make-believe adventure is a product of her book reading: "At that time, I was quite young, in an age that should have witnessed the flowering of my youth; but all I possessed were a few translations of novels that

I had bought in a bookstore and a prince on a white horse who existed only in my dreams."[6] Thus the young author frankly acknowledges how, in her exceedingly anemic adolescent life, foreign literary texts provided the only source of exotic imagination and romantic fantasy. Sure enough, the girl's whim to search for a Christmas tree is inspired by an illustration in a picture book—"On the last page a prince and princess stood under a hugh Christmas tree holding hands and smiling" (127). And her fantasies have their blueprints in Western literature and film: the "white" Christmas (Taiwan has no snow except in the mountains); princes, princesses, and forest nymphs; and scenes from French movies.

The story can thus be taken as reflective of the cultural landscape of the time, as the influx of Western cultural texts dominated the literary imagination of young writers, providing them with vicarious fulfillment and emotional escape from sociopolitical constraints and cultural isolation. The narrator of "Flower Season" invites the reader to indulge in a celebration of freedom; although no one expects anything really to happen, the flight of the imagination that the bicycle trip allows is infinitely more exciting than a routine day at school. Unfortunately, however, the drab reality of the author's semiopen society, like the anemic-looking chrysanthemum bushes found in the florist's garden, inevitably returns. The disheartening effect of this realization is recaptured by Li Ang in the title page of *Nien-hua* [Youthful years] (1988), which contains the following words: "THE END OF THE SIXTIES. Nothing happens; no one comes, and no one leaves; it's truly horrifying!—*Waiting for Godot.* Beckett" (23).

Such signs indicating a half-conscious uneasiness about the dominance of Western cultural texts as exhibited by the young author of "Flower Season" undercut the modernist discourse. They at the same time betray the fact that the "complacency with borrowed facts" (Kwan-Terry 197) among Modernist writers of the 1960s was not after all complete.

Just as the sociohistorical conditions of the 1960s left perceptible imprints on "Flower Season," the impact of the cultural transition at the end of the sixties and the beginning of the seventies was recorded in *Youthful Years* (which was written in the early 1970s but not immediately published), in which the author shows a mixture of enthusiasm and doubt about the new intellectual trend of the "nativist return." A decade later, in 1984, Li wrote another story, "I-feng wei-chi te ch'ing-shu" [An unmailed love letter], which deals with almost the same subject, only with an added note of nostalgia. Looking back at the idealism of the "rebellious, Westernized" sixties from the vantage point of the eighties, a decade marked by rampant materialism and bourgeois complacency, Li regrets that the rebellious spirit and globalism introduced by Westernization has been "replaced by a nativism so inflated that it sometimes became a blind spot" and by "arrogance, self-content, and utilitarianism" (Nien-hua x).[7]

Thus, throughout her career, Li has been simultaneously reflective and self-reflective about the dominant cultural trends. She has embodied a typical "schizophrenic" position that characterizes Westernized third-world intellectuals, who are constantly disturbed that the very conceptual frameworks they use to critique the cultural condition of their own countries are inevitably borrowed from a foreign tradition. This dilemma is again reflected in one of Li's later works, An-yeh [Dark nights] (1986).

Dark Nights, as Howard Goldblatt puts it, "describes the complex, and sometimes slightly contrived, social and sexual relationships of a group of middle- and upper-class men and women living in the intensely materialistic environment of Taipei's financial circles" ("Sex and Society" 189). Of particular interest for the present discussion is the frame story of the novel. Ch'en T'ien-jui, a graduate student in philosophy and a self-styled moralist, pays an unexpected visit to the capitalist Huang Ch'eng-te, a member of Taiwan's self-made nouveaux riches, for the purpose of exposing the illicit affair between Huang's wife and Huang's own best friend, Yeh Yüan. That Ch'en tries to provoke Huang into punishing his wife and her lover turns out to be selfishly motivated in that Ch'en was formerly rejected by Yeh's new mistress, Ting Hsin-hsin. Therefore, while other characters' psychological motives for participating in sexual affairs are traced to their childhood experiences and family backgrounds, thus earning them considerable sympathy from the reader, Ch'en alone is portrayed as utterly self-righteous and ludicrous, as he is directly identified with a misconceived moralism that condemns without understanding.

One central weakness of this novel, however, is that crucial messages about the society's moral degeneration are conveyed through an essentially negative character, Ch'en T'ien-jui. On the one hand, Ch'en's pedantic preaching about the notion of "false consciousness" as a means of persuading Huang into action betrays his muddleheadedness. By showing that he frequently feels elated about his own eloquence, the author is apparently satirizing progressive intellectuals and their elite discourse, replete with neo-Marxist jargon. On the other hand, Li obviously gives credence to the critical notions Ch'en has expressed through his jargons. In her critical essay, Michelle Yeh, for example, has quoted Ch'en's definition of "false consciousness" in full and demonstrated how it appropriately sums up the characters' "self-conceit, moral cowardice, and hypocrisy" (87). An even stronger piece of evidence is that Ch'en's discussion of women's socially prescribed role in traditional Chinese culture (78) closely reflects Li's real views expressed on other occasions.

There is nothing wrong with an author's voicing his or her own opinions through an untrustworthy mouthpiece. The dubious moral quality of the critic Ch'en T'ien-jui does not automatically invalidate his criticism of the other characters. What is bothersome, however, is that the author cleverly avoids putting Ch'en's discourse in a theoretical perspective, either directly or indirectly. Simply discrediting the speaker in personal terms rather than problematizing the content of the speech unwittingly betrays Li's profound ambivalence toward the Western-imported theoretical discourse. (In contrast, the criticism of the Chinese family system in terms of the Western value of bourgeois individualism in Family Crisis is deeply problematized by Fan Yeh's complex, self-contradictory character.) Li's tacit acknowledgment of the validity of Ch'en's "borrowed" theoretical formulations makes her satirization of the intellectual elite pointless—as if she disapproves only of their pretentious manner and not of any part of their ideology. This lack of critical perspective enervates her intended criticism of society, since there is no way of really distinguishing her and Ch'en's ways of appropriating such notions as "false consciousness" for cultural criticism.[8]

Just as Li has absorbed certain traits of existentialist literature in her early work without really subscribing to its philosophical tenets, she now seems to be complying to some extent with poststructuralist cultural criticism without fully committing herself in ideological terms. Her ambivalence, skepticism, and inability to offer a cogent critique of Western-influenced, current intellectual discourse point to a syndrome common among modern Taiwan intellectuals, from which few are immune, including the hardcore Nativists. Ch'en Ying-chen, for example, while denouncing the imported literary trend of Western modernism, nevertheless extols "nineteenth-century European realism" as an ideal literary model. Even in their attempt to resist a domineering Western influence, Chinese intellectuals frequently resort to another influence, one that is also of Western origin, for spiritual support.

Veteran Modernists in the 1980s

One of the major theses of this study is that the liberal Modernists preceded the socialistically-inclined Nativists in challenging the ideological constraints of the hegemonic culture in Taiwan's post-1949 era. In the political sphere, too, before the rise of the radical Nativists, the liberal reformers posed a real threat to hegemony. With the liberalization of the ruling regime itself and the complex regional and factional elements surrounding the oppositional forces, the foundation of the liberals' contesting position seemed to have been eroded, and many of them were actually incorporated into the mainstream bureaucracy. Nonetheless, as demonstrated by the most recent events—especially those that have occurred since 1990, after the rifts within the Nationalist party were brought into the open—the liberal contestation of the authoritarian government gained momentum again, this time involving largely a younger generation of liberal scholars.[9]

Although Modernist writers apparently supported the liberal reforms and had endorsed liberal views in their works, few of them directly participated in political discussions. The trajectory the Modernists traveled, however, had certain parallels with that of the liberal reformist discourse. As Wang Wen-hsing seems to be recognized as the most "authentic" Chinese modernist,[10] I would like to conclude with a brief examination of his relationship with Taiwan's liberal reformist discourse. Having contributed to the *Literary Star* in the early 1960s, he also joined the editorial board of *The Intellectuals* in the early 1970s, both of them leading liberal magazines with a radical political image. After Wang returned from a one-year visit to the United States in 1970, his open endorsement of the progressive student movements in the West for a while caused some uneasiness in the government, which, sensing the subversive edge of his novel *Family Crisis*, took some cautionary steps by limiting public discussion of the novel.

Ironically enough, in just a few years, as the Modernists became the targets of radical Nativist attacks, their relationship with the rightist government visibly improved. In retrospect, there seems to be a justification for the Modernists' close alliance with the government, as both envisioned Taiwan's future in a Western-style democracy and in the development of a capitalist economy. In his 1977 speech at Tien Education Center, Wang went out of his way to indicate his support for a market economy and suggested that foreign countries' capital investment in Taiwan was "mutually beneficial." Daniel Bell once said: "Bourgeois capitalism, as the sociological form of the modern economy, and avant-garde modernism, as the victorious feature of the culture, had common roots in their repudiation of the past, in their dynamism, in the search for novelty and sanction of change" (xv). The Enlightenment values promoted in the Modernists' works essentially contributed to the nation-state's modernization efforts following the Western model.

Nevertheless, the coalition of modernism and bourgeois capitalism is inevitably precarious. In the more advanced stage of capitalist development, conflicts between cultural and societal modernism become unavoidable.[11] The incredible speed with which bourgeois values spread in Taiwan's society has made many people of the Modernist generation profoundly uneasy. As an interesting coincidence, both Ch'en Ying-chen and Wang Wen-hsing published works in 1987 that betrayed a deep sense of alarm and apprehension toward the society's rampant materialism. Ch'en's novella *Chao Nan-tung*,[12] takes off from the critique of creature comforts in "Mountain Path" and portrays the younger generation raised in Taiwan's new social affluence as lost in an animalistic indulgence in sensual gratification. Wang Wen-hsing's humorous short play M *ho* W [M and W], apparently a product of spontaneity, insinuates that the senseless way in which people are infatuated with money games will eventually lead them to destruction, just as the woman in the play is finally snatched away by a faceless phantom, the personification of death.

The alienation of such a Modernist as Wang in Taiwan's society of the 1980s goes beyond his disapproval of the insatiable greed for material gain. A travelogue by Wang, written during a trip to the mainland in the summer of 1989 and published under the title "Wu-sheng yin-hsiang" [Impressions of five Chinese provinces] (1990), again aroused considerable controversy.

In this work, Wang's stylistic experimentation reaches a new stage of maturity; poetic subjectivity and objective landscape description are interfused and rendered in an exquisite style vividly recalling traditional Chinese lyrical prose, which also reflects Wang's interest in that tradition over the last ten years. Although the work may well become a milestone in Wang's personal stylistic evolution, its unreserved expression of Wang's positive impressions of the Chinese mainland is so outlandish that even the editor of *Lien-ho wen-hsüeh* [Unitas], in which the work was published, felt obliged to add parenthetical notes to certain parts of the work, stating that they "solely represent Wang's personal opinions."

On close scrutiny, Wang's remarks on the "marvelous" social achievements in the People's Republic of China, such as orderly traffic, state construction, and a healthy economy, have resulted from the fact that Wang had seriously underestimated what the Chinese government has managed to accomplish in the last forty years. With all his original insights into phenomena that may have escaped the eyes of an ordinary tourist, Wang has betrayed a deficit of historical information readily available in Taiwan in the last few years. Wang's distrust of secondhand information and his invincible faith in personal observation are perhaps at once a holdover from the "New Critical" syndrome and a radical reaction to the information explosion in modern society. In other words, they are part and parcel of his voluntarily chosen aesthetic-cognitive mode. Wang's limitation in historical knowledge is therefore self-imposed, a logical consequence of his deep immersion in modernist ideology. Interestingly, this self-induced limitation in historical knowledge provides a contrast to what Ch'en Ying-chen has delineated through the life story of Ts'ai Ch'ien-hui in "Mountain Path." The shock that comes with the belated revelation of the "truth" about the contemporary People's Republic of China proves to be a deadly blow to political idealists such as Ts'ai and, in a sense, to Ch'en himself, as revealed in his other writings. To Wang Wen-hsing, however, who is no romantic idealist and has never believed in the utopia promised by the Chinese Communists, this same reality ironically has generated positive feelings for very different reasons.

That members of Taiwan's Modernist generation found themselves so soon left behind by their times is a consequence of the compressed timetable of the entire Modernist literary movement and may not be a unique phenomenon in non-Western appropriations of literary modernism. Undoubtedly, in terms of both quantity and quality of literary works produced, none of the three waves of the Chinese modernist literary movement can compare with the modernist movements that occurred in the West in the first quarter of the century. The historical implications of these works in both global and national contexts, however, are not bound by their artistic accomplishments. This study, by trying to offer an account of the ambitions and achievements, pretensions and presuppositions of Taiwan's Chinese writers in their appropriation of literary modernism, hopes to pave the way for future exploration of these significant implications.

Notes

Preface

1. In this study, the term "Modernist literary movement" with a capital M will be used specifically in reference to Taiwan's Hsien-tai wen-hsüeh yün-tung, in contradistinction to the more general implications of the noncapitalized "modernism."

1. Introduction

1. The modern Chinese literary tradition was established in the so-called New Literary Movement (Hsin wen-hsüeh yün-tung), or Vernacular Literary Movement (Pai-hua wen-hsüeh yün-tung), between 1917 and 1919. During the following decades, literature written in the modern Chinese vernacular (pai-hua) and heavily influenced by Western literary forms replaced the traditional literary forms, which used the literary language (wen-yen), to become the mainstream of modern Chinese literature.
2. Its founders have grown into outstanding writers, critics, and literary scholars. Pai Hsien-yung, Wang Wen-hsing, Ou-yang Tzu, Ch'en Jo-hsi, Shui Ching, and Wang Chen-ho became recognized as the country's leading fiction writers; Wai-lim Yip and Tai T'ien as highly esteemed poets; and Leo Ou-fan Lee, Joseph Shiu-ming Lau, Wai-lim Yip, and Ou-yang Tzu as distinguished literary scholars and critics.
3. Throughout modern Chinese history, the efforts of liberal intellectuals to play a determinant role in China's long and convoluted course of modernization have been frequently overshadowed or defeated by the conservatives on the one hand and the radicals on the other. In *The Great Chinese Revolution: 1800–1985* (1986), John King Fairbank devoted one entire chapter, titled "The New Culture and the Sino-Liberal Education," to the liberal reforms in the Republican era (1911–1949) which largely involved American-trained returned students. Whereas the liberals' gradualist approach apparently failed in China before the Communist Revolution, it has

proven to be a great success in Taiwan's post-1949 era. As Fairbank observed, "Taiwan after 1949 harbored that part of the Chinese Republic's Sino-liberal leadership that chose not to take its chances with the CCP. Although the warlord wing of the Nationalist regime began by slaughtering the Taiwanese Chinese elite in February 1947, the Sino-liberal wing thereafter had its chance" (268). The emergence in Taiwan of a Modernist literary movement heavily characterized by Anglo-American influences reveals the legacy of the pre-1949 "sino-liberal" tradition in the literary realm. It is readily observable that ideas of important literary figures of post-1949 Taiwan, such as Liang Shih-ch'iu, former member of the Crescent Moon Society, T. A. Hsia, mentor of a core group of Modernists, and Yen Yüan-shu, leading critic of the 1960s who introduced New Criticism to Taiwan, are all fundamentally rooted in the Western liberal-humanist tradition. Yen Yüan-shu's proposition that "literature has the dual function of being the dramatization and criticism of life," in particular, closely echoes both Matthew Arnold and the Association for Literary Studies' famous tenet "art for life's sake."

4. Public advocacy by reformist intellectuals for "wholesale Westernization" broke out several times in modern Chinese history, and the initial stage of Taiwan's Modernist literary movement significantly coincided with one of them—the *Chung-hsi wen-hua lun-chan* (Chinese-Western cultural debate) in the early 1960s, with the liberal magazine *Wen-hsing* [Literary star] as its major forum. In this debate, young intellectuals—the best known among them is Li Ao—launched ferocious attacks on the establishment and the academic conservatives. Such radical liberal attacks typically ended with a government crackdown. Although the largely apolitical Modernist writers had at best an indirect involvement with the debate (Wang Wen-hsing, for example, contributed to *Literary Star* magazine), they apparently shared some of its important assumptions. Other large-scale outbursts of intellectual debate over the relative strengths of Chinese and Western cultures occurred during the May Fourth Movement, in the late 1930s, and most recently in the People's Republic of China in the mid-1980s. The last of these culminated with the famous 1987 television series *Ho-shang* [River elegy].

5. Leo Lee, speaking as a member of the Modernist generation, has remarked: "In Taiwan during the 1960s, however, the consciousness of cultural crisis was noticeably absent. The ideological battles against tradition had been fought long ago and 'won'; tradition and modernity were no longer sharply polarized in Taiwan as in May Fourth China, despite the spurious slogans of 'total Westernization'" ("'Modernism'" 19–20).

6. During the years following the retreat from the mainland, as the recently defeated Nationalist government struggled to build Taiwan into an island-nation under the prevalent material scarcity and immediate military threat from a powerful enemy across the Taiwan Strait, the Communist-ruled People's Republic of China, social stability and economic growth were frequently sought at the expense of intellectual freedom. The political myth of regaining the Chinese mainland, while

serving to boost the morale of the mainlander émigrés, in effect intensified people's latent anxiety about the inevitability of an impending war. When the situation gradually began to relax in the 1960s, as economic development gained momentum, the society at large continued to suffer under various constraints from the conservative, authoritarian government as well as remnant feudal social values. The atmosphere of stagnation, confinement, and isolation is vividly captured in a group of articles published in *The China Quarterly* in 1963 that were later collected in *Formosa Today* (Mancall).

7. Because of the lack of such discontent, primitivism, one major theme of Western literary modernism that indirectly attacked modern civilization, has been conspicuously absent from Taiwan's Modernist literature.

8. The following words by Arnold, quoted by Trilling, seem to characterize the ideal modern world envisioned by Taiwan's liberal intellectuals: "A society . . . is a modern society when it maintains a condition of repose, confidence, free activity of the mind, and the tolerance of divergent views. A society is modern when it affords sufficient material well-being for the conveniences of life and the development of taste. And, finally, a society is modern when its members are intellectually mature, by which Arnold means that they are willing to judge by reason, to observe facts in a critical spirit, and to search for the law of things" (70).

9. *Hung-lou meng* [Dream of the red chamber] was written by Ts'ao Hsüeh-ch'in (1715?–1763) of the Ch'ing dynasty. The latest and best translation of the novel, by David Hawkes and John Minford, has a different title, *The Story of the Stone*.

10. The quotation is from J. Habermas, "Bewusstmachende oder rettende Kritik—die Aktualität Walter Benjamins," in S. Unseld, ed., *Zur Aktualität Walter Benjamins* (Frankfurt: Suhrkamp, 1972), 190.

11. Judging from recent developments in Taiwan, the liberals have apparently made a forceful return by actively involving themselves in the campus student movement.

12. That Taiwan's Modernists should find in capitalism a spirit congenial to their own matches this description by Daniel Bell in his book *Winding Passage*: "Bourgeois capitalism, as the sociological form of the modern economy, and avant-garde modernism, as the victorious feature of the culture, had common roots in their repudiation of the past, in their dynamism, in the search for novelty and sanction of change," even though, as Bell remarked elsewhere, the relationship between the two is a precarious one and is bound to change as mass culture develops in the capitalist society (xv).

13. In Peter Bürger's own words, the establishment of such central categories of "artistic means" and "procedures" shows that "the artistic process of creation can be reconstructed as a process of rational choice between various techniques, the choice being made with reference to the effect that is to be attained. Such a reconstruction of artistic production not only presupposes a relatively high degree of rationality in artistic production; it also presupposes that means are freely available, i.e., no longer part of a system of stylistic norms where, albeit in mediated

form, social norms express themselves." Shortly after this passage, he continues, "From the point of view of production aesthetics, this dominance of form in art since about the middle of the nineteenth century can be understood as command over means; from the point of view of reception aesthetics, as a tendency toward the sensitizing of the recipient. It is important to see the unity of the process; means become available as the category 'content' withers" (17–18).

14. Schulte-Sasse has summarized Bürger's view in more specific terms: "Aestheticism's intensification of artistic autonomy and its effect on the foundation of a special realm called aesthetic experience permitted the avant-garde to clearly recognize the social inconsequentiality of autonomous art and, as the logical consequence of this recognition, to attempt to lead art back into social praxis" (xiv).

15. The conflict between the social missions of literature conceived by Chinese intellectuals and the generic attributes of realist fiction as developed in the West has received full treatment in Marston Anderson's *The Limits of Realism* (1990). The titles of Anderson's chapters revealingly suggest that moral and social "impediments" are the major forces preventing a full development of the realist conventions inherent in this Western literary form. The antisocial quality of realistic fiction as a bourgeois literary form, he argues, contradicts Chinese intellectuals' deep-seated views of literature.

16. See Liang's essays collected in *Liang Shih-ch'iu lun wen-hsüeh*. Although members of the Creation Society, a rival of the Association for Literary Studies, supposedly advocated the "art for art's sake" principle, their turning to the extremely utilitarian, leftist view of literature proves that their original claims were more romantic than aesthetic. By contrast, the Association's ideal of "literature for life's sake" leaves more room for artistic freedom.

17. This remark was made by Wang in private conversations.

18. In her essay "I-shu yü jen-sheng" [Art and life], Ou-yang Tzu says that she approves of the Texas state government's decision to remove Jonathan Swift's "A Modest Proposal" from a middle-school textbook and suggests that mature literary works should be targeted specifically at readers of literary magazines (292–294).

19. See *Chou Tso-jen wen-hsüan* [Collected works of Chou Tso-jen] (1983). Also see David E. Pollard's excellent discussion in the section "Utilitarianism," in *A Chinese Look at Literature: The Literary Values of Chou Tso-jen in Relation to the Tradition* (41–46).

2. The Rise of the Modernist Trend

1. Literary scene in Taiwan during the fifties was virtually dominated by mainlander writers. After Taiwan was returned to China in 1945, Mandarin Chinese replaced the Taiwanese dialect and Japanese as the official spoken language of the province. Creative activities of middle-aged native Taiwanese writers were then greatly hampered by this language barrier. Political fear was another factor that silenced native Taiwanese writers. Taiwanese intellectuals were brutally persecuted follow-

ing the "February 28 Incident" of 1947, in which a Taiwanese riot was violently suppressed by the Nationalist army.
2. For the resurgence of the familiar essay in wartime Shanghai and Peking, see chapter 4 of Edward Gunn's *Unwelcome Muse*.
3. *San-ching yu meng shu tang chen* (1975).
4. Lin Hai-yin, for example, in the years she edited the literary supplement of the *United Daily News* and *Ch'un wen-hsüeh* [The literary magazine], promoted a number of important writers of the Modernist generation, including Ch'i-teng Sheng and Huang Ch'un-ming. P'eng Ko, a novelist, was the champion of the government's official views during the Nativist literary movement of the 1970s. In the late 1970s and early 1980s, the prolific fiction writer Chu Hsi-ning gathered around him a group of talented young writers of the baby-boom generation. They subsequently formed a publishing house, the Double-Three Bookclub, which became a forum for writers with a self-conscious "China complex." Ya-hsien, a poet, for more than twenty years has served as the editor of the literary supplement of the *United Daily News*. The annual fiction contests sponsored by this newspaper and its rival *China Times* between the mid-1970s and mid-1980s literally boosted the market value of creative writers.
5. Joseph Lau in his writing repeatedly talks about this mentality of Taiwan's mainlander expatriates.
6. Chu has been especially articulate about the nostalgic sentiments of mainlander expatriates in Taiwan and has tried very hard to urge the government to lift its ban on pre-1949 literature in the 1970s.
7. Chu's euphoric view of Chinese culture seems to have been influenced b, such works as *Shan-ho sui-yüeh* [Mountains, rivers, and human life] (1975) and *Chin-sheng chin-shih* [This life, this world] (1976) by Hu Lan-ch'eng, an erudite journalist who collaborated with the Japanese during the Sino-Japanese War in occupied Shanghai and was the former husband of Chu's favorite writer, Eileen Chang.
8. For a more detailed discussion of this phenomenon, please see my two articles "Yuan Qiongqiong and the Rage for Eileen Zhang among Taiwan's 'Feminine' Writers" and "Chu T'ien-wen and Taiwan's Recent Cultural and Literary Trends."
9. The father in both the novel *My Cousin Lien-i* and a later story by P'an, "Yu-ch'ing wa" [A pair of socks with love] (1985), seems to be modeled on P'an's own father in real life.
10. Chu Hsi-ning has made an interesting comment on the similarity between P'an and Eileen Chang in *Wei-yen p'ien* (37).
11. Here is a summary of the story: Ch'u-chia, the youngest son of a jade shop owner, receives a telegram from his father before he leaves for home after eight years. The telegram asks him to find a pair of real jade cups. After a laborious search, he finally purchases from a connoisseur merchant a pair of precious cups of fine white jade. Arriving at home, Ch'u-chia is told by his father that this was actually a test: the father has realized that the new wife of Ch'u-chia's brother is someone Ch'u-chia

was formerly in love with, and thus it has become impossible for both brothers to coinherit his antique shop. He therefore ordered both of them to bring back a pair of precious jade cups to determine which one is better qualified for the family business. When Ch'u-chia is about to open the box triumphantly, he discovers that he has erroneously brought another pair of cups that he had bought before he found the real goods. The cups had been placed in similar containers. This pair is obviously inferior to a third pair his father then takes out, which presumably was bought by Ch'u-chia's brother. Father is apparently disappointed, for he has always loved this youngest son much more than his brother. Ch'u-chia suppresses his urge to correct the mistake when he realizes that his unemployed brother and his pregnant wife need the shop more. The brother inherits the shop, never having heard about the jade cup test. Apparently, the father has lied to Ch'u-chia in order to justify an emotionally difficult decision.

12. As Průšek observed, along with their lyrical, subjective tendency, the May Fourth writers made serious efforts "to introduce broader and new spheres of personal life into higher literature" (10).
13. Most of the stories in *Na ch'ang t'ou-fa te nü-hai* have been revised and published under a different title, *Ch'iu-yeh* [Autumn leaves] (1971).
14. Given that T. A. Hsia was a contemporary of such modernistic Chinese writers of the 1940s as Ch'ien Chung-shu, Eileen Chang, and Yüan K'o-chia, it may be reasonable to assume that he was familiar with, if not a participant in, the trend that reacted against the romantic style of the May Fourth writers. See the chapter on "antiromanticism" in Edward Gunn's *Unwelcome Muse*.
15. Most of the Modernists studied in graduate schools in the United States, in particular the International Writers' Workshop at the University of Iowa.
16. It is interesting to note that the PRC writer Kao Hsing-chien's (Gao Xingjian) *Hsientai hsiao-shuo chi-ch'iao ch'u-t'an* [A preliminary discussion of the techniques of modern fiction] (1981), a book that stirred heated debate on literary modernism in the early 1980s, contains ideas strikingly similar to those propagated by Taiwan's Modernists in the 1960s.
17. See Ou-yang's "Kuan-yü wo tzu-chi—hui-ta Hsia Tsu-li nü-shih te fang-wen" [About myself—reply to an interview by Ms. Hsia Tsu-li], appendix to *I-chih te ying-hua* [A transplanted oriental cherry] (187).
18. Sally Lindfors' dissertation, "Private Lives," has an excellent discussion of Ou-yang Tzu's preoccupation with the problem of identity.
19. For a related discussion of this feature of pre-1949 modern Chinese literature, see Marston Anderson, *The Limits of Realism*.
20. This refers to the film directed by Kurosawa, which is adapted from Akutagawa's short story "In the Bamboo Grove."
21. During the 1980s, however, there was a resurgence of the lyrical essay form among the baby-boom generation, and such well-known writers as Ch'en Hsing-hui, Ai-

ya, and Lin Ch'ing-hsüan have written primarily in this form. This trend went hand in hand with a sudden rage for imitating Eileen Chang's style, which features a self-conscious elevation of lyrical sentimentality. A preliminary discussion of the close connection between this strand of baby-boom-generation literature with writings of the older generation can be found in my article "Yuan Qiongqiong and the Rage for Eileen Zhang among Taiwan's 'Feminine' Writers."

22. This conclusion is based on both personal interviews and publicly expressed opinions over the last fifteen years.

3. Appropriations of Literary Modernism

1. Leo Lee once commented that "the decision to feature Kafka in the first issue [of *Modern Literature*]—a daring act of Wang Wen-hsing—and the subsequent highlighting . . . of Mann, Joyce, and Lawrence must be considered as an impressive feat and a tribute to the intellectual precocity of Wang Wen-hsing and his classmates" ("'Modernism'" 14). Although writers of the *Modern Literature* group were responsible for initially introducing Kafka to readers in Taiwan and were themselves fascinated by certain existentialist themes, in practice, they demonstrated a greater restraint in mimicking his enigmatic style.

2. In Kwan-Terry's own words: "In all of them, we find a host of examples where communication between poet and reader seems to fail on two planes; both on the plane of reference, all that is ordinarily called the 'sense' of the poem; and on the plane of feeling, the emotional attitude towards the situation presented. Whatever tradition recent Chinese poetry may have recalled us to, the most important tradition of all, that of a natural community of understanding between poet and reader, is absent" ("Modernism" 194–195).

3. How Ch'i-teng Sheng stubbornly demanded such personal rights has been demonstrated by Kao Ch'üan-chih in his excellent study "Ch'i-teng Sheng te tao-te chia-kou" [The moral context of Ch'i-teng Sheng], with copious textual references to Ch'i-teng Sheng's works.

4. Commenting on Ortega's theory about modernist dehumanization, Poggioli said: "In short, the principle of dehumanization comes to take on much more valid and precise meaning insofar as it is at least partially synonymous with the vaster and less approximate stylistic concept of *deformation*. The principle of deformation is nothing new in the history of art. Avant-garde art certainly rediscovered it in primitive or archaic art. Thus, for example, avant-garde sculpture has attentively studied Etruscan and Egyptian statuary, as well as statues from pre-Columbian America, pre-Classical Greece, and Negro Africa. And we might perhaps say that what Ortega calls dehumanization is nothing other than neoprimitivist deformation, or a conscious replication of the authentic and ingenuous deformation of all that barbaric and exotic art" (176–177).

5. Depicting repressive elements in society has been popular in artistic works of Taiwan since the 1970s, especially in films.
6. Translated by Timothy A. Ross and Dennis T. Hu.
7. In "My First Case," Ch'en compares the past and the present with lights at the two ends of a bridge, one burnt out, one still working. See my discussion in Chapter 5.
8. In such writings, Ch'i-teng Sheng has particularly stressed a few incidents in which he rejected social indoctrination. Once, as an art student at the normal school, he jumped onto the dining table and danced with chopsticks in his hands to protest the quality of the food served in the cafeteria. The incident resulted in his nearly being dismissed from school. Another time, during his first few years as an elementary school teacher, he slapped the face of a colleague supposedly out of indignation. Ch'i-teng Sheng eventually quit his teaching job, so that between 1965 and 1970, he was frequently struggling in poverty as a self-supporting artist. He finally resumed teaching and settled in his hometown, T'ung-hsiao.
9. The stories referred to here were first collected in *Hun-sheng ho-ch'ang* [Mixed chorus] (1975) before they were published in *Hua-chi* [Flower season] (1985).
10. See the afterword to *Li-ch'eng chi* [Leaving the city] (68). The suggestions were made by Hu Yao-heng, editor of the prestigious *Chung-wai wen-hsüeh* [Chung-wai literary monthly].
11. Leo Lee has taken special pains to coin a new Chinese term, *fan-feng*, to capture fully the nuance connotated by the English work "irony."
12. See the section on "Heteroglossia in the Novel" in Bakhtin's "Discourse in the Novel" (301–331).
13. In the late 1970s, Nativist critics frequently referred to this disturbing phenomenon as the "vulgarization" of Nativist literature.
14. Pai has replaced this language with more natural everyday speech in his later novel *Crystal Boys*, whose indebtedness to traditional literature is more thematic and structural than linguistic.
15. Ch'en's sentimentality frequently was excessive. This may be what Joseph Lau meant by his observation that Ch'en's fictional style is at times "embarrassing" ("'How Much Truth . . .'") (632).
16. Translated by Wang Chen-ho and Jon Jackson.
17. Although Li Yung-p'ing was brought up in Southeast Asia, he received his college education in Taiwan, in the Department of Foreign Languages and Literatures at National Taiwan University. He has therefore been closely associated with the same literary tradition as the *Modern Literature* group.
18. See Wang's preface to the 1978 Hung-fan shu-tien edition of *Family Crisis* (2).
19. According to Wang himself, this language experiment began at an even earlier date.
20. This section is based on my personal interview of Wang in 1982.
21. This idea seems to be similar to what is proposed in Bakhtin's discussion of "the artistic image of a language" in artistic prose, in the section on "The Speaking Person in the Novel" in "Discourse in the Novel." In essence, Bakhtin argues that

the novelist makes no effort to achieve a linguistically exact reproduction of the empirical data of languages that he incorporates into his text; instead, a distinctive social language in the novel becomes "the object of a re-processing, reformulation and artistic transformation that is free and oriented towards art . . . departures from the empirical reality of the represented language may . . . be highly significant, not only in the sense of their being biased choices or exaggerations of certain aspects peculiar to the given language, but even in the sense that they are a free creation of new elements—which, while true to the spirit of the given language, are utterly foreign to the actual language's empirical evidence" (336).

22. While changes in Wang's style may be taken as symbolically connoting the mood of the story—besides the previously mentioned example of *Family Crisis*, Edward Gunn has pointed out that the more natural language in the last episode of *Backed Against the Sea* coincided with the appearance of the only positive character in the book, the Healthy Happy Hooker ("Process" 38)—it is also frequently mimetic in a realistic sense. An interesting example is that, when the protagonist-narrator in *Backed Against the Sea* drinks alone at night, his speech becomes increasingly entangled, frequently trailing off with "*te te te te le ke.*" Later, when he goes out to urinate, the utterance of "*te te te*" seems to be the result of shivering in the chilly night air. After returning to the room, however, he seems to have sobered up, and his language also becomes more natural.

23. Another passage in Jameson's book expresses this point even more clearly: "Modernism can at one and the same time be read as a Utopian compensation for everything reification brings with it. We stressed the semi-autonomy of the fragmented senses, the new autonomy and intrinsic logic of their henceforth abstract objects such as color or pure sound; but it is precisely this new semi-autonomy and the presence of these waste products of capitalist rationalization that open up a life space in which the opposite and the negation of such rationalization can be, at least imaginatively, experienced" (236–237).

24. Of course, sometimes both phonetic and semantic elements are explored. For example, Wang used two different k'ung characters in the words k'ung-ch'i, k'ung-ch'i, to call attention to the sound of the train. The semantic element of the Chinese characters—the first k'ung means "empty," and the second k'ung means "control"—may also suggest something about the young hero's mood when listening to the train. In Susan Dolling's translation of the novel (in progress), the words are brilliantly rendered as "humptch-dumptch, humptch-dumptch," which may arouse in the reader's mind the fantasy world of Humpty Dumpty. At other times, however, the native reader may find it awkward to have to disregard the semantic reference of the character in order to "hear" it, as Wang clearly expects him or her to do.

25. He has done so at least twice: once at a panel held at National Taiwan University in 1973, following the publication of *Family Crisis*, and another time at the Conference on Literature and Religion held at Fu-jen University in 1986, where Wang was one of three featured writers.

26. This view is succinctly summarized by Fredric Jameson as follows: "In the commercial universe of late capitalism the serious writer is obliged to reawaken the reader's numbed sense of the concrete through the administration of linguistic shocks, by restructuring the overfamiliar or by appealing to those deeper layers of the physiological which alone retain a kind of fitful unnamed intensity" (Marxism and Form 20).
27. See chapter 2, "Metaphysical Theories," of James J. Y. Liu's *Chinese Theories of Literature*.
28. These views were expressed by Wang in a private conversation in 1982. Also see chapter 4 of James Liu's *Chinese Theories of Literature* on technical theories in traditional China.

4. Modernists Reaching Maturity

1. The full title of Pai's own English translation of *Taipei jen* is *Wandering in the Garden, Waking from a Dream: Tales of Taipei Characters*.
2. Ou-yang has expounded the universalist implication of *Tales* rather explicitly: "The struggle between the soul and the flesh is the same as that between the past and the present, since, in the world of *Tales of Taipei Characters*, 'soul' is reflected in the 'past' and 'flesh' is identified with the 'present.' The soul is love, the ideal and the spirit, while the flesh is sexuality, reality and the body" ("Fictional World" 174). In fact, the direct correspondence between the two sets of values is not found in all the tales; it is absent, for example, in "Hua-ch'iao jung-chi" [Glory's by Blossom Bridge] (1970), "Na hsüeh i-pan te tu-chüan hua" [A sea of bloodred azaleas] (1969), and "I-pa ch'ing" [A touch of green] (1966). Yet similar contrasts are also found in Pai's other works. In his early stories, the past is a deluding, phantasmal, imaginary state of bliss: "Yüeh-meng" [Moon dream] (1960), "Ch'ing-ch'un" [Youth] (1961), and "Nei-wan te yüeh-kuang" [The moonlight on that night] (originally titled "Pi-yeh" [Graduation]) (1961). In the later *Niu-yüeh k'o* [New Yorker] series, the past stands for a time prior to the characters' loss of "self" and personal identity: "Chih-chia-ko chih ssu" [Death in Chicago] (1964), "Che-hsien chi" [Li T'ung: a Chinese girl in New York] (1965), "Che-hsien yüan" [The grievances of a celestial in mundane exile] (1969).
3. As many scholars have observed, there are some apparent points of convergence between traditional Chinese aesthetics and the modernist one, despite their fundamental differences at the level of generic conception, social origin, and metaphysical belief systems.
4. This idea is suggested by the well-known Confucianist dictum "Every individual citizen must be held responsible for the prosperity and decline of the state."
5. See Ou-yang Tzu's discussion of the symbolic implication of k'un-ch'ü in *Wang-Hsieh* (262–266).
6. These two lines are taken from the poem "Po Ch'in-huai" [Mooring at Ch'in-huai

River] by the famous late-T'ang poet Tu Mu (803–852). The allusion appears intentional as the Ch'in-huai River is also located in today's Nanking, where the story "Wandering in the Garden" took place.

7. For example, the scheme loses its analytical power when used to explicate such a story as "A Sea of Bloodred Azaleas." The story features a somewhat abnormal relationship between a middle-aged male servant, Wang Hsiung, who has an apelike appearance and a simple heart like that of a child, and the mistress' spoiled ten-year-old daughter Li-erh. Wang's devotion to Li-erh, the author suggests, has a subconscious sexual implication, as Wang has taken Li-erh as a substitute for the childhood lover whom he left behind on the mainland when following the Nationalists to Taiwan. Applying her flesh-soul opposition, Ou-yang interprets what happens in the story as such: As Li-erh grows older and rejects Wang's affection, the "spiritual" relationship is ruined and Wang's illusory world of innocence—symbolized by the azalea garden he carefully tends behind the house—threatens to collapse. One day, all of a sudden, Wang commits suicide. Before doing so, he rapes and mutilates the house's sexy maid Hsi-mei, who has been getting on his nerves. With strained logic, Ou-yang contends that Wang's attack of Hsi-mei and his subsequent suicide represents "a final revenge and victory of his 'soul' against 'flesh'" (102).

8. Ou-yang's idea is summarized in chapter 1 of *Swallows*: As a result of inevitable human mortality, "love" only becomes eternal when it is crystallized in the individual's memory. Those characters who embrace the soul and reject the flesh can only end in self-destruction, as the obsession with the spiritual often turns out to be beyond human capacity. In order to cope with the reality of practical life, which is dominated by the needs of the flesh, one can only occasionally revisit those precious moments, preserved by the memory of one's youth, when the soul was not yet contaminated by corporeal desires. The ability to reflect, then, has a redemptive value for individuals forced to compromise with the flesh (22–23).

9. It is through the erotic lyrics of the play that Pai registers Mme. Ch'ien's inner disturbance, which is the result of repressed sexuality and an impoverished emotional life. Influenced by the erotic associations of the play and the effects of alcohol, Mme. Ch'ien recalls her illicit affair with her husband's aide-de-camp, which Pai presents in a brilliant stream-of-consciousness passage replete with poetic sexual allusions. This act of transgression is not something that Mme. Ch'ien would normally perform.

10. Extracts from the novel *Crystal Boys* are taken from Howard Goldblatt's English translation.

11. In a public lecture that I attended in the early 1970s at National Taiwan University, Pai openly expressed his admiration for the free spirit of the hippie movement. Pai has lived in the United States since 1962.

12. Note that it is not the masculine, vulgar energies of *The Water Margin*, preserved in the Chinese folk tradition and consequently in vernacular fiction, that serves as

the prototype of the repressed *ch'ing* for Pai. Rather, the model seems to be taken from the more "feminine" type of *ts'ai-tzu chia-jen* (talents and beauties) stories in fiction and drama.

13. See the following passage in *Dream*: "As a consequence of all this, Vanitas, starting off in the Void (which is Truth) came to the contemplation of Form (which is Illusion); and from Form engendered Passion; and by communicating Passion, entered again into Form; and from Form awoke to the Void (which is Truth). He therefore changed his name from Vanitas to Brother Amor, or the Passionate Monk, (because he had approached Truth by way of Passion), and changed the title of the book from *The Story of the Stone* to *The Tale of Brother Amor*" (51).

14. Hsia uses the following words: "He neither avoids nor emphasizes his homosexual inclination, and in his recent works he seems to have entirely adopted the ethical norms of society in judging the behavior of his characters, even though, as soon as he touches on love (such as in "A Sea of Bloodred Azaleas"), he still maintains his own unique view of the most complex and miraculous phenomenon of human life" ("Pai" 308).

15. Somewhat disapprovingly, Ou-yang thus sums up Pai's supposedly "superstitious" view of life: "Pai seems to believe that the *nieh* in human life mainly comes from one's ancestors, predestined at birth, impossible for anyone to escape" (Wang-Hsieh 28).

16. There is another interpretation of the title *Nieh-tzu* that pertains to contemporary Chinese history. That A-qing was chased out of the family and Dragon Prince out of the country and that Papa Fu's son committed suicide, more as a protest against his father's failure to understand than out of shame, may be taken, at a highly symbolic level, as the collective plight of a generation of modern Chinese who have been exiled from their own homeland for different, mostly political, reasons, as the phrase "ku-ch'en nieh-tzu" usually connotes. One may recall that in one story in *Tales*, "Tung-yeh" [Winter night] (1970), Pai suggests that during the May Fourth Movement, as the Chinese intellectuals denounced their own tradition, they made themselves sinners who must forever carry with them the stigma of patricide, an ultimate form of *nieh*. It is tempting to see in *Crystal Boys* an implicit comment on this political theme. Since *Tales* sees the tradition from the perspective of an older generation, there is deep remorse about its decline. *Crystal Boys*, however, sees the tradition from the perspective of the younger generation—who are compared to "typhoons and earthquakes on the island" or to young birds "flying over the ocean" that "do not know where to end"—and the austere father figure, the law of the state, is shown to be fundamentally in the wrong.

17. Feng Tsu-sheng [Feng Zusheng], a critic from Fukien, China, has voiced an objection to the theme of *Family Crisis* in a manner almost indistinguishable from that of the Nativist attack on the novel. See the section on *Family Crisis* in Feng's *Ta'i-wan hsiao-shuo chu-yao liu-p'ai ch'u-t'an* [Preliminary study of the major schools of fiction in Taiwan] (198–200).

18. Page references for James Shu's article are taken from J. Faurot, ed., *Chinese Fiction from Taiwan*.
19. This self-consciousness can be safely assumed because Wang Wen-hsing is among the few Chinese writers in Taiwan who perceive themselves as modernist writers in the global context and because he has made self-conscious attempts to engage in a dialogue with the literary tradition of the Western world. For instance, Wang has revealed that, inspired by Camus' *The Plague*, he deliberately concealed the identity of the narrator of *Family Crisis*, intending it to be discovered by "future readers." For a discussion of the narrator in *Family Crisis*, see my article "Language, Narrator, and Stream-of-Consciousness: The Two Novels of Wang Wen-hsing."
20. See Fredric Jameson's discussion in *The Political Unconscious* on the aestheticizing strategy that "for whatever reason seeks to recode or rewrite the world and its own data in terms of perception as a semi-autonomous activity" (230).
21. In a published interview, Shan Te-hsing asks Wang if he agrees with some critics that Fan Yeh's lengthy criticism of the Chinese family system is a technical flaw. Wang replies: "I thought about that when I wrote it. But I decided to choose this incongruity, for I felt that only by inserting such an incongruous passage could the idea of this book be fully expressed. I still hold this opinion today. It's the only essay passage in the novel. This was a quite common method in the eighteenth and nineteenth centuries and has been regarded as immature. But I would rather adopt it. What's more, I made some alterations. In the essay passages of the eighteenth- and nineteenth-century novels, the novelists freely expressed their opinions. In *Chia pien*, this essay passage was fictionalized. It's the expression of the character's idea, not mine. It makes all the difference" (63).
22. Edward Gunn has made a comparison of Wang's views and those found in the four Western classics ("Process" 39).
23. In the published interview conducted by Shan Te-hsing, Wang discussed his interest in such literary techniques as stream of consciousness, serious comedy, interior monologue, low comedy, farce, burlesque, and symbolic realism—all in the context of Western literature.
24. Wang acknowledged the influence of Beckett on this novel in an interview (Shan 63).
25. On several occasions, Wang mentioned that black humor, which reveals a special truth about life, is absent from traditional Chinese narrative and qualitatively different from the macabre, sensational comic treatment frequently used by novelists of the late Ch'ing. He made a similar remark in Shan Te-hsing's interview, that the technique of burlesque "has never been used in Chinese fiction before, but it is very common in European fiction" (64).
26. Wang says in Shan's interview that *Backed Against the Sea* "is the most symbolic among all my works" (Shan 62). Much of the symbolism in this novel has deep existentialist import. For example, Wang says: "Throughout the work, the emphasis is on the placing of a tiny man before an indifferent natural backdrop" (Shan 64).

My discussion, however, is not primarily intended to explicate such existentialist themes (although references to them are inevitable) but rather explores the work's sociological implications in the historical context of contemporary Taiwan. All page references are based on the original Chinese version of *Pei-hai te jen* (Taipei: Hung-fan shu-tien, 1981).

27. Jameson has argued against Lukacs' perceiving modernism as "ideological distraction" by saying that "the modernist project is more adequately understood as the intent, following Norman Holland's convenient expression, to 'manage' historical and social, deeply political impulses, that is to say, to defuse them, to prepare substitute gratifications for them, and the like. But we must add that such impulses cannot be managed until they are aroused; this is the delicate part of the modernist project, the place at which it must be realistic in order in another moment to recontain that realism which it has awakened" (*Political Unconscious* 266).
28. Wang once mentioned that the section about the Dialect Research Bureau office was modeled on Thomas Mann's *Magic Mountain*. However, whereas Mann deals with the upper or upper-middle class, Wang states: "Here in this section I want to collect the garbage of the whole of China. It's a garbage can" (Shan 64).
29. Page references here are based on the 1973 edition of *Chia-pien*.
30. Wang himself said that he made the narrator of *Backed Against the Sea* an extrovert to contrast with Fan Yeh's introverted personality.
31. Translated by Philip Yampolsky, in *The Platform Sutra of the Sixth Patriarch* (132).
32. Once Wang said that he had developed many strange habits in the actual process of writing. For example, he must use a short pencil in order to "strike" the paper with physical energy.

5. The Nativist Resistance to Modernism

1. For example, the liberal magazine *Ta-hsüeh tsa-chih* [The Intellectuals] had such well known, outspoken liberals as Ch'en Ku-ying, Yang Kuo-shu, and Chang Chünhung, on its editorial board. Wang Wen-hsing was also an editor for a time.
2. Interestingly, one finds in Kwan-Terry's argument about a Chinese "cultural crisis" strong echoes of A. J. Toynbee's criticism of Western modernism, especially the avant-garde trend, as evidenced by the passage by Toynbee cited in Renato Poggioli's famous book *The Theory of the Avant-Garde* (178):

    The prevailing tendency to abandon our Western artistic traditions . . . the decline which betrays itself in this revolutionary change in aesthetic taste is not technical but is spiritual. In repudiating our own native Western tradition of art and thereby reducing our aesthetic faculties to a state of inanition and sterility in which they seize upon the exotic and primitive art of Dahomey and Benin as though this were manna in the wilderness, we are confessing before all men that we have forfeited our spiritual birthright. Our abandonment

of our traditional artistic technique is manifesting the consequence of some kind of spiritual breakdown in our Western Civilization. (Toynbee 4: 52) As Kwan-Terry also refers to Poggioli's book in his article, such similarities in both vocabulary and conception may not be accidental.
3. In the first two decades after 1949, there were disproportionately more mainlanders than native Taiwanese occupying high-ranking official positions in the Nationalist government. As the postwar generation of Taiwanese intellectuals came of age, however, the demand for redistribution of political power became increasingly strong. Although the government had promoted a T'ai-wan pen-t'u-hua (Taiwanization) program since the early 1970s, its pace was felt to be unsatisfactory. Much of the political resentment of the Taiwanese intellectuals was a direct result of a historical event, the Nationalists' bloody suppression of a Taiwanese riot in the February 28 Incident of 1947.
4. The impact was felt strongly because T'ang published several essays in different journals within a short period of time pressing the same issue. The short essay "Chiang-pi te hsien-tai shih" [The ossified modern poetry] published in *Chung-wai Literary Monthly* serves as a good example of his terse and forceful style.
5. Ch'en's 1977 essay "Wen-hsüeh fan-ying she-hui, hui-tao she-hui" [Literature reflects society, returns to society] represented the major contentions of his camp.
6. Important articles written during the debate were collected by Yü T'ien-ts'ung in *Hsiang-t'u wen-hsüeh t'ao-lun chi* [A collection of discussions on Nativist literature].
7. Hsü is an eminent scholar of traditional Chinese literature. Hu is a liberal Marxist and editor of *Chung-hua tsa-chih* [China magazine]. The magazine often criticizes the government but has for years had an ambivalently close relationship with the top echelon of the Nationalist party. Both Hsü and Hu apparently saw in the Nativists' criticism of society a revival of May Fourth ideals. According to Ch'en Ying-chen, the Nativist activists at the time genuinely feared that political arrests were imminent, so they sought protection from such established members of the literati as Hsü and Hu. With his prestige and personal connections with the government, Hu allegedly did manage to stop the anticipated arrests.
8. An extreme example is Hou Li-ch'ao's calling the antifamily motif in Wang Wen-hsing's *Family Crisis* and Pa Chin's *Family* "Wang-Pa literature," a pun on *wang-pa*, a profanity equivalent to the English "bastard" (Hou). Joseph Lau has offered a nice summary of Hou's and others' attacks on the Modernists in his article "The Tropics Mythopoeticized."
9. Faced with undisguised hostility, Ou-yang Tzu, who had the advantage of living in the United States, chose not to reply to the militant criticism but instead expounded her views of literature in a book on Pai Hsien-yung's *Tales of Taipei Characters*, which turned out to be a wise strategy. By contrast, Wang Wen-hsing paid dearly for the public speech he gave at Tien Education Center in 1978, in which he expressed fundamentally liberal views on literary and economic issues. He

was criticized harshly by the *Summer Tide* group; a farmers' union in T'ai-chung protested his views in newspapers; and an entire volume of essays containing negative criticism of Wang, *Che-yang te chiao-shou Wang Wen-hsing* [Such a "professor," Wang Wen-hsing], was published in the same year (P'an and Hsiao).

10. Jing Wang, for example, describes Nativist literature in the following words: "Hsiang-t'u literature could thus be best defined in the idiom of dichotomy: it is nationalistic literature set against colonial literature; plebeian literature against aristocratic literature; the literature of society against that of individualism and escapism; realist literature as opposed to avant-garde literature" (62).

11. Liu specifically identified 1967 as the year in which Huang Ch'un-ming bade farewell to modernism with the publication of "Ch'ing-fan Kung te ku-shih" [The story of Grandpa Ch'ing-fan] (228).

12. Howard Goldblatt, for example, has rightly praised Huang's stories of this period for their essential humanist import and an "intrinsic universality" ("Introduction" xiii, xi).

13. The use of pathological symbols for social problems reminds one of Lu Hsün's "Medicine," in which the old man's attempt to use the bread soaked in the blood of an executed revolutionary to cure his son's tuberculosis is motivated by ignorance and superstition. The contrast of ringworms, a stubborn but hardly fatal disease, with Lu Hsün's tuberculosis reveals a much less bleak social outlook on Huang Ch'un-ming's part.

14. Although Ch'en says he is not concerned with artistry, but rather with "what to say" in literature, he concedes that great art is the work of genius. He also argues that "techniques are basic" and that "good artists adopt whatever techniques are available to them." In a 1987 interview he further qualifies his negative assessment of Taiwan's Modernists and praises the imaginary vitality of the "magical realism" of Latin American writers. That he founded a pictorial magazine *Jen-chien* [Human world] (1985–1989) and employed visual images and journalistic reporting to communicate his beliefs seems to be a tacit acknowledgment that, because of the greater indeterminacy of literary works, literature is a less effective tool for dissemination of ideas in modern society.

15. For a sample of Ch'en's views of postwar Taiwan literature, see "Ssu-shih nien lai te T'ai-wan wen-i ssu-ch'ao" [Taiwan's literary currents in the last forty years], a lecture note published in Hong Kong's *Pa-fang wen-i ts'ung-k'an*. A shorter version of this lecture is included in *Ch'en Ying-chen tso-p'in chi*.

16. These two short essays may very well be, as Ch'en himself has suggested, the earliest criticism of Modernist literature in Taiwan.

17. A neo-Marxist magazine published by promising younger scholars.

18. Ch'en Ying-chen, to be sure, has come to understand the complex relationship between societal modernization and modernist culture. In his 1987 Hong Kong lecture, he said he was aware of certain writers who tried to use the obscurity of modernism to express a kind of resistance that could not be made openly in a

period of white terror. But he goes on to deny the further development of this tendency ("Ssu-shih-nien" 17).
19. The Nativists were divided into northern and southern factions in around 1982 and 1983, more or less along the lines of Ch'en's prounification stance (the northern) and a pro–Taiwan independence stance (the southern).
20. Ch'en may be one of the few exceptions among his generation in Taiwan who have been directly exposed to Chinese literature of the early modern period under the ban, which has only been gradually revoked since the mid-1980s. In a recent essay Ch'en mentions that at the age of twelve or thirteen he chanced upon a story collection that contained "The True Story of Ah Q," which made a real impact on him, awakening in him a sense of Chinese history.
21. Ch'en once associated his acute sense of history with several incidents in his adolescent years. For example, a young woman who lived next door was taken away by the secret police and every day, on his train rides to middle school in Taipei, he used to read execution notices on the train station wall.
22. The existentialist theme is symbolically presented by the image of an arched bridge outside a hotel window, which reminds Hu of a bridge he saw while fleeing from his mainland home. The repeated mention that for some reason only the light on one side of the bridge is working bears a thematic message: the broken light comes to symbolize the loss of meaning in the hero's present life and confirms his decision to take his own life. It is interesting that whereas the torch image in Ch'i-teng Sheng's "I Love Black Eyes" suggests that only the present is real and one should live only for the present, Ch'en's bridge image suggests that the present is no longer meaningful. These two authors seem to have interpreted the existentialist metaphysics in diametrically different ways.
23. The settings of the two stories "Ou, Su-shan-na" [Oh! Susannah] (1966) and "The Last Summer Days" (1966) reflect more realistically the contemporary social milieu. The characters are modeled on people in Ch'en's life, young intellectuals caught between the temptation of a decadent lifestyle and the practical choice of going abroad in pursuit of a successful career. The stories remind one of Pai Hsien-yung's New Yorker series written between 1964 and 1969 about people he met in his first few years in the United States.
24. Chiefly in the section entitled "An Exemplary Issue: Representation."
25. The "Hua-sheng-tun ta-lou" [Washington Tower] series (1978–1982) treats the life of Chinese employees in Taiwan's transnational corporations. The stories completed so far are "Yeh-hsing huo-ch'e" [The night freight] (1978), "Shang-pan tsu te i-jih" [One day of a white-collar employee] (1978), "Yün" [Clouds] (1980), and "Wan-shang ti-chün" [Emperor of all trades] (1982). Jefferey C. Kinkley has offered an excellent analysis of this series in "From Oppression to Dependency: Two Stages in the Fiction of Chen Yingzhen."
26. The canon of the Chinese "realist" tradition, to be sure, does not include many artistically successful works. One of their characteristic features is the coexistence

of disparate discourses under an ostensibly ideological frame, which also seems to be the case in Ch'en's work. While Ch'en tries to diagnose and propose solutions for social problems along certain ideological lines, as Leo Lee has perceptively pointed out, his stories often contain "subtexts," betraying influences from his modernist period, which then tend to undermine the intended ideological messages.

27. The story is part of a series in which Ch'en intends to deal with the problem of political prisoners. The finished stories of the series are "Ling-tang hua" [Bell flowers] (1983), "Mountain Path" (1984), and the novella *Chao Nan-tung* (1987).

28. Although the Nativists have favored more transparent narrative representation primarily on political rather than aesthetic grounds, as they value literature's intelligibility to the masses, some writers—notably Yang Ch'ing-ch'u, Wang T'o, and Sung Tse-lai—have employed a "naturalistic" method of incorporating statistics and other devices to enhance the credibility of their historical representation. As these writers themselves soon became more eclectic in their use of artistic modes, no significant work or theorization regarding this method seems to have appeared. Yet the naturalistic method has left some imprints on Ch'en's works of the later period, such as the use of documentary mode (the medical reports in "Brother Hopper," the diary in "Mountain Path," and the case history in *Chao Nan-tung*) and transparent imagery (the roses in the transitional story "Liu-yüeh li te mei-kuei hua" [The roses of June] (1967), the cloisonné accessories with a Chinese design in "The Night Freight," and the waving caps in blue, yellow, and white in "Clouds").

29. This theme was further developed in *Chao Nan-tung*, which will be briefly discussed in the next section. Ch'en frequently cites Herbert Marcuse's "one-dimensional man" in essays written in the mid-1980s.

30. This particular theme of the story carries a personal note. The leftist's sacrifice rendered vain by the unexpected turn in history has Ch'en's own biography as a frame of reference. Ch'en once described his disillusionment with the Chinese Communists in an interview: "I originally thought that the Communist card would be a good one to bet on; who would have expected that it turned out to be a lousy card. By contrast, the card originally thought to be a bad one now doesn't look that bad any more . . . it is truly ironical" (6: 9).

6. Conclusion: Entering a New Era

1. The Nativist activists themselves regard this phenomenon as "a vulgarization of the Nativist literature." The media, however, have played a complicated role in the Nativist literary movement. Ch'en Ying-chen once said that the Nativist literary debate of the 1970s might not have spread so broadly without the media, especially the literary supplement of *China Times* under the editorship of Kao Hsin-chiang. Partly as a marketing strategy in its competition with the pro-Modernist

United Daily News, China Times promoted "reportage literature" to explore social problems along Nativist lines, which had the effect of both popularizing Nativist causes and diluting their radical image.
2. Chüan-ts'un refers to government housing compounds built during the early decades following the Retreat for dependents of military personnel, mostly Nationalists from the mainland. A distinct subculture was developed around such areas, which was shared by a large number of second-generation mainlanders.
3. A group of writers revolving around T'ai-wan wen-i [Taiwan literature] (1964–) has continued and even further radicalized the political tradition of the Nativist literature and advocated "human rights literature," "resistance literature," as well as "Taiwanese nativist literature" (T'ai-wan pen-t'u wen-hsüeh).
4. Wang made such remarks in a private conversation in 1988.
5. For instance, in Lin Yao-te's remarks one reads: "How to maintain a balance between actual reality and its presentation is all a matter of the writers' philosophical attitudes" and "I don't indulge myself in the fantasy of searching for my ultimate value in life" (Free China Review 23, 24).
6. Howard Goldblatt's translation (Carver and Chang 126).
7. This motif has recurred in several of her later works, such as An-yeh [Dark nights] (1986) and stories collected in I-feng wei-chi te ch'ing-shu [An unmailed love letter] (1986).
8. Li's ambivalence may partially recall such works as Ch'en Ying-chen's story "The Comedy of T'ang Ch'ien," written in 1967, which satirizes young intellectuals' craze for existentialist philosophy and neopositivism, the 1960s counterpart of neo-Marxism, poststructuralism, and postmodernism.
9. Liberal professors have been directly involved in the burgeoning student movement in Taiwan in recent years. Inspired by the T'ien-an-men Incident, students had a hunger strike in front of the Chiang Kai-shek Memorial in March 1990, in protest of the National Assembly's (the nation's electoral college) political blackmail on the eve of the presidential election. Then, in May 1991, a protest against political persecution, caused by the on-campus arrest of a student at Ch'ing-hua University for pro–Taiwan independence activities, involved a larger group of liberal intellectuals in the academy and resulted in the abolition of the article on Punishment of Traitors by the Legislative Yuen.
10. Leo Lee said: "If I were compelled to nominate a true modernist on both sides of the Taiwan Straits, I would not hesitate to single out Wang Wenxing [Wang Wen-hsing]." ("Beyond Realism" 74).
11. Bell has also warned about the vulnerable nature of the modernism-capitalism coalition: "Yet, inevitably, the different axial principles of these reals (the techno-economic realm segmenting a person into 'roles,' the culture emphasizing the achievement of the whole person) brought the bourgeois economic system into sharp conflict with the modernist culture" (xv).
12. Chao Nan-tung, the son of a martyred woman intellectual, is portrayed as a victim

of Taiwan's social affluence. Good-natured, irresponsible, and keen on sensuous pleasures, Chao seems to have no moral sense or goal in life other than constantly seeking gratification of physical desires. After his father's death, Yeh Ch'un-mei, his deceased mother's cellmate, finally decides to take Chao with her to her home in the country before he sinks deeper in Taipei.

Select Bibliography

Anderson, Marston. *The Limits of Realism: Chinese Fiction in the Revolutionary Period*. Berkeley and Los Angeles: University of California Press, 1990.
Arac, Jonathan. *Critical Genealogies: Historical Situations for Postmodern Literary Studies*. New York: Columbia University Press, 1989.
Bakhtin, M. M. "Discourse in the Novel." *The Dialogic Imagination*. Ed. Michael Holquist. Austin: University of Texas Press, 1981. 259–422.
———. *Problems of Dostoersky's Poetics*. Trans. R. W. Rotsel. Ann Arbor: Ardis, 1973.
Barthes, Roland. S/Z. New York: Hill and Wang, 1974.
Bell, Daniel. *The Winding Passage*. New York: Basic Books, 1980.
Birch, Cyril. "Images of Suffering in Taiwan Fiction." Faurot 71–85.
Booth, Wayne. *The Rhetoric of Fiction*. Chicago: University of Chicago Press, 1961.
Bradbury, Malcolm, and James McFarlane. "The Name and Nature of Modernism." *Modernism: 1890–1930*. Ed. Malcolm Bradbury and James McFarlane. New York: Penguin Books, 1976. 19–55.
Bürger, Peter. *Theory of the Avant-Garde*. Minneapolis: University of Minnesota Press, 1984.
Carver, Ann, and Sung-sheng Yvonne Chang, eds. *Bamboo Shoots after the Rain: Contemporary Stories by Women of Taiwan*. Introduction by Sung-sheng Yvonne Chang. New York: Feminist Press, 1990.
Chang Han-liang. "Ch'ien-t'an Chia-pien te wen-tzu" [Some thoughts on the language of *Family Crisis*]. *Chung-wai wen-hsüeh* [Chung-wai literary monthly], 1.12 (1973): 122–141.
———. "Wang Wen-hsing Pei-hai te jen te yü-yen hsin-yang" [The "religion of language" and Wang Wen-hsing's *Backed Against the Sea*]. *Fu-jen ta-hsüeh* 438–457.
Chang Heng-hao, ed. *Huo-yü te tzu-fen* [Burning oneself in purgatorial flames]. Taipei: Yüan-hsing ch'u-pan she, 1977.
Chang, Sung-sheng Yvonne. "Chu T'ien-wen and Taiwan's Recent Cultural and Literary Trends." *Modern Chinese Literature* 6.1–2 (1992).
———. "Elements of Modernism in Fiction from Taiwan." *Tamkang Review* 19.1–4 (Autumn 1988–Summer 1989): 591–606.

---. "Hsien-tai chu-i yü T'ai-wan hsien-tai p'ai hsiao-shuo" [Modernism and the Modernist school of fiction in Taiwan]. *Wen-i yen-chiu* [Aesthetic studies], 4 (July 1988): 69–80.

---. "Language, Narrator, and Stream-of-consciousness: The Two Novels of Wang Wen-hsing." *Modern Chinese Literature* 1.1 (1984): 43–55.

---. "Modernism and Contemporary Fiction of Taiwan." *Proceedings of the XIIth Congress of the International Comparative Literature Association: Space and Boundaries*. Ed. Roger Bauer and Douwe Fokkema. Munich: Iudicium Verlag Press, 1988. 285–290.

---. "Ts'ung Chia-pien te hsing-shih she-chi t'an ch'i" [Formal devices in the novel *Family Crisis*]. *Lien-ho wen-hsüeh* [Unitas, a literary monthly] 32 (1987): 196–199.

---. "Wang Wen-hsing hsiao-shuo chung te i-shu ho tsung-chiao tsui-hsün" [The quest for art and religion in the fiction of Wang Wen-hsing]. Trans. Hsieh Hui-ying. *Chung-wai wen-hsüeh* 15.6 (1986): 108–119. Rpt. in *Fu-jen ta-hsüeh* 421–437.

---. "Yuan Qiongqiong and the Rage for Eileen Zhang among Taiwan's 'Feminine' Writers." *Modern Chinese Literature* 4.1–2 (Spring-Fall 1988): 201–223.

Chatman, Seymour. *Story and Discourse: Narrative Structure in Fiction and Film*. Ithaca and London: Cornell University Press, 1978.

Chen, Chang-fang, and Mei-hwa Sung. "Elements of Change in the Fiction of Taiwan of the 1980s." *The Chinese Pen* Summer 1989: 31–42.

Ch'en Kuo-ch'eng. "Tzu-wo shih-chieh te tsui-ch'iu" [Quest for the self]. Chang, Heng-hao 77–89.

Ch'en Ying-chen. *Ch'en Ying-chen tso-p'in chi* [Collected works of Ch'en Ying-chen]. 15 vols. Taipei: Jen-chien ch'u-pan she, 1988.

---. "Ssu-shih nien lai te T'ai-wan wen-i ssu-ch'ao" [The literary currents in Taiwan in the last forty years]. *Pa-fang wen-i ts'ung-k'an* 6 (1987): 3–36. A shorter version of the lecture is included in *Ch'en Ying-chen tso-p'in chi* 8: 207–223.

Cheng Heng-hsiung. "Ts'ung chi-hao hsüeh te kuan-tien k'an *Pei-hai te jen* te tsung-chiao kuan" [A semiotic study of the religious view in *Backed Against the Sea*]. *Fu-jen ta-hsüeh* 393–420.

---. "Wen-t'i te yü-yen te chi-ch'u: lun Wang Wen-hsing te *Pei-hai te jen* te" [The linguistic foundation of style: on *Backed Against the Sea* by Wang Wen-hsing]. *Chung-wai wen-hsüeh* 15.1 (1986): 128–157.

Cheng Ming-li. *Hsien-tai san-wen lei-hsing lun* [On the typology of the modern essay]. Taipei: Ta-an ch'u-pan she, 1987.

---. *Hsien-tai san-wen tsung-heng lun* [A general study of the modern essay]. Taipei: Ch'ang-an ch'u-pan she, 1986.

Cheng Shu-sen (William Tay). Introduction. *Hsien-tai Chung-kuo hsiao-shuo hsüan*. Ed. Shu-sen Cheng. Vol. 3. Taipei: Hung-fan shu-tien, 1989. iii–xviii.

---. "Ssu-shih-nien lai te Chung-kuo hsiao-shuo" [Chinese fiction in the last forty years]. *Lien-ho pao* [United daily news], 11–12 (Aug. 1989): 27.

Cheng, Stephen. "Jamesian Techniques in 'Delirious Mutterings at Midnight.'" *Tamkang Review* 11.1 (Fall 1980): 43–64.

Ch'i-chün. Ch'i-chün hsiao-p'in [Familiar essays of Ch'i-chün]. Taipei: San-min shu-chü, 1967.

———. Ch'i-chün tzu-hsüan chi [Stories of Ch'i-chün selected by the author]. Taipei: Li-ming wen-hua kung-ssu, 1975.

———. Ch'i-yüeh te ai-shang [The sorrow of July]. Taipei: Ching-sheng wen-wu kung-ying kung-ssu, 1971.

———. Ch'in-hsin [The heart of the harp]. Taipei: Kuo-feng she, 1953.

———. Ching chieh [Sister Ching]. 1956. Taipei: Erh-ya ch'u-pan she, 1981.

———. Hung-sha teng [Red-gauze lantern]. Taipei: San-min shu-chü, 1969.

———. Shan-chiao shih pa hsiao-shih [Eight hours in the copy room]. Taipei: Shang-wu yin-shu kuan, 1968.

———. San-ching yu meng shu tang chen [When I had a dream at midnight, I took a book as my pillow]. Taipei: Erh-ya ch'u-pan she, 1975.

———. Yen-ch'ou [Melancholy smoke]. Taipei: Kuang-ch'i ch'u-pan she, 1963.

Chi, Pang-yuan (Ch'i Pang-yüan). "Moving Beyond the Boudoir" [Kuei-yüan chih wai]. Trans. Susan Ku. *Free China Review* 41.4 (Apr. 1971): 26–32.

Ch'i-teng Sheng. Chiang-chü [Quandary]. Taipei: Lin-pai ch'u-pan she, 1969.

———. Ching-shen ping-huan [The mental patient]. Taipei: Ta-lin ch'u-pan she, 1970.

———. Ch'ing yü ssu [Feelings and thoughts]. Taipei: Yüan-hsing ch'u-pan she, 1977.

———. Chü-hsieh chi [Giant crab]. Taipei: Hsin-feng ch'u-pan she, 1972.

———. Ch'ung-hui Sha-ho [Return to Sandy River]. Taipei: Yüan-ching ch'u-pan kung-ssu, 1986.

———. Hsiao-shou te ling-hun [The emaciated soul]. Taipei: Yüan-ching ch'u-pan she, 1976.

———. "I Love Black Eyes." Trans. Timothy A. Ross and Dennis T. Hu. Lau, *Chinese Stories* 63–73.

———. Lai-tao hsiao-chen te Ya-tzu-pieh [Ya-tzu-pieh who came to a small town]. Taipei: Yüan-ching ch'u-pan she, 1976.

———. Lao fu-jen [The old lady]. Taipei: Hung-fan shu-tien, 1984.

———. Li-ch'eng chi [Leaving the city]. Taipei: Ch'en-chung ch'u-pan kung-ssu, 1973.

———. Pai-ma [White horse]. Taipei: Yüan-hsing ch'u-pan she, 1977.

———. San-pu ch'ü Hei-ch'iao [Strolling to the Black-bridge]. Taipei: Yüan-ching ch'u-pan she, 1978.

———. Sha-ho pei-ko [The sad music from Sandy River]. Taipei: Yüan-hsing ch'u-pan she, 1976.

———. T'an-lang te shu-hsin [Love letters from T'an]. Taipei: Yüan-shen ch'u-pan she, 1985.

———. Wo ai Hei Yen-chu [I love black eyes]. Taipei: Yüan-hsing ch'u-pan she, 1976.

———. Yin-po ch'ih-pang [Wings over the silver waves]. Taipei: Yüan-ching ch'u-pan she, 1980.

———. Yin-tun che [The hidden character]. Taipei: Yüan-hsing ch'u-pan she, 1976.

Ch'i I-shou. "Hsiang-t'u wen-hsüeh chih wo-chien" [My personal views of Nativist literature]. 1978. Yü T'ien-ts'ung 578–595.
Chou Tso-jen. *Chou Tso-jen wen-hsüan* [Collected works of Chou Tso-jen]. Ed. Yang Mu. 2 vols. Taipei: Hung-fan shu-tien, 1983.
Chu Hsi-ning. *Chu Hsi-ning tzu-hsüan chi* [Stories of Chu Hsi-ning selected by the author]. Taipei: Li-ming wen-hua kung-ssu, 1975.
———. *Lang* [Wolf]. 1963. Taipei: Huang-kuan ch'u-pan she, n.d.
———. *Mao* [Cat]. Taipei: Huang-kuan ch'u-pan she, 1966.
———. *P'o-hsiao shih-fen* [At daybreak]. 1963. Taipei: Huang-kuan ch'u-pan she, 1967.
———. *Ta huo-chu te ai* [Love of the great torch]. Taipei: Ch'ung-kuang wen-i ch'u-pan she, 1952.
———. *T'ieh-chiang* [Soup of melted iron]. Taipei: Wen-hsing shu-tien, 1963. Taipei: Huang-kuan ch'u-pan she, 1980.
———. *Wei-yen p'ien* [Chapters of minced words]. Taipei: San-san shu-fang, 1981.
———. *Yeh-chin che* [The gold smelter]. Taipei: Hsien-jen-chang ch'u-pan she, 1970.
Chu Hsi-ning et al. *Hsiao-shuo chia-tsu* [A family of fiction writers]. Taipei: Hsi-tai ch'u-pan kung-ssu, 1986.
Chu Tzu-ch'ing. *Pei-ying* [Reflections of my father]. Hong Kong: Chung-liu ch'u-pan she, 1976.
Chu Yen. "Wo tu 'Jih-t'ou yü'" [My reading of "The rain from the sun"]. *Lien-ho pao liu-pa nien-tu tuan-p'ien hsiao-shuo chiang tso-p'in chi* [1979 prize-winning short stories from the United Daily News]. Taipei: Lien-ho pao-she, 1979. 335–343.
Eagleton, Terry. *The Ideology of the Aesthetic*. Oxford and Cambridge, MA: Basil & Blackwell, 1990.
Fairbank, John King. *The Great Chinese Revolution, 1800–1985*. New York: Harper and Row, 1986.
Faurot, Jeannette L., ed. *Chinese Fiction from Taiwan: Critical Perspectives*. Symposium on Taiwan Fiction, University of Texas at Austin, 1979. Bloomington: Indiana University Press, 1980.
Feng Tsu-sheng (Feng Zusheng). *Ta'i-wan hsiao-shuo chu-yao liu-p'ai ch'u-t'an* [A preliminary study of the major schools of Taiwan fiction]. Fu-chou: Fu-chien jen-min ch'u-pan she, 1983.
Fokkema, Douwe W. *Literary History, Modernism and Postmodernism*. Amsterdam and Philadelphia: John Benjamins Publishing Company, 1984.
Foster, Hal, ed. *The Anti-Aesthetic: Essays on Postmodern Culture*. Port Townsend, Washington: Bay Press, 1983.
Free China Review Seminar. "Reflections on Reality." Trans. Merisa Lin and Winnie Chang. *Free China Review* 41.4 (April 1991): 20–25.
Fu-jen ta-hsüeh wai-yü hsüeh-yüan [College of Foreign Languages at Fu-jen University], eds. *Wen-hsüeh yü tsung-chiao* [Literature and religion]. Taipei: Shih-pao wen-hua ch'u-pan kung-ssu, 1987.

Gold, Thomas B. *State and Society in the Taiwan Miracle.* Armonk, New York and London: M. E. Sharpe, 1986.
Goldblatt, Howard. Introduction. *The Drowning of an Old Cat and Other Stories.* By Hwang Chun-ming [Huang Ch'un-ming]. xi–xiv.
———. "The Rural Stories of Hwang Ch'un-ming." Faurot 110–133.
———. "Sex and Society: The Fiction of Li Ang." Goldblatt, *Worlds Apart* 150–165.
———, ed. *Worlds Apart: Recent Chinese Writing and Its Audiences.* Armonk, New York and London: M. E. Sharpe, 1990.
Gunn, Edward. "The Process of Wang Wen-hsing's Art." *Modern Chinese Literature* 1.1 (Sept. 1984): 29–41.
———. *Unwelcome Muse: Chinese Literature in Shanghai and Peking, 1937–1945.* New York: Columbia University Press, 1980.
Habermas, Jürgen. "Modernity—an Incomplete Project." Foster 3–15.
Hassan, Ihab. "Pluralism in Postmodern Perspective." *Critical Inquiry* 12.3 (Spring 1986): 503–520.
Hawkes, David, and John Minford. *The Story of the Stone.* 5 vols. Middlesex, England: Penguin Books, 1973–1982.
Hegel, Robert E. "The Search for Identity in Fiction from Taiwan." *Expressions of Self in Chinese Literature.* Ed. Robert E. Hegel and Richard C. Hessney. New York: Columbia University Press, 1985. 343–360.
Ho Hsin. "Ou-yang Tzu shuo le hsieh she-mo?" [What has Ou-yang Tzu said]? 1973. Yip, ed., *Chung-kuo hsien-tai tso-chia lun* 419–438.
Hou, Chien. "Irving Babbitt and Chinese Thought." *Tamkang Review* 5.2 (Oct. 1974): 135–185.
Hou Li-ch'ao. "Lien-ching chi-t'uan san-pao i-k'an te wen-hsüeh pu-tui—ts'ung Ou-yang Tzu te tzu–pai k'an t'a-men te pei-ching" [The literary troop of three newspapers and one magazine—an examination of their background based on Ou-yang Tzu's confession]. 1978. Yü T'ien-ts'ung 666–684.
Howe, Irving. "The Idea of the Modern." Howe, ed., *Literary Modernism* 11–40.
———, ed. *Literary Modernism.* NY: Fawcett, 1967.
Hsia, C. T. (Hsia Chih-ch'ing). Appendix 1. "Obsession With China: The Moral Burden of Modern Chinese Literature." *A History of Modern Chinese Fiction.* By C. T. Hsia. 2d ed. New Haven: Yale University Press, 1971. 533–554.
———. "The Continuing Obsession with China: Three Contemporary Writers." *Review of National Literatures* 6.1 (1975): 76–99.
———. Foreword. *Chinese Stories from Taiwan: 1960–1970.* Ed. Joseph Lau. ix–xxvii.
———. "Pai Hsien-yung lun" [On Pai Hsien-yung]. 1969. Pai, *Taipei jen* 291–312.
———. Preface to the Second Edition. *A History of Modern Chinese Fiction.* By C. T. Hsia. 2d ed. New Haven: Yale University Press, 1971. v–viii.
Hsü Chin-ch'iao and Ts'ai Shih-p'ing, eds. 1986 *T'ai-wan nien-tu p'ing-lun* [Annual selection of critical essays on Taiwan: 1986]. Taipei: Yüan-shen ch'u-pan she, 1987.

Hsü Fu-kuan. "P'ing T'ai-pei yu kuan 'Hsiang-t'u wen-hsüeh' chih cheng" [Remarks on the debate on Nativist literature in Taipei]. 1977. Yü T'ien-ts'ung 332–333.
Hu Ch'iu-yüan. "Lun Wang Wen-hsing te nonsense chih sense" [The "sense" of Wang Wen-hsing's "nonsense"]. 1978. Yü T'ien-ts'ung 731–758.
Hu Lan-ch'eng. *Chin-sheng chin-shih* [This life, this world]. Taipei: Yüan-ching ch'u-pan kung-ssu, 1976.
———. *Shan-ho sui-yüeh* [Mountains, rivers, and human life]. Taipei: Yüan-ching ch'u-pan she, 1975.
Huang Ch'un-ming (Hwang, Chun-ming). *Ch'ing-fan Kung te ku-shih* [The story of Grandpa Ch'ing-fan]. Taipei: Huang-kuan ch'u-pan she, 1985.
———. *The Drowning of an Old Cat and Other Stories.* Trans. Howard Goldblatt. Bloomington: Indiana University Press, 1980.
———. *Erh-tzu te ta wan-ou* [His son's big doll]. Taipei: Ta-lin ch'u-pan she, n.d.
———. *Hsiao kua-fu* [Little widows]. Taipei: Yüan-ching ch'u-pan she, 1975.
———. *Lo* [The gong]. Taipei: Yüan-ching ch'u-pan she, 1974.
———. *Sha-yu-na-la, tsai-chien* [Sayonara, good-bye]. Taipei: Yüan-ching ch'u-pan she, 1974.
Huang, I-min. "A Postmodernist reading of *Rose, Rose I Love You*." *Tamkang Review* 17.1 (Autumn 1986): 27–45.
Jameson, Fredric. *The Ideologies of Theory: Essays, 1971–1986*, Vol. 1, *Situations of Theory*. Minneapolis: University of Minnesota Press, 1988.
———. "Literary Innovation and Modes of Production: A Commentary." *Modern Chinese Literature* 1 (1984): 67–77.
———. *Marxism and Form: Twentieth-Century Dialectical Theories of Literature.* New Jersey: Princeton University Press, 1971.
———. *The Political Unconscious: Narrative as a Socially Symbolic Act.* Ithaca, NY: Cornell University Press, 1981.
K'ang Lai-hsin. "Wang Wen-hsing ju-shih shuo" [Thus spake Wang Wen-hsing] *Chung-yang jih-pao* [The central daily], 30 Dec. 1987.
———, ed. *Wang Wen-hsing te hsin-ling shih-chieh* [The spiritual world of Wang Wen-hsing]. Taipei: Ya-ko ch'u-pan she, 1990.
Kao Ch'üan-chih. "Ch'i-teng Sheng te tao-te chia-kou" [The moral context of Ch'i-teng Sheng]. Chang Heng-hao 91–112.
Kao Hsing-chien (Gao Xingjian). *Hsien-tai hsiao-shuo chi-ch'iao ch'u-t'an* [A preliminary discussion of the techniques of modern fiction]. Kuang-chou: Hua-ch'eng ch'u-pan she, 1981.
Kinkley, Jeffrey C. "From Oppression to Dependency: Two Stages in the Fiction of Chen Yingzhen [Ch'en Ying-chen]." *Modern China* 16.3 (July 1990): 243–268.
Ku Chi-t'ang. *Ching-t'ing na hsin-ti te hsüan-lu: T'ai-wan wen-hsüeh lun* [Listen quietly to that rhythm of the heart]. Peking: Kuo-chi wen-hua ch'u-pan kung-ssu, 1989.
Kuo Feng. "Heng-hsing te i-hsiang jen—hsü Chü-hsieh chi ping t'an hsin hsiao-shuo"

[The stranger—preface to *Giant Crab* and a commentary on the new fiction]. Chang Heng-hao 23–28.
Kwan-Terry, John. "Modernism and Tradition in Some Recent Chinese Verse." *Tamkang Review* 3.2 (1972): 189–202.
Lau, Joseph Shiu-ming. "Celestials and Commoners: Exiles in Pai Hsien-yung's Stories." *Monumenta Serica* 36 (1984–1985): 409–423.
———, ed. *Chinese Stories from Taiwan: 1960–1970*. New York: Columbia University Press, 1976.
———. "Ch'i-teng Sheng 'hsiao-erh ma-p i' te wen-t'i" [Ch'i-teng Sheng's style of "infantile paralysis"]. Chang Heng-hao 39–41.
———. "The Concepts of Time and Reality in Modern Chinese Fiction." *Tamkang Review* 4.1 (1973): 25–40.
———. "'Crowded Hours' Revisited: The Evocation of the Past in *Taipei Jen*." *Journal of Asian Studies* 35.1 (1975): 31–47.
———. "Death in the Void: Three Tales of Spiritual Atrophy in Ch'en Ying-chen's Post-Incarceration Fiction." *Modern Chinese Literature* 2.1 (Spring 1986): 21–28.
———. "Echoes of the May Fourth Movement in Hsiang-t'u Fiction." *Mainland China, Taiwan, and U.S. Policy*. Ed. Hung-mao Tien. Cambridge, MA: Oelgeschlager, Gunn and Hain, 1983. 135–150.
———. Foreword. *Hsien-tai wen-hsüeh* 1 (1960): 2.
———. "'How Much Truth Can a Blade of Grass Carry?': Ch'en Ying-chen and the Emergence of Native Taiwan Writers." *Journal of Asian Studies* 32.4 (1973): 623–638.
———. "Obsession with Taiwan: The Fiction of Chang Hsi-kuo." Faurot 148–165.
———. "San-ku Ch'i-teng Sheng" [Review Ch'i-teng Sheng for the third time]. Chang Heng-hao 141–151.
———. "Shih nien lai te T'ai-wan hsiao-shuo: 1965–75—chien lun Wang Wen-hsing te *Chia pien*" [Taiwan fiction during the last ten years: 1965–75—with a commentary on Wang Wen-hsing's *Family Crisis*]. *Chung-wai wen-hsüeh* 4.12 (May 1976): 4–16.
———. "Text and Context: Toward a Commonwealth of Modern Chinese Literature." Goldblatt, *Worlds Apart* 11–28.
———. "The Tropics Mythopoetized: The Extraterritorial Writing of Li Yung-p'ing in the Context of the Hsiang-t'u Movement." *Tamkang Review* 12.1 (Fall 1981): 1–26.
———. *The Unbroken Chain: An Anthology of Taiwan Fiction since 1926*. Bloomington: University of Indiana Press, 1983.
Lee, Leo Ou-fan. "Beyond Realism: Thoughts on Modernist Experiments in Contemporary Chinese Writing." Goldblatt, *Worlds Apart* 64–77.
———. "Chung-kuo hsien-tai wen-hsüeh te hsien-tai chu-i—wen-hsüeh shih te yen-chiu chien pi-chiao" [Modernism in modern Chinese literature—a comparative study of literary history]. Trans. Wu Hsin-fa. *Hsien-tai wen-hsüeh fu-k'an* 14 (June 1981): 7–33.
———. "'Modernism' and 'Romanticism' in Taiwan Literature." Faurot 6–30.

Li Ang (Shih Shu-tuan). *Ai-ch'ing shih-yen* [Experiments of love]. Taipei: Hung-fan shu-tien, 1982.
———. *An-yeh* [Dark nights]. Taipei: Shih-pao wen-hua ch'u-pan kung-ssu, 1985.
———. "Flower Season." Trans. Howard Goldblatt. *Carver and Chang* 125–133.
———. "Hsin na-jui-ssu chieh-shuo: Li Ang te tzu-p'o yü tzu-hsing—Shih Shu-tuan fang Li Ang" [A new narcissism: Li Ang's self-analysis and self-reflection—a personal interview with Li Ang by Shih Shu-tuan]. *An-yeh* 155–179.
———. *Hua-chi* [Flower season]. Taipei: Hung-fan shu-tien, 1985.
———. *Hun-sheng ho-ch'ang* [Mixed chorus]. Taipei: Chung-hua wen-i yüeh-k'an she, 1975.
———. "I-feng wei-chi te ch'ing-shu" [An unmailed love letter]. *I-feng wei-chi te ch'ing-shu* 3–37.
———. *I-feng wei-chi te ch'ing-shu* [An unmailed love letter]. Taipei: Hung-fan shu-tien yu-hsien kung-ssu, 1986.
———. *Nien-hua* (Youthful years). Taipei: Shih-pao wen-hua ch'u-pan ch'i-yeh yu-hsien kung-ssu, 1988.
———. *Sha-fu: Lu-kang ku-shih* [The butcher's wife: stories about Lu-kang]. Taipei: Lien-ho pao-she, 1983.
———. *T'a-men te yen-lei* [Their tears]. Taipei: Hung-fan shu-tien, 1984.
———. "Wo te ch'uang-tso kuan" [My view of literary creation]. *An-yeh* 181–187.
Li Feng-mao. "Hsü-lun" [Introduction]. *Chung-kuo hsien-tai san-wen hsüan-hsi* [Selection and commentary of modern Chinese essays]. Ed. Li Feng-mao et al. Taipei: Ch'ang-an ch'u-pan she, 1985. 1–24.
Li Yung-p'ing. *Chi-ling ch'un-ch'iu* [Chronicle of Chi-ling]. Taipei: Hung-fan shu-tien, 1986.
———. *La-tzu fu* [A La-tzu woman]. Taipei: Hua-hsin ch'u-pan kung-ssu, 1976.
Liang Shih-ch'iu. "Hsien-tai Chung-kuo wen-hsüeh chih lang-man te ch'ü-shih" [The romantic tendency in modern Chinese literature]. *Liang Shih-ch'iu lun wen-hsüeh* [Essays on literature by Liang Shih-ch'iu]. Taipei: Shih-pao wen-hua ch'u-pan shih-yeh yu-hsien kung-ssu, 1978.
Lin Hai-yin. *Ch'eng-nan chiu-shih* [Old stories of south Peking]. Taipei: Kuang-ch'i ch'u-pan she, 1960.
———. *Chu-hsin* [Candlewick]. 1965. Taipei: Ai-mei wen-i ch'u-pan she, 1971.
———. *Hun-yin te ku-shih* [Stories of marriage]. Taipei: Wen-hsing shu-tien, 1963.
———. *Lin Hai-yin tzu-hsüan chi* [Stories of Lin Hai-yin selected by the author]. Taipei: Li-ming wen-hua kung-ssu, 1975.
———. *Lü-tsao yü hsien-tan* [Green seaweed and salted eggs]. Taipei: Hsüeh-sheng shu-chü, 1958.
Lin I-chieh. "P'an-ni yü chiu-shu—Li Ang kuei-lai te hsün-hsi" [Rebellion and redemption—the message of Li Ang's homecoming]. Appendix. *T'a-men te yen-lei*. By Li Ang. 203–228.
Lindfors, Sally Ann. "Private Lives: An Analysis of the Short Stories of Ouyang Tzu, a Modern Chinese Writer." Diss. University of Texas at Austin, 1983.

Liu Ch'un-ch'eng. *Huang Ch'un-ming ch'ien-chuan* [A prebiography of Huang Ch'un-ming]. Taipei: Yüan-shen ch'u-pan she, 1987.

Liu, James J. Y. *Chinese Theories of Literature*. Chicago and London: University of Chicago Press, 1975.

Lü Cheng-hui et al. "Mei yu ch'u-lu te fan-p'an ying-hsiung—Wang Wen-hsing lun" [A rebellious hero without an outlet—on Wang Wen-hsing]. *Wen-hsing* [Literary star] 102 (Dec. 1986): 112–129.

———. "Wang Wen-hsing te pei-chü—sheng ts'o le ti-fang, hai shih shou ts'ao le chiao-yü" [The tragedy of Wang Wei-hsing—either he was born in the wrong place or he received the wrong kind of education]. *Wen-hsing* 102 (Dec. 1986): 113–117.

Lu Hsün. *Na-han* [Outcry]. Beijing: Jen-min wen-hsüeh ch'u-pan she, 1973.

———. *P'ang-huang* [Hesitation]. Beijing: Jen-min wen-hsüeh ch'u-pan she, 1973.

Lung Ying-t'ai. "I-ko Chung-kuo hsiao-chen te su-hsiang" [Portrait of a Chinese small town]. *Tang-tai* [Contemporary Monthly], 2 (June 1986): 166–172.

———. *Lung Ying-t'ai k'an hsiao-shuo* [Criticism of fiction by Lung Ying-t'ai]. Taipei: Erh-ya ch'u-pan she, 1985.

Mancall, Mark, ed. *Formosa Today*. New York and London: Frederick A. Praeger, 1964.

McFadden, Susan. "Tradition and Talent: Western Influence in the Works of Pai Hsien-yung." *Tamkang Review* 9.3 (Spring 1979): 315–344.

Miller, Lucien. "A Break in the Chain: The Short Stories of Ch'en Ying-chen." Faurot 86–109.

———. Introduction. *Exiles at Home: Stories by Ch'en Ying-chen*. By Ch'en Ying-chen. Trans. Lucien Miller. Ann Arbor: University of Michigan, Center for Chinese Studies, 1986. 1–26.

Ng, Sheung-Yuan Daisy. "The Labyrinth of Meaning: A Reading of Li Ang's Fiction." *Tamkang Review* 18.1–4 (Autumn 1987–Summer 1988): 141–150.

———. "Li Ang's Experiments with the Epistolary Form." *Modern Chinese Literature* 3.1–2 (Spring–Fall 1987): 91–106.

Ou-yang Tzu. Appendix. "Kuan-yü wo tzu-chi—hui-ta Hsia Tsu-li nü-shih te fang-wen" [About myself—reply to an interview by Ms. Hsia Tsu-li]. *I-chih te ying-hua*. By Ou-yang Tzu. 153–201.

———. *Ch'iu-yeh* [Autumn leaves]. Taipei: Ch'en-chung ch'u-pan she, 1971.

———. "The Fictional World of Pai Hsien-yung." Faurot 166–178.

———, ed. *Hsien-tai wen-hsüeh hsiao-shuo hsüan chi*. 2 vols. Taipei: Erh-ya ch'u-pan she, 1977.

———. *I-chih te ying-hua* [A transplanted oriental cherry]. Taipei: Erh-ya ch'u-pan she, 1978.

———. "I-shu yü jen-sheng" [Art and life]. 1979. Ou-yang, *Ou-yang Tzu tzu-hsüan chi* 269–294.

———. "Lun Chia-pien chih chieh-kou, hsing-shih, yü wen-tzu chü-fa" [A discussion of

the structure, form, language, and syntax in Family Crisis]. Chung-wai wen-hsüeh 1.12 (1973): 51–63. Rpt. in Ou-yang, Ou-yang Tzu tzu-hsüan chi 295–319.
———. Na ch'ang t'ou-fa te nü-hai [The girl with long hair]. Taipei: Wen-hsing shu-tien, 1967; Ta-lin ch'u-pan she, 1978.
———. Ou-yang Tzu tzu-hsüan chi [Stories of Ou-yang Tzu selected by the author]. Taipei: Li-ming wen-hua kung-ssu, 1982.
———. Sheng-ming te kuei-chi [Tracks of life]. Taipei: Chiu-ko ch'u-pan kung-ssu, 1988.
———. Wang-Hsieh t'ang ch'ien te yen-tzu: T'ai-pei jen te yen-hsi yü so-yin [Swallows in front of the noble mansions of Wang and Hsieh: an analysis of Tales of Taipei Characters]. Taipei: Erh-ya ch'u-pan she, 1976.
Pai Hsien-yung. Che-hsien chi [Celestials in mundane exile]. Taipei: Ta-lin ch'u-pan she, 1967.
———. Chi-mo te shih-ch'i sui [Lonely seventeen]. Taipei: Yüan-ching ch'u-pan she, 1976.
———. Crystal Boys: A Novel by Pai Hsien-yung. Trans. Howard Goldblatt. San Francisco: Gay Sunshine Press, 1990.
———. Ming-hsing k'a-fei kuan: Pai Hsien-yung lun-wen tsa-wen chi [The Star Café: collected essays of Pai Hsien-yung]. Taipei: Huang-kuan tsa-chih she, 1984.
———. Mo-jan hui-shou [Suddenly looking back]. Taipei: Erh-ya ch'u-pan she, 1978.
———. Nieh-tzu [Crystal boys]. Taipei: Yüan-ching ch'u-pan shih-yeh kung-ssu, 1983.
———. Niu-yüeh k'o [New Yorkers]. Hong Kong: Wen-hsüeh shu-chü, 1975.
———. Taipei jen [Tales of Taipei characters]. Taipei: Ch'en-chung ch'u-pan she, 1971.
———. "T'an hsiao-shuo p'i-p'ing te piao-chun—tu T'ang Chi-sung 'Ou-yang Tzu te Ch'iu-yeh' yu kan" [Criteria for the criticism of fiction—after reading "Ou-yang Tzu's Autumn Leaves," by T'ang Chi-sung]. Mo-jan hui-shou [Suddenly turning back my head]. Taipei: Erh-ya ch'u-pan she, 1978. 33–53.
———. "The Wandering Chinese: The Theme of Exile in Taiwan Fiction." The Iowa Review 7. 2–3 (Spring–Summer 1976): 205–212.
———. Wandering in the Garden, Waking from a Dream: Tales of Taipei Characters. Trans. Pai Hsien-yung and Patia Yasin. Bloomington: Indiana University Press, 1982.
Pai Shao-fan et al., eds. Hsien-tai T'ai-wan wen-hsüeh shih [Modern Taiwanese literary history]. Shen-yang: Liao-ning ta-hsüeh ch'u-pan she, 1987.
P'an Jen-mu. Ai-le hsiao t'ien-ti [Sorrow and happiness in a small world]. Taipei: Ch'un wen-hsüeh ch'u-pan kung-ssu, 1981.
———. Lien-i piao-mei [My cousin Lien-i]. 1952. Taipei: Ch'un wen-hsüeh ch'u-pan kung-ssu, 1985.
P'an Jung-li and Hsiao Kuo-ho, eds. Che-yang te chiao-shou Wang Wen-hsing [Such a "professor," Wang Wen-hsing]. Taipei: Tun-li ch'u-pan she, 1978.
P'eng Ko. Pu t'an jen-hsing, ho yu wen-hsüeh [Where is literature, if one does not talk about "human nature"?]. Taipei: Lien-ho pao-she, 1978.
Poggioli, Renato. The Theory of the Avant-Garde. Trans. Gerald Fitzgerald. Cambridge, MA: Belknap Press of Harvard University Press, 1968.

Pollard, David E. *A Chinese Look at Literature: The Literary Values of Chou Tso-jen in Relation to the Tradition*. Berkeley and Los Angeles: University of California Press, 1973.
Prusek, Jaroslav. *The Lyrical and the Epic: Studies of Modern Chinese Literature*. Ed. Leo Ou-fan Lee. Bloomington: Indiana University Press, 1980.
Robinson, Lewis Stewart. "Double-edged Sword: Christianity and Twentieth-Century Chinese Fiction." *Tamkang Review* 13.2 (Winter 1982): 161–184.
Said, W. Edward. *Orientalism*. New York: Vintage Books, 1978.
Schulte-Sasse, Jochen. Foreword. "Theory of Modernism versus Theory of the Avant-Garde." *Theory of the Avant-Garde*. By Peter Burger. vii–xlvii.
Shan, Te-hsing. "The Stream-of-Consciousness Technique in Wang Wen-hsing's Fiction." *Tamkang Review* 15.1–4 (Autumn 1984–Summer 1985): 523–545.
———. "Wang Wen-hsing on Wang Wen-hsing." *Modern Chinese Literature* 1.1 (Sept. 1984): 57–65.
Shih Shu. "Yen-wu—tai hsü" [Salted room—in lieu of preface]. Li Ang, *Hua-chi*. 5–18.
Shih Shu-ch'ing. *Liu-li wa* [Glazed tile]. Taipei: Shih-pao wen-hua ch'u-pan kung-ssu, 1976.
———. "Na-hsieh pu-mao te jih-tzu" [The barren years]. *Hsien-tai wen-hsüeh* 42 (Dec. 1970): 182–197. Rpt. in Shih Shu-ch'ing, *Shih-to na-hsieh jih-tzu* 1–25.
———. *Shih-to na-hsieh jih-tzu* [Gather those days]. Taipei: Chih-wen ch'u-pan she, 1971.
———. *T'ai-wan yü* [Taiwanese jade]. Fu-chou: Hai-hsia wen-i ch'u-pan she, 1987.
———. *Yüeh-po te mo-i* [The last descendants of Job]. Taipei: Hsien-jen-chang ch'u-pan she, 1969.
Ssu-t'u Wei. *Wu-shih nien-tai wen-hsüeh lun-p'ing* [Critical essays on literature of the fifties]. Taipei: Ch'eng-wen ch'u-pan she, 1979.
Shu, James C. T. "Iconoclasm in Taiwan Literature: 'A Change in the Family.'" *Chinese Literature: Essays, Articles and Reviews* 2.1 (Jan. 1980): 73–85. Rpt. as "Iconoclasm in Wang Wen-hsing's Chia-pien." Faurot 179–193.
Shui Ching. See Yang, Robert Yi.
Steinberg, Erwin R. *The Stream of Consciousness and Beyond in Ulysses*. Pittsburgh: University of Pittsburgh Press, 1973.
T'ang Chi-sung. "Ou-yang Tzu te Ch'iu-yeh" [Ou-yang Tzu's Autumn Leaves]. *Chung-hua jih-pao*, 17–19 May 1972.
T'ang Wen-piao. "Chiang-pi te hsien-tai-shih" [Ossified modern poetry]. *Chung-wai wen-hsüeh* 2.3 (1973): 18–20.
———. Preface. "I-chiu-pa-ssu nien te T'ai-wan ching-yen" [Taiwan experience in 1984]. T'ang Wen-piao, ed., *I-chiu-pa-ssu T'ai-wan hsiao-shuo hsüan* [Selected Stories from Taiwan: 1984]. Taipei: Ch'ien-wei ch'u-pan she, 1985. 1–11.
———. "Yin-tun te hsiao chiao-she" [The insignificant hidden character]. Chang Heng-hao 185.
Toynbee, A. J. *A Study of History*. London: Oxford University Press, 1935–1961.
Trilling, Lionel. "On the Modernist Element in Modern Literature." 1961. Howe, ed., *Literary Modernism* 59–82.

Ts'ai Yüan-huang. *Hai-hsia liang-an hsiao-shuo te feng-mao* [The outlooks of fiction from both sides of the Taiwan Strait]. Taipei: Ya-tien ch'u-pan she, 1989.

Ts'ao, Hsüeh-ch'in. *Hung-lou meng* [Dream of the red chamber].

T'ung Wan-tou. "Ts'ung 'p'i-p'ing te tao-te' tao 'tao-te-hua te p'i-p'ing': wen-hsüeh lun-chan ho cheng-chih fan-lan" [From 'the morality of criticism' to 'moralistic criticism': literary debate and political contamination]. *Nan-fang* [The south] 9 (1987): 8–13.

T'ung Wan-tou et al. "Hsiang-t'u wen-hsüeh lun-chan shih-nien: wen-hua pa-ch'üan te ching-chu" [Ten years after the Nativist literary debate: a contest for cultural hegemony]. *Nan-fang* 9 (1987): 6–37.

Wang Chen-ho. *Chia-chuang i niu-ch'e* [An oxcart for dowry]. Taipei: Yüan-ching ch'u-pan she, 1975.

———. *Hsiang-ko-li-la: Wang Chen-ho tzu-hsüan chi* [Shangri-la: stories by Wang Chen-ho selected by the author]. Taipei: Hung-fan shu-tien, 1980.

———. *Jen-sheng ko-wang* [The time of your life]. Taipei: Lien-ho wen-hsüeh tsa-chih she, 1987.

———. *Mei-jen t'u* [A portrait of the "beautiful people"]. Taipei: Hung-fan shu-tien, 1982.

———. *Mei-kuei mei-kuei wo ai ni* [Rose, rose, I love you]. Taipei: Yüan-chin ch'u-pan shih-yeh kung-ssu, 1984.

———. *San-ch'un chi* [The third spring]. Taipei: Ch'en-chung ch'u-pan she, 1975.

Wang, C. H. (Wang Ching-hsien). "Fancy and Reality in Ch'i-teng Sheng's Fiction." Faurot 194–205.

Wang Ching-shou. *T'ai-wan hsiao-shuo tso-chia lun* [On fiction writers from Taiwan]. Beijing: Pei-ching ta-hsüeh ch'u-pan she, 1984.

Wang, David Der-wei. *Ts'ung Liu O tao Wang Chen-ho: Chung-kuo hsien-tai hsiao-shuo san-lun* [From Liu O to Wang Chen-ho: essays on modern Chinese fiction]. Taipei: Shih-pao wen-hua ch'u-pan kung-ssu, 1986.

———. *Tsung-sheng hsüan-hua: san-ling yü pa-ling nien-tai te Chung-kuo hsiao-shuo* [Polyphonic clamor: Chinese fiction in the thirties and the eighties]. Taipei: Yüan-liu ch'u-pan kung-ssu, 1988.

———. "Radical Laughter in Lao She and His Taiwan Successors." Goldblatt, *Worlds Apart* 44–63.

Wang, Jing. "Taiwan Hsiang-t'u Literature: Perspectives in the Evolution of a Literary Movement." Faurot 43–70.

Wang T'o. "Shih 'Hsien-shih chu-i' wen-hsüeh, pu shih 'hsiang-t'u wen-hsüeh'" [It's "literature of the present reality," not "nativism"]. 1977. Yü T'ien-ts'ung 100–119.

Wang Wen-hsing. *Chia-pien* [Family crisis]. Taipei: Huan-yü ch'u-pan she, 1973. Taipei: Hung-fan shu-tien, 1978.

———. "Hsiang-t'u wen-hsüeh te kung yü kuo" [Merits and mistakes of Nativist literature]. 1978. Yü T'ien-ts'ung 515–546.

———. "Hsien-tai wen-hsüeh i-nien" [One year of *Modern Literature*]. *Hsien-tai wen-hsüeh* 7 (March 1961): 4–6.

———. *Lung-t'ien lou* [Dragon tower]. Taipei: Ta-lin ch'u-pan she, 1967.
———. *M ho W* [M and W]. *Lien-ho wen-hsüeh* [Unitas, a literary monthly], 4.5 (March 1988): 80–89.
———. *Pei-hai te jen* [Backed against the sea]. Taipei: Hung-fan shu-tien, 1981.
———. "Shih wei chih-chi che ssu te wen-hsüeh" ["A gentleman dies for those who appreciate his talents"—a subgenre of literature]. Lecture notes. Fu-jen ta-hsüeh 463–474.
———. *Shih-wu p'ien hsiao-shuo* [Fifteen stories]. Taipei: Hung-fan shu-tien, 1979.
———. "Shou-chi hsü-ch'ao" [Notes continued]. *Lien-ho wen-hsüeh* 13 (Nov. 1985): 98–107.
———. *Shu ho ying* [Books and shadows]. Taipei: Lien-ho wen-hsüeh ch'u-pan she, 1988.
———. *Wan-chü shou-ch'iang* [Toy pistol]. Taipei: Chih-wen ch'u-pan she, 1970.
———. "Wu hsiu-chih te chan-cheng" [A never-ending battle]. *Wen-hsing* [Literary star], 104 (Jan. 1987): 104–105.
———. "Wu-sheng yin-hsiang" [Impressions of five Chinese provinces]. *Lien-ho wen-hsüeh* 6.4 (1990): 35–47, and 6.5 (1990): 21–31.
Wang, Yeujin. "Mixing Memory and Desire: Red Sorghum, A Chinese Version of Masculinity and Femininity." *Public Culture* 2.1 (Fall 1989): 31–53.
Wen Yen. Introduction. *T'ai-wan tso-chia hsiao-shuo hsüan chi* [Selected stories of Taiwan writers], 1. By Chung-kuo she-hui k'o-hsüeh yüan wen-hsüeh yen-chiu suo tang-tai wen-hsüeh yen-chiu shih [Contemporary literature research group at the Chinese Academy of Social Sciences]. Beijing: Chung-kuo she-hui k'o-hsüeh ch'u-pan she, 1982. 1–20.
Williams, Raymond. *Marxism and Literature*. Oxford and New York: Oxford University Press, 1977.
Yampolsky, Philip, trans. *The Platform Sutra of the Sixth Patriarch*. New York: Columbia University Press, 1967.
Yang Chiang. *Kan-hsiao liu chi* [Six chapters of my life in the cadre school]. Hong Kong: Kuang-chiao-ching ch'u-pan she, 1981.
Yang, Robert Yi (Shui Ching). *Ch'ing-se te cha-meng* [The green grasshopper]. Taipei: Wen-hsing shu-tien, 1967.
———. "Form and Tone in Wang Chen-ho's Satires." Faurot 134–147.
Yeh, Michelle. "Shapes of Darkness: Symbols in Li Ang's Dark Night." *Modern Chinese Women Writers, Critical Appraisals*. Ed. Michael S. Duke. Armonk, NY, and London: M.E. Sharpe, 1989. 78–95.
Yeh Shih-t'ao. "Lun Ch'i-teng Sheng te Chiang-chü" [On *Quandary* by Ch'i-teng-sheng]. Chang Heng-hao 9–22.
———. "T'ai-wan hsiang-t'u wen-hsüeh shih tao-lun" [An introduction to the history of Taiwanese Nativist literature]. 1977. Yü T'ien-ts'ung 69–92.
Yen Yüan-shu et al. "Chia-pien tso-t'an hui" [Symposium on Family Crisis]. *Chung-wai wen-hsüeh* 2.1 (1973): 164–177.

———. "K'u-tu hsi-p'ing t'an *Chia-pien*" [An arduous reading and careful savoring of *Family Crisis*]. *Chung-wai wen-hsüeh* 1.11 (1973): 60–85.

Yin Ti. *Ch'i-chün te shih-chieh* [The world of Ch'i-chün]. Taipei: Erh-ya ch'u-pan she, 1980.

Yip, Wai-lim. *Chung-kuo hsien-tai hsiao-shuo te feng-mao* [Style and form of contemporary Chinese fiction]. Taipei: Ssu-chi ch'u-pan kung-ssu, 1977.

———, ed. *Chung-kuo hsien-tai tso-chia lun* [On modern Chinese writers]. Taipei: Lien-ching ch'u-pan kung-ssu, 1976.

Yü Kuang-chung. "Lang lai le" [The wolf is here]. 1977. *Yü T'ien-ts'ung* 264–267.

———. "Shih-erh pan te kuan-yin lien—wo tu *Chi-ling ch'un-ch'iu*" [A Bodhisattva lotus with twelve petals—my reading of *Chronicle of Chi-ling*]. Li, *Chi-ling ch'un-ch'iu* 1–9.

Yü T'ien-ts'ung. *Hsiang-t'u wen-hsüeh t'ao-lun chi* [A collection of discussions on Nativist literature]. Taipei: Yüan-liu, Ch'ang-ch'iao lien-ho fa-hsing pu, 1978.

Yüan Liang-chün. *Pai Hsien-yung lun* [A study of Pai Hsien-yung]. Taipei: Erh-ya ch'u-pan she, 1991.

Yüan Tse-nan. "Ch'ih-erh liao-ch'üeh kung-chia shih: ch'ien-t'an Pai Hsien-yung te chin-tso *Nieh-tzu*" [The political obsession: on Pai Hsien-yung's recent novel *Crystal Boys*]. *Hsien-tai wen-hsüeh fu-k'an* 20 (June 1983): 7–18.

Sources of English Translations of Literary Works from Taiwan

Translation Journals

Chinese Pen. Taipei: Chinese Center, International P.E.N.
Renditions. Hong Kong: Chinese University of Hong Kong, Research Centre for Translation.

General Collections That Include Writers from Taiwan

Carver, Ann, and Sung-sheng Yvonne Chang. *Bamboo Shoots After the Rain: Contemporary Stories by Women of Taiwan*. Introduction by Sung-sheng Yvonne Chang. New York: Feminist Press, 1990.
Cheung, Dominic. *An Isle Full of Noises: Modern Chinese Poetry from Taiwan*. New York: Columbia University Press, 1987.
Cheung, Dominic, and Michelle Yeh, eds. *Exiles and Native Sons, Modern Chinese Stories from Taiwan*. Taipei: National Institute for Compilation and Translation. 1991.
Chi, Pang-yuan, et al., eds. *An Anthology of Contemporary Chinese Literature: Taiwan, 1949–1976*. 2 vols. Taipei: National Institute for Compilation and Translation, 1975.
Contemporary Chinese Women Writers, eds. *The Muse of China: A Collection of Prose and Short Stories*. 2 vols. Taipei: Chinese Women Writers' Association, 1974.
Contemporary Taiwan Literature. Renditions 35–36. Hong Kong: Chinese University of Hong Kong, Research Centre for Translation, 1991.

Contemporary Women Writers. Renditions 27–28. Hong Kong: Chinese University of Hong Kong, Research Centre for Translation, 1987.
Duke, Michael S. *Worlds of Modern Chinese Fiction: Short Stories and Novellas from the People's Republic, Taiwan, and Hong Kong.* Armonk, NY, and London: M. E. Sharpe, 1991.
Hsia, C. T., ed. *Twentieth-Century Chinese Stories.* New York: Columbia University Press, 1971.
Hsu, Vivian Ling, ed. *Born of the Same Roots: Stories of Modern Chinese Women.* Bloomington: Indiana University Press, 1981.
Ing, Nancy, ed. *New Voices: Stories and Poems by Young Chinese Authors.* Rev. ed. Taipei: Chinese Materials Center, 1980.
——. *Summer Glory: A Collection of Contemporary Chinese Poetry.* Taipei: Chinese Materials Center, 1982.
——. *Winter Plum: Contemporary Chinese Fiction.* Taipei: Chinese Materials Center, 1982.
Lau, Joseph S. M., ed. *The Unbroken Chain: An Anthology of Taiwan Fiction since 1926.* Bloomington: Indiana University Press, 1983.
Nieh, Hua-ling, ed. *Eight Stories by Chinese Women.* Taipei: Heritage Press, 1962.
Rexroth, Kenneth, and Ling Chung, eds. *The Orchid Boat: Women Poets of China.* New York: McGraw Hill, 1972.
Soong, C. Stephen, and John Minford, eds. *Trees on the Mountain: An Anthology of New Chinese Writing.* A Renditions Book. Hong Kong: Chinese University Press, 1984.
Palandri, Angela C. Y. Jung, and Robert J. Bertholf, eds. and trans. *Modern Verse from Taiwan.* Berkeley: University of California Press, 1972.
Yip, Wai-lim. *Modern Chinese Poetry: Twenty Poets from the Republic of China, 1955–1965.* Iowa City: University of Iowa Press, 1970.
Yip, Wai-lim, and William Tay, eds. *Chinese Women Writers Today.* Occasional Papers/Reprint Series in Contemporary Asian Studies, no. 4. College Park: University of Maryland, School of Law, 1979.
Yu, Kwang-chung (Yü Kuang-chung), *New Chinese Poetry.* Taipei: Heritage Press, 1970.

Translations of Individual Writers from Taiwan

Chen, Jo-hsi. *The Execution of Mayor Yin and Other Stories from the Great Cultural Revolution.* Bloomington: Indiana University Press, 1978.
—— [Chen Ruoxi]. *The Old Man and Other Stories.* Renditions paperback. Hong Kong: Chinese University of Hong Kong, Research Centre for Translation, 1986.
——. *Spirit Calling: Tales about Taiwan.* Taipei: Heritage Press, 1962.
Ch'en Ying-chen. *Exiles at Home: Stories by Ch'en Ying-chen.* Trans. Lucien Miller. Ann Arbor: University of Michigan, Center for Chinese Studies, 1986.
Hwa Yen. *Lamp of Wisdom.* Taipei: Woman Magazine, 1974.
Hwang Chun-ming. *The Drowning of an Old Cat and Other Stories.* Trans. Howard Goldblatt. Bloomington: Indiana University Press, 1980.
Kuo, Gloria Liang-hui. *Taipei Women.* Hong Kong: New Enterprise Company, 1983.

Li, Ang. *The Butcher's Wife: A Novel by Li Ang*. Trans. Howard Goldblatt and Ellen Yeung. San Francisco: North Point Press, 1986.

Lin, Hai-yin. *Green Seaweed and Salted Eggs*. Taipei: Heritage Press, 1963.

Nieh, Hua-ling, ed. *Eight Stories by Chinese Women*. Taipei: Heritage Press, 1962.

———. *Mulberry and Peach: Two Women of China*. London: Women's Press, 1986, c1981.

Pai, Hsien-yung. *Crystal Boys: A Novel by Pai Hsien-yung*. Trans. Howard Goldblatt. San Francisco: Gay Sunshine Press, 1990.

———. *Wandering in the Garden, Waking from a Dream: Tales of Taipei Characters*. Trans. Pai Hsien-yung and Patia Yasin, ed. George Kao. Bloomington: Indiana University Press, 1982.

Peng, Ko. *Black Tears, Stories of War-Torn China*. Trans. Nancy Ing. Introduction by C. T. Hsia. Taipei: Chinese Materials Center, 1986.

Shih, Shu-ch'ing. *The Barren Years and Other Short Stories and Plays*. Trans. John M. Mclellan. San Francisco: Chinese Materials Center, 1975.

Wang, Wen-hsing. *Backed Against the Sea*. Trans. Edward Gunn. Ithaca: Cornell East Asia Program. Forthcoming.

Glossary

ai er pu shang
哀而不傷

Ai Ya
愛亞

Ch'an
禪

Chang Ai-ling
張愛玲

   Yang-ko
   秧歌

Chang Chün-hung
張俊宏

Chang Han-liang
張漢良

Chang Hsiao-feng
張曉風

Chang Hsiu-ya
張秀亞

Chang Ta-ch'un
張大春

Che-yang te chiao-shou Wang Wen-hsing
這樣的教授王文興

Ch'en Hsi-ying
陳西瀅

   Ti-ts'un chuan
   狄村傳

Ch'en Hsing-hui
陳幸蕙

Ch'en Jo-hsi
陳若曦

Ch'en Ku-ying
陳鼓應

Ch'en Ying-chen
陳映真

   Chao Nan-tung
   趙南棟

Ch'en Ying-chen tso-p'in chi
陳映真作品集

"Ch'i-ts'an te wu-yen te tsui"
淒慘的無言的嘴

"Chiang-chün tsu"
將軍族

"Chih-shih jen te p'ien-chih"
知識人的偏執

"Ho ta-ko"
賀大哥

"Hsiang-ts'un te chiao-shih"
鄉村的教師

   Wu Chin-hsiang
   吳錦翔

"Hsien-tai chu-i te tsai k'ai-fa"
現代主義的再開發

"Hua-sheng-tun ta-lou"
華盛頓大樓

"I lü-se chih hou-niao"
一綠色之候鳥

"Ku-hsiang"
故鄉

"Lieh-jen chih ssu"
獵人之死

"Ling-tang hua"
鈴鐺花

"Liu-yüeh li te mei-kuei hua"
六月裏的玫瑰花

"Mao t'a-men te tsu-mu"
貓牠們的祖母

"Mien-t'an"
麵攤

"Mou i-ko jih-wu"
某一個日午

"Na-mo shuai-lao te yen-lei"
那麼衰老的眼淚

"Ou! Su-shan-na"
哦！蘇珊娜

"P'ing-kuo shu"
蘋果樹

"Shan-lu"
山路

  Li Kuo-k'un
  李國坤

  Li Kuo-mu
  李國木

  Ts'ai Ch'ien-hui
  蔡千惠

"Shang-pan tsu te i jih"
上班族的一日

"Shih lun Ch'en Ying-chen"
試論陳映真

"Ssu-che"
死者

"Ssu-shih nien lai te T'ai-wan wen-i ssu-ch'ao"
四十年來的台灣文藝思潮

"T'ang Ch'ien te hsi-chu"
唐倩的喜劇

"Ti i-chien ch'ai-shih"
第一件差事

  Hu Hsin-pao
  胡心保

"Tsu-fu ho shan"
祖父和傘

"Tsui-hou te hsia-jih"
最後的夏日

"Wan-shang ti-chün"
萬商帝君

"Wen-hsüeh fan-ying she-hui, hui-tao she-hui"
文學反映社會，回到社會

"Wen-shu"
文書

"Wo te ti-ti K'ang-hsiung"
我的弟弟康雄

  K'ang-hsiung
  康雄

"Wu-tzu chao-yao che te t'ai-yang"
兀自照耀著的太陽

"Yeh-hsing huo-ch'e"
夜行貨車

"Yün"
雲

"Yung-heng te ta-ti"
永恒的大地

ch'eng
誠

Ch'i-chün
琦君

  "Ah Yü"
  阿玉

  "Chi"
  髻

Ch'i-chün te shih-chieh
琦君的世界

"Ch'i-yüeh te ai-shang"
七月的哀傷

Glossary

Ching chieh
菁姐

"Chü-tzu hung le"
橘子紅了

"San-ching yu meng shu tang chen"
三更有夢書當枕

Ch'i I-shou
齊益壽

Ch'i-teng Sheng
七等生

  Chiang-chü
  僵局

  Ching-shen ping-huan
  精神病患

  Chü-hsieh chi
  巨蟹集

  Ch'ung-hui Sha-ho
  重回沙河

  "Fang-wen"
  訪問

  Li ch'eng chi
  離城記

  Lai-tao hsiao-chen te Ya-tzu-pieh
  來到小鎮的亞茲別

  "Lai-tao hsiao-chen te Ya-tzu-pieh"
  來到小鎮的亞茲別

  Lao fu-jen
  老婦人

  San-pu ch'ü Hei-ch'iao
  散步去黑橋

  Sha-ho pei-ko
  沙河悲歌

  "Ssu-kua pu"
  絲瓜布

  T'an-lang te shu-hsin
  譚郎的書信

  "T'iao-yüan hsüan-shou t'uei-hsiu le"
  跳遠選手退休了

  "Wo ai Hei Yen-chu"
  我愛黑眼珠

Ch'ing-tzu
晴子

Yin-po ch'ih-pang
銀波翅膀

Chiang Ching-kuo
蔣經國

Chiang Kai-shek
蔣介石

Chiang Kuei
姜貴

  Hsüan-feng
  旋風

Ching-ling
竟陵

ch'ing
情

Chou Tso-jen
周作人

  Chou Tso-jen wen-hsüan
  周作人文選

Chu Li-min
朱立民

Chu Hsi-ning
朱西寧

  "Hsiao Ts'ui yü Ta Hei-niu"
  小翠與大黑牛

  Lang
  狼

  "Lang"
  狼

  "Lo-ch'e shang"
  驛車上

  P'o-hsiao shih-fen
  破曉時分

  "P'o-hsiao shih-fen"
  破曉時分

  T'ieh-chiang
  鐵漿

  "T'ieh-chiang"
  鐵漿

Wei-yen p'ien
微言篇

"Yeh shih tzu-wei"
也是滋味

Chu T'ien-hsin
朱天心

Chu T'ien-wen
朱天文

Chu Tzu-ch'ing
朱自清

"Pei-ying"
背影

Chu Yen
朱炎

chüan-ts'un
眷村

Chuang Yin
莊因

Ch'un wen-hsüeh
純文學

chung
忠

Chung Chao-cheng
鍾肇政

Chung-hsi wen-hua lun-chan
中西文化論戰

Chung-hua tsa-chih
中華雜誌

Chung Mei-yin
鍾梅音

Chung-wai wen-hsüeh
中外文學

C. T. Hsia
夏志清

fan-feng
反諷

fan-kung ta-lu
反攻大陸

Fang Yü
方瑜

Feng Tsu-sheng
封祖盛

T'ai-wan hsiao-shuo chu-yao liu-p'ai ch'u-t'an
台灣小說主要流派初探

fu-k'an
副刊

Ho-shang
河殤

Hou Li-ch'ao
侯立朝

hsi-hua
西化

Hsia-ch'ao
夏潮

Hsia Chi-an
夏濟安

Hsia Ch'eng-t'ao
夏承燾

hsiang-t'u
鄉土

hsiao
孝

Hsiao Sa
蕭颯

hsieh-shih
寫實

hsien-shih
現實

Hsien-tai wen-hsüeh
現代文學

Hsien-tai wen-hsüeh yün-tung
現代文學運動

hsin
心

Hsin-shih lun-chan
新詩論戰

Hsin wen-hsüeh
新文學

Hsin-yüeh she
新月社

hsing
性

hsing-fu i-shih
幸福意識

hsing-ssu
形似

hsiu-ts'u li ch'i ch'eng
修辭立其誠

Hsü Chung-p'ei
徐鍾珮

Hsü Fu-kuan
徐復觀

Hsü Hsing
徐星

hsün-fu
尋父

Hu Ch'iu-yüan
胡秋原

Hu Lan-ch'eng
胡蘭成

  Chin-sheng chin-shih
  今生今世

  Shan-ho sui-yüeh
  山河歲月

hua-pu
花部

Huang Ch'un-ming (Hwang Chun-ming)
黃春明

  "Ch'ing-fan Kung te ku-shih"
  青番公的故事

  "Erh-tzu te ta wan-ou"
  兒子的大玩偶

    K'un-shu
    坤樹

  "Hsiao Ch'i te nei i-ting mao-tzu"
  小琪的那一頂帽子

  "Hsien"
  癬

    Ah-fa
    阿發

"Lo"
鑼

Kam Kim-ah
憨欽仔

"Ni-ssu i-chih lao-mao"
溺死一隻老猫

  Uncle Ah-sheng
  阿盛伯

"P'ing-kuo te tzu-wei"
蘋果的滋味

"Yü"
魚

  Ah-ts'ang
  阿蒼

Huang Fan
黃凡

hui-kuei hsiang-t'u
回歸鄉土

hung-kuei
紅龜

i (p. 122)
伊

i (p. 227)
義

i-k'u
憶苦

i-yang tun-ts'uo
抑揚頓挫

Jen-chien
人間

Joseph Shiu-ming Lau
劉紹銘

Kao Ch'üan-chih
高全之

  "Ch'i-teng Sheng te tao-te chia-kou"
  七等生的道德架構

Kao Hsin-chiang
高信疆

Kao Hsing-chien
高行健

Hsien-tai hsiao-shuo chi-ch'iao ch'u-t'an
現代小說技巧初探

ku-ch'en nieh-tzu
孤臣孽子

kuan-yin
觀音

k'un-ch'ü
崑曲

Kung-an
公安

k'ung-ch'i k'ung-ch'i
空其控奇

Kuo Feng
郭楓

Lao She
老舍

Leo Ou-fan Lee
李歐梵

Li Ang
李昂

  An-yeh
  暗夜

    Ch'en T'ien-jui
    陳天瑞

    Huang Ch'eng-te
    黃承德

    Ting Hsin-hsin
    丁欣欣

    Yeh Yüan
    葉原

"Hua-chi"
花季

Hun-sheng ho-ch'ang
混聲合唱

"I-feng wei chi te ch'ing-shu"
一封未寄的情書

Nien-hua
年華

Sha-fu
殺夫

Li Ch'iao
李喬

Li Yung-p'ing
李永平

  Chi-ling ch'un-ch'iu
  吉陵春秋

  "Hao i-p'ien ch'un-yü"
  好一片春雨

  "Jih-t'ou yü"
  日頭雨

  "Man-t'ien hua-yü"
  滿天花雨

  "Ssu-nien"
  思念

  "Ta shui"
  大水

  "Wan-fu hsiang li"
  萬福巷裏

    Ch'ang-sheng
    長笙

    Ch'iu-t'ang
    秋棠

    Ch'un-hung
    春紅

    Hsiao Lo
    小樂

    Liu Lao-shih
    劉老實

    Sun Ssu-fang
    孫四房

    Yen-niang
    燕娘

Liang Ch'i-ch'ao
梁啟超

Liang Shih-ch'iu
梁實秋

  Liang Shih-ch'iu lun wen-hsüeh
  梁實秋論文學

Liao Hui-ying
廖輝英

lien
蓮、憐

Lin Ch'ing-hsüan
林清玄

Lin Hai-yin
林海音

    Ch'eng-nan chiu-shih
    城南舊事

    "Chin Li-yü te pai-chien ch'ün"
    金鯉魚的百襉裙

    "Chu"
    燭

    "Ch'un-chiu"
    春酒

    "Hsün"
    殉

    "Lü-tsao yü hsien-tan"
    綠藻與鹹蛋

Lin Huai-min
林懷民

Lin Wen-yüeh
林文月

Lin Yao-te
林耀德

ling
靈

Liu Ch'un-ch'eng
劉春城

    Huang Ch'un-ming ch'ien-chuan
    黃春明前傳

Liu So-la
劉索拉

Liu Ta-jen
劉大任

Liu Yü-hsi
劉禹錫

    "Wu-i hsiang"
    烏衣巷

Lu Hsün
魯迅

"Ah Q cheng-chuan"
阿Q正傳

"K'uang-jen jih-chi"
狂人日記

"K'ung I-chi"
孔乙己

Na-han
吶喊

"Yao"
藥

Lu-kang
鹿港

Lü Cheng-hui
呂正惠

Lung Ying-t'ai
龍應台

Mao Tun
茅盾

Miao-li
苗栗

Meng Yao
孟瑤

nieh
孽

Nieh Hua-ling
聶華苓

nin
您

Ou-yang Tzu
歐陽子

    "Chin huang-hun shih"
    近黃昏時

    Chi-wei
    吉威

    Li-fen
    麗芬

    Yü Pin
    余彬

    "Hua-p'ing"
    花瓶

I-chih te ying-hua
移植的櫻花

"I-shu yü jen-sheng"
藝術與人生

"Kuan-yü wo tzu-chi—hui-ta Hsia Tsu-li nü-shih te fang-wen"
關於我自己——回答夏祖麗女士的訪問

"Mo-nü"
魔女

Na ch'ang t'ou-fa te nü-hai
那長頭髮的女孩

"Pan-ko wei-hsiao"
半個微笑

"Tsui-hou i-chieh k'o"
最後一節課

"Wang"
網

Wang-Hsieh t'ang ch'ien te yen-tzu
王謝堂前的燕子

Pa Chin
巴金

Pa-fang wei-i ts'ung-k'an
八方文藝叢刊

Pai Hsien-yung
白先勇

"Che-hsien chi"
謫仙記

"Che-hsien yüan"
謫仙怨

"Chih-chia-ko chih ssu"
芝加哥之死

"Ch'ing-ch'un"
青春

"Hua-ch'iao jung-chi"
花橋榮記

"Hsiang-kang, 1960"
香港——一九六〇

"I-pa ch'ing"
一把青

"Ku-lien hua"
孤戀花

Chüan-chüan
娟娟

K'o Lao-liu
柯老六

Wu Pao
五寶

"Na hsüeh i-pan te tu-chüan hua"
那血一般的杜鵑花

Hsi-mei
喜妹

Li-erh
麗兒

Wang Hsiung
王雄

"Nei-wan te yüeh-kuang"
那晚的月光

Nieh-tzu
孽子

  A-qing (Ah-ch'ing)
  阿青

  Chief Yang (Yang Chiao-t'ou)
  楊教頭

  Fu Wei
  傅衛

  Heavensent Fu (Fu T'ien-ts'u)
  傅天賜

  Little Jade (Hsiao Yü)
  小玉

  Luo Ping (Lo P'ing)
  羅平

  Mousey (Lao-shu)
  老鼠

  Papa Fu (Fu Lao-yeh-tzu)
  傅老爺子

  Peach Boy (T'ao T'ai-lang)
  桃太郎

  Phoenix Boy (Ah Feng)
  阿鳳

  Wang Kuilong, Dragon Prince
  (Wang K'uei-lung, Lung-tzu)
  王夔龍,龍子

Wu Min
吳敏

Niu-yüeh k'o
紐約客

"Pi-yeh"
畢業

Taipei jen
台北人

"Tung-yeh"
冬夜

"Yu-yüan ching-meng"
遊園驚夢

 Cheng Yen-ch'ing
 鄭彥青

 Fu-tzu miao
 夫子廟

 Mme. Ch'ien
 錢夫人

 "Yüeh-meng"
 月夢

 "Yung-yüan te Yin Hsüeh-yen"
 永遠的尹雪艷

pai-hua
白話

Pai-hua wen-hsüeh yün-tung
白話文學運動

P'an Jen-mu
潘人木

 Ai-le hsiao t'ien-ti
 哀樂小天地

 "Ai-le hsiao t'ien-ti"
 哀樂小天地

 Lien-i piao-mei
 蓮漪表妹

 "Nao she chih yeh"
 鬧蛇之夜

 "Yeh-kuang pei"
 夜光杯

  Ch'u-chia
  楚嘉

"Yu-ch'ing wa"
有情襪

P'eng Ko
彭歌

Ping Hsin
冰心

Shan Te-hsing
單德興

Shang-nü pu chih wang-kuo hen, ko chiang yu ch'ang Hou-t'ing hua"
商女不知亡國恨，隔江猶唱後庭花

shen
神

shen-ssu
神似

Shen Ts'ung-wen
沈從文

 "Hsiao Hsiao"
 蕭蕭

sheng-chi wen-t'i
省籍問題

Shih Shu-ch'ing
施叔青

 "Yüeh-po te mo-i"
 約伯的末裔

Shui Ching
水晶

 "Mei-yu lien te jen"
 沒有臉的人

Ssu-ma Chung-yüan
司馬中原

Su Ch'ing
蘇青

Sun Yat-sen
孫逸仙

Sung Tse-lai
宋澤萊

T. A. Hsia
夏濟安

ta
她

Ta-hsüeh tsa-chih
大學雜誌

Ta shuo-huang chia
大說謊家

tai
代

Tai T'ien
戴天

T'ai-chung
台中

T'ai-wan pen-t'u-hua yün-tung
台灣本土化運動

T'ai-wan wen-i
台灣文藝

T'ang Wen-piao
唐文標

"Chiang-pi te hsien-tai shih"
僵斃的現代詩

te te te te le ko
的的的的了個

T'ien-an-men
天安門

t'ien-li
天理

Ting Ling
丁玲

tsai-tao
載道

t'sai-tzu chia-jen
才子佳人

Ts'an-hsüeh
殘雪

Ts'ao Hsüeh-ch'in
曹雪芹

  Hung-lou meng
  紅樓夢

    Nü-wa
    女媧

    Pao-yü
    寶玉

Tai-yü
黛玉

Ying-lien
英蓮（應憐）

ts'u
詞

Tsung-sheng hsüan-hua
眾聲喧嘩

Ts'ung Shu
叢甦

Tu Mu
杜牧

"Po Ch'in-huai"
泊秦淮

Tuan Ts'ai-hua
段彩華

Tzu-yu Chung-kuo
自由中國

Wai-lim Yip
葉維廉

wan-neng
萬能

Wang Chen-ho
王禎和

  "Chi-mo hung"
  寂寞紅

  "Chia-chuang i niu-ch'e"
  嫁粧一牛車

    Ah-hao
    阿好

    Chien
    簡

    Wan-fa
    萬發

  "Hsiang-ko li-la"
  香格里拉

  "K'uai-le te jen"
  快樂的人

  Mei-kuei mei-kuei wo ai ni
  玫瑰玫瑰我愛你

Tung Ssu-wen
董斯文

"Su-lan hsiao-chieh yao ch'u-chia"
素蘭小姐要出嫁

"Wu-yüeh shih-san chieh"
五月十三節

Wang Hsiao-lien
王孝廉

wang-pa
王八

Wang T'o
王拓

"Shih 'Hsien-shih chu-i' wen-hsüeh, pu shih 'hsiang-t'u wen-hsüeh' "
是"現實主義"文學，不是"鄉土文學"

wang-tzu ch'eng-lung
望子成龍

Wang Wen-hsing
王文興

   Chia-pien
   家變

      Fan Yeh
      范曄

"Ch'ien-ch'üeh"
欠缺

"Hai-pin sheng-mu chieh"
海濱聖母節

"Han-liu"
寒流

"Hei-i"
黑衣

"Hsiang-t'u wen-hsüeh te kung yü kuo"
鄉土文學的功與過

"Jih-li"
日曆

"Lung-t'ien lou"
龍天樓

"Ming-yün te chi-hsien"
命運的跡線

"Mu-ch'in"
母親

Pei-hai te jen
背海的人

Healthy Happy Hooker (Yeh Yeh Yeh)
葉葉葉

Shen-k'eng ao
深坑澳

yeh
爺

Yü Shih-liang
虞世樑

"Tsui k'uai-le te shih"
最快樂的事

"Wan-chü shou-ch'iang"
玩具手槍

"Wu hsiu-chih te chan-cheng"
無休止的戰爭

"Wu-sheng yin-hsiang"
五省印象

wen
文

Wen-chi
文季

Wen-hsing
文星

wen-hua fu-hsing
文化復興

wen-jou tun-hou
溫柔敦厚

wen-yen
文言

Wu Chin-fa
吳錦發

Wu Tsu-hsiang
吳組緗

   "Kuan-kuan te pu-p'in"
   官官的補品

Ya Hsien
瘂弦

Yang Chiang (Yang Jiang)
楊絳

   Kan-hsiao liu chi
   幹校六記

Yang Ch'ing-ch'u
楊青矗

Yang Kuo-shu
楊國樞

Yeh Shih-t'ao
葉石濤

Yen Yüan-shu
顏元叔

yen-chih
言志

yin
淫

yü
慾

Yü Kuang-chung
余光中

   "Lang lai le"
   狼來了

Yü T'ien-ts'ung
尉天聰

   Hsiang-t'u wen-hsüeh t'ao-lun chi
   鄉土文學討論集

yüan
緣

Yüan Ch'iung-ch'iung
袁瓊瓊

Yüan K'o-chia
袁可嘉

yüan-nieh
冤孽

Yün-men wu-chi
雲門舞集

Index

Aestheticism, 16, 191–192 n.13, 192 n.14; modernist aesthetic strategy, 78, 117–120, 124, 201 n.20, 202 n.27; Modernists and, 16–17, 61, 73–87, 157–158
Anti-Communism: in works, 23–24, 29, 36–37; writers and, 100, 152. See also "Combat literature"
Arnold, Matthew, 9, 19, 190 n.6, 191 n.8
Artistic autonomy, 7, 12–22; Pai Hsien-yung and, 90
Artistic reorientation: Modernists and, 3–4, 6, 25–26, 38–49
Avant-gardism: discussion of, 17, 53–54, 60, 161–162, 195 n.4; Modernists and, 17, 50–62, 181; reaction against, 17, 51, 148–149. See also Existentialism, theme of; Romantic avant-garde writers

Baby-boom generation writers, 3, 49, 177–178, 179–180
Bakhtin, M. M., 22, 64–65, 68, 69, 71, 127, 136, 196 n.21
Barthes, Roland, 120
Beckett, Samuel, 125, 182
Bell, Daniel, 186, 191 n.12, 207 n.11
Booth, Wayne, 64
Bourgeois complacency (hsing-fu i-shih), 164, 178; theme of, 174–176, 183–184, 186
Bradbury, Malcolm and James MaFarlane, Modernism—1890–1930, 86
Bürger, Peter, Theory of the Avant-Garde, 15–17, 60 , 191 n.13, 191 n.4

Camus, Albert, 123
Chang Han-liang, 113
Chang Hsiu-ya, 27, 39
Chang Ta-ch'un, 179
Chatman, Seymour, 64, 84
Ch'en, Hsi-ying, 30
Ch'en Jo-hsi, 38, 48, 61
Ch'en Ying-chen, 42, 48, 54, 57, 61, 69–70, 101, 136, 151, 153, 184, 186–187; life and work, 160–176
Ch'i-chün, 26–29
Ch'i-teng Sheng, 52–62, 121, 151, 172
Chiang Ching-kuo, 1
Chiang, Kai-shek, 1
Chiang Kuei, 30
Ch'ing (sentimentality) 14, 94–96, 97–98, 101–111
"Combat literature," 23
Chu Hsi-ning, 30, 33–36, 85
Chu, Li-min, 40, 63
Chu Yen, 84

Chung (loyalty) and hsiao (filial piety), 14, 103, 110–111
Chung-kuo shih-pao [China times], 49, 81, 177
Chung-wai wen-hsüeh (Chung-wai literary monthly), 78
Classical literary tradition: artistic assumptions, 10–11, 21–22, 24–26, 28–29, 45, 49; "censorship of beauty," 25; critical concepts, 79–80; traditionalist critics, 49; traditionalist prose, 24–29; writers' appropriation of, 10–11, 91–93, 146–147, 187. See also Allusions in Hung-lou meng
Cold war: spirit, 36; U.S. policy, 164. See also Anti-Communism
Compassion, human capacity for, 71–73, 132–138, 172–173
"Critical realism," 1, 171; failure of, 32–33, 33–36
Cultural imperialism, 2, 6, 7, 114–115, 179–185; nativist resistance of, 148–150, 153–154, 159–160, 160–164
"Cultural nostalgia," 36, 193 n.8. See also Imaginary nostalgia; Mainlander émigrés.
Cultural sinocentrism, 34–36

"Deautomatization" or "dehabitualization," 74, 113
"Double-Three Bookclub," 35

Enlightenment rationality, 10, 13, 14–15, 117, 124, 186; limitations of, 138–140
Existentialism, theme of, 55–58, 121–124, 124–147, 156, 165–169, 173, 205 n.22
Exoticism: Chinese, 85–86; occidental, 53–55

Fairbank, John King, 189–190 n.3
Father-son relationship, theme of, 13–14, 26, 97–98, 103, 109–111, 111–124

Feminist protest, theme of, 31–32
Filial piety, 26, 117
Formalist criticism, 13, 39, 113–114; departure from, 114, 160–161
Fu-k'an (Literary supplement to newspaper), 24

Goldblatt, Howard, 180, 183, 204 n.12, 199 n.10, 207 n.6
Gunn, Edward, 116, 138–139, 194 n.14, 197 n.22, 201 n.22

Habermas, Jürgen, 10, 13, 15, 191 n.10
Homosexuality, theme of, 14, 45–46, 96–111
Howe, Irving, 12, 80, 200 n.14
Hsia, C. T., 3, 12, 37, 43, 89, 99, 100, 108, 169
Hsia-ch'ao [Summer tide], 152
Hsia, Ch'eng-t'ao, 28
Hsia, T. A., 4, 39, 42, 49, 63, 189–190 n.3
Hsien-tai wen-hsüeh [Modern literature], 4–5, 7, 8, 38, 52, 63, 166
Hsin (heart), 105–108
Hsü Fu-kuan, 152
Hu Ch'iu-yüan, 152
Huang Ch'un-ming, 48, 65–66, 151, 153–159
Humanitarianism, 70–73, 174–176; Modernist skepticism of, 132–138
Hung-lou meng [Dream of the red chamber], 11, 14, 20, 69, 95, 191 n.9; allusions in Crystal Boys, 101–108; Prospect Garden (Ta-kuan yüan), 14, 103

Impersonal narration, 64–66, 83–84
"Intellectual poverty," 164, 170, 176

Jameson, Fredric, 22, 77, 117, 120, 124, 130, 197 n.23, 198 n.26, 201 n.20, 202 n.27
Jen-chien [Human world], 164

Kao Chüan-chih, 55, 58
Kwan-Terry, John, 51, 149, 163, 195 n.2
K'un-ch'ü, 11, 94–95

Lau, Joseph Shiu-ming, 8, 51–52, 53, 55, 58, 61, 84, 87, 88, 89, 90, 112, 153, 163, 189 n.2
Leavis, F. R., 19
Lee, Leo Ou-fan, 38, 125, 189 n.2, 190 n.5
Li Ang, 23, 49, 60, 80, 179, 180–185
Li Yung-p'ing, 16, 17, 23, 61, 73, 181; *Chronicles of Chi-ling*, 80–87
Liang Ch'i-ch'ao, 18
Liang Shi-ch'iu, 19, 62, 189–190 n.3
Liberal-humanism, 19–22, 89–90, 98–101, 105–108
Lien-ho pao [United daily news], 52, 83, 177
Lien-ho wen-hsüeh [Unitas], 187
Lin Hai-yin, 30–33, 34
Lin Huai-min, 54, 179
Lin Yao-te, 179
Liu Ch'un-ch'eng, 154
Liu, James J. Y., 79, 198 n.27
Lü Cheng-hui, 114–115, 124
Lukacs, Georg, 6, 115
Lyrical-sentimental strand, 1–2, 25–26, 26–29, 39, 49; resurgence of, 3, 178, 194–195 n. 21. *See also* Sentimentalism

Mainlander émigrés: dominant culture and, 23–24, 192 n.1; nostalgia, 27, 30, 34–36, 90–93, 190–191 n.6; second-generation, 36, 193 n.8; theme of, 88–96, 111, 127, 165–166, 168, 169–171; "transit passenger" mentality, 30, 193 n.5
Mainlander-Taiwanese relationship, 2, 150–151; theme of, 168, 169–171
Marcuse, Herbert, 100, 206 n.29
Materialism: in the eighties, 177–178; "philistine" spirit, 115; theme of, 130–132, 174–176, 183–184, 186, 207–208 n.12
"Middle brow" literature, 24, 37, 177–178
Middle-class mentality, 30–31, 36–37, 44, 177–178; criticism of, 171, 174–176
Modernist literary movement (Hsien-tai wen-hsüeh yün-tung), vii, 2–7, 189 n.1; compressed timetable, 16, 187; criticism of, 5–6, 114–115, 148–149, 151–152, 153–154, 160–163, 204 n.14, 204–205 n.18; scholarly treatment of, 3–4
Mu-tan t'ing [The peony pavilion], 95

Nan-fang [The south], 162
Nativist literary movement (Hsiang-t'u wen-hsüeh yün-tung), 2, 149–153, 204 n.10; criticism of, 153, 163; in global context, viii, 161
Naturalistic techniques, 175, 206 n. 28
Neo-Confucianist ethics, 13–15; critique of, 101–108; discontent with, 94–96; partriarchy and, 14, 104, 109–111. *See also* Father-son relationship; Chung (loyalty) and hsiao (filial piety); Neotraditionalist cultural discourse; Traditionalist worldviews
Neotraditionalist cultural discourse; critique of, 2, 13–15, 22, 127–128, 130–132; dominant culture and, 10, 24–25, 27–29, 34–36, 93, 112
New Literature (Hsin wen-hsüeh), 1, 7, 189 n.1
New Poetry debate, 51, 148–149
Nieh (cyclical retribution, inherited evil, predestined suffering), 85–87, 108–110; nieh-tzu, 109, 200 n.16
Nostalgia, imaginary, 69, 165–166. *See also* "Cultural nostalgia"

"Objective form," 38–41, 44–48

Oedipus complex, theme of, 46, 119, 121–122
Ou-yang Tzu, 19, 24, 38, 39–47, 49, 65–66, 67, 86, 88, 101, 113, 124, 152; interpretation of Pai Hsien-yung's work, 90, 92–95, 108, 189 n.2, 198 n.2, 199 n.7, 199 n.8

Pai Hsien-yung, 4, 11, 13–14, 19, 38, 42, 43, 52, 54, 63, 68, 69, 80, 87, 112, 121, 152, 162, 165–166, 169; *Crystal Boys*, 96–111; *Tales of Taipei Characters*, 88–96
P'an Jen-mu, 30; *Lien-i piao-mei* [My cousin Lien-i], 36–38
Poggioli, Renato, *The Theory of the Avant-Garde*, 53, 54, 60, 195 n.4
Pollard, David E., 21, 192 n.19
"Postmodern" trend, 179–180
Poverty, theme of: in *Backed Against the Sea*, 128, 132–133; in Ch'en Ying-chen's fiction, 172–173; in *Crystal Boys*, 98; in *Family Crisis*, 111; in Huang Ch'un-ming's fiction, 156–157; in "An Oxcart for Dowry," 71–73
Pre-1949 liberal tradition: Modernists and, 7, 19–22, 31, 189 n.3
Pre-1949 literary societies: Association for Literary Studies (Wen-hsüeh yen-chiu she), 31, 189–190 n.3, 191 n.16; Crescent Moon Society (Hsin-yüeh she), 19, 31, 191 n.16
Pre-1949 realist tradition: writers of the fifties and, 29–38, 89; Modernist generation and, 71–73, 115–116, 157, 171
Pre-1949 writers: Chang, Eileen, 29, 37, 87, 193 n.8, 193 n.10; Chou Tso-jen, 21, 192 n.19; Chu Tzu-ch'ing, 25–26, 28; Hsü Chih-mo, 25; Lao She, 29; Ling Shu-hua, 31; Lu Hsün, 19, 29, 34, 45, 71, 87, 115, 157, 164, 166, 167, 204 n.13; Mao Tun, 29, 33, 36, 171; Pa Chin, 29, 115; Ping Hsin, 39; Shen Ts'ung-wen, 35, 37; Su Ch'ing, 37; Ting Ling, 36, 171; Wu Tsu-hsiang, 33, 71, 73
Professional artistry, Flaubertian, 16, 21
"Provincial identity problem" (sheng-chi wen-t'i), 150
Průšek, Jaroslav, 25 194 n.12

Reader-text dynamics: "ambivalent laughter," 72, 136; "arbitrary narrator," 66–67
"Realism": "canceled realism," 120; Nativist concepts of, 159, 169; Wang Wen-hsing's higher mode of, 76, 197 n.22, 197 n.24
"Regain the mainland" (fan-kung ta-lu), 150, 190 n.6
Representation of history: Ch'en Ying-chen's battle for, 164–171; Modernists' universalist approach, 89–96; writers of the fifties and, 33–34, 36–37
"Return to the native" (hui-kuei hsiang-t'u), 148, 179, 182–183
Romantic avant-garde writers, 50–62

Sentimentalism: May Fourth, 11, 39; criticism of, 39–40; in works, 70, 172, 175, 196 n.15
"Seriocomic" mode, 125, 137
Shih Shu-ch'ing, 52, 54, 60, 121, 151, 179
Shu, James, 114, 115–116, 124
Shui Ching, 42, 43, 52, 63
Shui-hu chuan [The water margin], 85
"Speech genre," incorporation of, 67–73
Stream-of-consciousness technique, 63–64
Sung Tse-lai, 160, 174

Ta-hsüeh tsa-chih [The intellectuals], 15, 185, 202 n.1
T'ang Wen-piao, 59; "Incident," 151–152
Traditionalist worldviews, 21–22, 26, 28–29; Confucianist scholar-official,

27, 37, 102–104 gentry class code, 18–19, 102–104; literati lifestyle, 21–22, 27. See also Chung (loyalty) and hsiao (filial piety)
Trilling, Lionel, 9, 191 n.8
Tzu-yu Chung-kuo [Free China], 15

"Underground naturalism," 81

Wang, C. H., 58, 59
Wang Chen-ho, 16, 22, 48, 61, 68, 74, 80, 81, 83, 151, 154, 162; arbitrary narrator, 66–67; "An Oxcart for Dowry," 70–73
Wang T'o, 153, 155, 159, 174
Wang Wen-hsing, 8, 10, 11, 13, 16, 17, 19, 20–21, 22, 26, 38–39, 42, 43, 48, 49, 52, 54, 61, 63, 70, 80, 83, 90, 155, 162, 169, 179, 181, 185–187; aesthetic views, 73–80; Backed Against the Sea, 124–147; Family Crisis, 111–124
Wen-chi [Literary quaterly], 151, 152, 154, 160
Wen-hsing [Literary star], 15, 185, 190 n.4
Western cultural texts, 53–55, 181–182; individual appropriation of, 41–43, 70, 123, 125, 167
Western intellectual frames: American countercultural movement, 14, 98–101, 103–105; bourgeois individualism, 14, 114; existentialism, 43, 50, 55–58, 120, 181; Frankfurt School critical theory, 115, 162, 176; Freudianism, 43, 119, 166; "new myths" in Family Crisis, 26, 121–124; poststructuralist cultural theory, 181, 183–184
Westernization: criticism of, 114; discourse, 7–8, 179–185, 190 n.4, 190 n.5; historical precondition, 8–9. See also Cultural imperialism
Williams, Raymond, 2

Yang Ch'ing-ch'u, 153, 155, 159
Yang Mu, 11
Yen Yüan-shu, 9, 19, 40, 63, 89, 113, 151, 153, 189–190 n.3
Yip, Wai-lim, 40, 189 n.2
Yü Kuang-chung, 11, 84, 85; "Lang lai le" [The wolf is here], 152
Yü T'ien-t'sung, 6, 151, 160, 203 n.6

Sung-sheng Yvonne Chang, Assistant Professor of Chinese and Comparative Literature at the University of Texas at Austin, is coeditor of *Bamboo Shoot after the Rain: Contemporary Stories by Women Writers of Taiwan.*

Library of Congress Cataloging-in-Publication Data
Chang, Sung-sheng, 1951–
Modernism and the nativist resistance :
contemporary Chinese fiction from Taiwan / by
Sung-sheng Yvonne Chang.
Includes bibliographical references and index.
ISBN 0-8223-1328-6.—ISBN 0-8223-1348-0 (pbk.)
1. Chinese fiction—Taiwan—History and criticism.
2. Chinese fiction—20th century—History and criticism.   I. Title.
PL3031.T3C447   1993
895.1'35209951249—dc20   92-41437

www.ingramcontent.com/pod-product-compliance
Lightning Source LLC
Chambersburg PA
CBHW071816230426
43670CB00013B/2473